9 95

CONCISE COLLEGE TEXTS

CW00894127

Green and Henderson: Land Law

OTHER BOOKS IN SERIES

"A" Level Law, B. Hogan, P. Seago and G. Bennett
"A" Level Law: Cases and Materials, B. Hogan, P. Seago and G. Bennett
Banking Law, C. Hamblin
Contract, F. R. Davies
Criminal Law, P. Seago
English Legal System, K. J. Eddey
GCSE and "O" Level Law, W. J. Brown
Grant and Levin: Family Law, Jennifer Levin
General Principles of Law, C. R. Newton
Hotel and Catering Law in Britain, David Field
Introduction to Commercial Law, C. Hamblin and F. B. Wright
Labour Law, C. D. Drake
Law of Arbitration, William H. Gill
Law for Retailers, Jennifer Brave
Patents, Trade Marks, Copyright and Industrial Designs,
    T. A. Blanco White and Robin Jacob
Press Law, Robin Callender Smith
Sale of Goods and Consumer Credit, A. P. Dobson
Shipping Law, R. Grime
Tort, C. D. Baker

AUSTRALIA AND NEW ZEALAND
The Law Book Company Ltd.
Sydney : Melbourne : Perth

CANADA AND U.S.A.
The Carswell Company Ltd.
Agincourt, Ontario

INDIA
N. M. Tripathi Private Ltd.
Bombay
and
Eastern Law House
Calcutta and Delhi
M.P.P. House
Bangalore

ISRAEL
Steimatzky's Agency Ltd.
Jerusalem : Tel-Aviv : Haifa

CONCISE COLLEGE TEXTS

Green and Henderson: Land Law

Fifth Edition

by

N. Henderson, B.A.,

Of the Middle Temple, Barrister,
a member of the Board of Management
of the College of Law

LONDON
SWEET & MAXWELL
1988

First Edition 1965
Second Edition 1970
Third Edition 1975
Fourth Edition 1980
Fifth Edition 1988

Published in 1988 by
Sweet & Maxwell Limited
11 New Fetter Lane, London.
Laserset by P.B. Computer Typesetting, N. Yorks.
Printed in Great Britain by
Page Bros. (Norwich) Ltd.

British Library Cataloguing in Publication Data

Green, E. Swinfen
    Green & Henderson land law.—5th ed.
    —(Concise college texts).
    1.   Real property — England
    I.   Title.   II. Henderson, N.   III.   Green,
    E. Swinfen. Land law
    344.2064'3   KD829

    ISBN 0–421–38440–9

Preface

English land law has the reputation, deserved in some respects, of being difficult. One of its advantages, however, is that as compared with the more volatile case-law subjects, such as contract and tort, it changes at a slower rate and in a more structured fashion. There is one exception, namely the law of landlord and tenant, and in particular security of tenure. In the previous edition the latter topic acquired a separate chapter to itself: since then there has been a fresh outburst of legislation, spawning further varieties of statutory protection for residential tenants; and as this new edition goes to press further changes are on their way. Inevitably Chapter 13 has been entirely rewritten. I am grateful to my colleague Andrew Gibson for his help in scrutinising its content.

Other important changes have been incorporated in this edition, including amendments made to the Wills Act 1837 by the Administration of Justice Act 1982. These affect the wills of testators dying after December 31, 1982: for the sake of simplicity references to the previous law as set out in previous editions have been omitted, but it should be borne in mind that wills of testators dying before January 1, 1983 remain subject to the unamended law.

Long experience of trying to explain the different functions of trusts for sale, in relation to settlements on the one hand, and co-ownership on the other, has indicated a need to amplify the treatment of both topics; and, although eyebrows raised by the Court of Appeal's decision in *Flegg* were lowered with relief following its reversal by the House of Lords, difficulties encountered in that case have suggested a similar need to re-examine some other basic concepts of property law, such as overreaching.

Contrary to the recent fashion for dealing with registration of title at the outset of books on land law, and referring to it continually thereafter, the topic has been left almost to the end, as in previous editions. The Land Registration Act 1925, unlike the Law of Property Act 1925 and the Settled Land Act 1925, was intended to modify the procedural, not the substantive, law of real property, by substituting a different method of proving and transferring title to land: to the extent that the Act has in the event affected substantive

v

law it has done so almost by inadvertence, which scarcely justifies giving it special prominence in an account of the basic principles of land law.

N.H.
February 1988

Extract from Preface to First Edition

This book is intended to give a practical outline of the land law, or, as it is otherwise known, the law of real property, including the law of wills and intestacy. Its primary purpose is to meet the needs of the many students who are now studying law as part of a wider syllabus. It is hoped that it will also be useful as an introductory book to those who require a more detailed knowledge of the subject: experience has shown that there is much advantage to be gained from studying a short book before proceeding to a more comprehensive work, particularly where the subject is as difficult as is the land law.

E.S.G.
March 1, 1965

Contents

Preface   v
Extract from Preface to First Edition   vi
Abbreviations   viii
Table of Cases   ix
Table of Statutes   xiii

1.   The Scope of Land Law   1
2.   Tenure and Estate   3
3.   Classification of Property   7
4.   Words of Limitation   9
5.   Rights of Beneficial Owners   12
6.   The Contribution of Equity   23
7.   Legal Estates and Interests since 1925   28
8.   Settlements   32
9.   Co-ownership   53
10. The Perpetuity Rule   66
11. Contracts for the Disposition of Land   80
12. Leases and Tenancies   82
13. Security of Tenure and Rent Restriction   101
14. Easements and Profits   112
15. Licences   129
16. Covenants Concerning Land   133
17. Rentcharges   143
18. Mortgages   146
19. Disabilities   162
20. Aquisition of Title under the Limitation Act 1980   165
21. Registration   175
22. Devolution on Death   189
23. Wills   193
24. Intestacy   206

Index   214

Abbreviations

AEA 1925	Administration of Estates Act 1925
LCA 1925	Land Charges Act 1925
LPA 1925	Law of Property Act 1925
LRA 1925	Land Registration Act 1925
M. & W.	Megarry and Wade, *The Law of Real Property* (5th ed. 1984)
SLA 1926	Settled Land Act 1925

Table of Cases

Abbey National Building Society
v. Maybeech 93
Acklom, *Re* 37
Addiscombe Garden Estates
Ltd. v. Crabbe 84
Alefounders' Will Trusts, *Re* 43
Allen v. Greenwood 115
Andrews v. Partington 203
Ankerson v. Connelly 127
Arlesford Trading Co. Ltd. v.
Servansingh 135
Ashe v. Hogan 174
Asher v. Whitlock 174

Ballard's Conveyance, *Re* 140
Bannister v. Bannister 129
Barclay v. Barclay 59
Barclay's Bank Ltd. v. Taylor 186
Barnes v. Barratt 83
Barton v. Morris 61
Baxter v. Four Oaks Properties
Ltd. 141
Beckett v. Lyons 128
Beesley v. Hallwood Estates
Ltd. 134
Berkley v. Poulett 14
Bernstein v. Skyviews & General
Ltd. 13
Besterman, *Re* 191
Beswick v. Beswick 137
Biggs v. Hoddinott 153
Binions v. Evans 131, 177
Borman v. Griffith 119
Boyer v. Warbey 94
Bridges v. Mees 183
Bridgett and Hayes Contract,
Re 44
Bristol & West Building Society
v. Henning 56
British Railways Board v.
Glass 116, 120
Brocklebank v. Thompson 128

Broomfield v. Williams 119
Browne v. Flower 96, 113
Bryant v. Lefever 113
Brunner v. Greenslade 141
Buchanan-Wollaston, *Re* 60
Bull v. Bull 56, 60
Burgess v. Rawnsley 63

Cable v. Bryant 113
Cadell v. Palmer 66
Calabar Properties Ltd. v.
Seagull Autos Ltd. 89
Caldy Manor Estate Ltd. v.
Farrell 16
Callaghan, *Re* 191
Cardigan v. Curzon-Howe 38
Carne's Settled Estates, *Re* 129
Caunce v. Caunce 57, 184
Celsteel Ltd. v. Alton House
Holdings Ltd. (No. 2) 95
Central Estates (Belgravia) Ltd.
v. Woolgar (No. 2) 89
Chambers v. Randall 140
Chandler v. Kerley 131
Chatsworth Estates Co. v.
Fewell 142
Cheese v. Lovejoy 196
Chowood's Registered Land,
Re 187
City of London Building Society
v. Flegg 58, 184
Cityland and Property v.
Dabrah 153
Clark v. Barnes 119
Clore v. Theatrical Properties
Ltd. 129
Colls v. Home and Colonial
Stores Ltd. 115
Cook, *Re* 64
Cook v. Mayor and Corpn. of
Bath 126
Cooper v. Critchley 60

Copeland v. Greenhalf 114
Coventry's Indentures, *Re* Earl
    of 71
Crabb v. Arun D.C. 131
Cuckmere Brick Co. Ltd. v.
    Mutual Finance Ltd. 156

Dalton v. Angus 120, 121
Davies v. Du Paver 122, 126
Davis v. Whitby 120
Dearle v. Hall 160
Dennis v. McDonald 60
D'Eyncourt v. Gregory 14
Dillwyn v. Llewelyn 131
Diment v. N.H. Foot Ltd. 120
Dolphin's Conveyance, *Re* 141
Duke v. Robson 155
Duffield v. Duffield 196
Dyer v. Dyer 56

Edmondson's Will Trusts, *Re* 204
Elias v. George Sahely & Co.
    (Barbados) Ltd. 80
Elias v. Mitchell 185
Ellenborough Park, *Re* 114
Elliston v. Reacher 141
Engels, *Re* 69
Epps v. Esso Petroleum Co.
    Ltd. 188
Errington v. Errington 84, 131
Esso Petroleum Co. Ltd. v.
    Harper's Garage 152, 153
——— v. Kingswood Motors
    (Addlestone) Ltd. 138
Expert Clothing Service & Sales
    v. Hillgate House 91

Facchini v. Bryson 84
Fairclough v. Swan Brewery Co.
    Ltd. 152
Fairweather v. St. Marylebone
    Property Co. 174
Farrar v. Farrars Ltd. 156
Federated Homes Ltd. v. Mill
    Lodge Properties Ltd. 141
Fish, *Re* 202
Formby v. Barker 140
Fox v. Mackreth 39
Freer v. Unwins Ltd. 187
Frewen, *Re* 35

Gallenga, *Re* 35
Gibson, In the Estate of 194
Gissing v. Gissing 56
Gonin, *Re* 81
Goodman v. Gallant 61

Goodman v. Mayor of Saltash 128
Gord v. Needs 202
Grant v. Edmonson 144
——— v. Edwards 56
Green v. Ashco Horticulturist 118
Green's Will Trusts, *Re* 72, 79
Griffiths v. Williams 87, 129
——— v. Young 80
Grigsby v. Melville 114

Halsall v. Brizell 138
Hampshire v. Wickens 98
Hardwick v. Johnson 131
Harmer v. Jumbil (Nigeria) Tin
    Areas Ltd. 96
Harris v. Chesterfield (Earl of) ... 125
——— v. Swick Securities Ltd. 108
Harvey v. Pratt 84
Healey v. Hawkins 120
Herklots, *Re* 33, 48
Hewitt v. Loosemoore 159
Higgs v. Nassauvian 172
Hill v. Tupper 113
Hodgkinson v. Crowe 98
Hodgson v. Marks 184
Hollington Bros. Ltd. v.
    Rhodes 177
Hollins v. Verney 120
Holmes, *Re* 160
Holmes v. Cowcher 148, 170
Horford Investments Ltd. v.
    Lambert 102
Hounslow L.B.C. v. Twick-
    enham Garden Develop-
    ments Ltd. 130
Hulbert v. Dale 121
Hunt v. Luck 27, 57
Hurst v. Picture Theatres Ltd. 130
Hutton v. Watling 74

Inns, *Re* 49
International Drilling Fluids Ltd.
    v. Louisville Investments
    (Uxbridge) Ltd. 100
Irani Finance Ltd. v. Singh 60
Inwards v. Baker 131
Itter, In the Goods of 198
Ives Investments Ltd. v. High 131,
                                      138, 176

Jackson, *Re* 202
Jones, *Re* 197
Jones v. Challenger 60
——— v. Jones 60

Kempthorne, *Re* 60

Kennedy v. De Trafford 156
Kenny v. Preen 96
King, *Re* 135
King v. David Allen Ltd. 129
Kingswood Estate Co. Ltd. v.
  Anderson 81
Kling v. Keston Properties Ltd. .. 183
Knightsbridge Estates Ltd. v.
  Byrne 152
Kreglinger v. New Patagonia 153

L.C.C. v. Allen 140
Lace v. Chantler 84
Landi, *Re* 168
Law v. Jones 80
Leach, *Re* (1948) 199
Leach, *Re* (1986) 191
Leicester (Earl of) v. Wells
  U.D.C. 140
Leigh v. Jack 173
——— v. Taylor 14
Lewis v. Frank Love Ltd. 152
Liverpool City Council v. Irwin .. 96,
                                       116, 117
London and County (A. & D.)
  Ltd. v. W. Sportsman Ltd. .90, 135
London, Corporation of v.
  Riggs 117
Luganda v. Service Hotels Ltd. .. 105
Lyus v. Prowsa Developments
  Ltd. 155, 177

McCarrick v. Liverpool Corpor-
  ation 97
Macleay, *Re* 16
Maddison v. Alderson 81
Marchant v. Charters 83
Markham v. Paget 96
Marten v. Flight Refuelling
  Ltd. 141
Mayo, *Re* 60
Midland Bank Ltd. v. Green 177
Midland Bank Trust Co. Ltd. v.
  Hett, Stubbs & Kemp 177
Midland Ry. Co.'s Agreement,
  Re 84, 86
Moore, *Re* 69
Moore v. Rawson 126
Morgan's Lease, *Re* 41
Moule v. Garrett 135
Multiservice Bookbinding Ltd.
  v. Marsden 153

National Provincial Bank Ltd. v.
  Ainsworth 132, 183
Nickerson v. Barraclough 117

90, Thornhill Road, *Re* 38
Nisbett and Potts' Contract, *Re* .. 173
Noakes & Co. Ltd. v. Rice 153

Old Grovesbury Manor Farm
  Ltd. v. W. Seymour Plant
  Sales & Hire Ltd. (No. 2) 100
Oliver v. Hinton 159
O'May v. City of London Real
  Property Co. Ltd. 109
Owen v. Gadd 96

Palk v. Shinner 123
Pascoe v. Turner 131
Payne v. Cardiff R.D.C. 155
Pearks v. Moseley 70
Peffer v. Rigg 186
Phelan, *Re* 195, 201
Phipps v. Pears 113, 118, 140
Pledge v. White 150
Poland v. Earl of Cadogan 108
Pooley, *Re* 199
Powell v. McFarlane 173
Prior's Case, The 137
Proctor v. Bishop of Bath and
  Wells 70
Pugh v. Savage 121, 123
Purchase v. Lichfield Brewery
  Co. 94

Quennell v. Maltby 154

Rapley, *Re* 195
Ray v. Fairway Motors
  (Barnstaple) Ltd. 127
Redland Brick Ltd. v. Morris 115
Reeve v. Lisle 152
Reeves, *Re* 203
Regent Oil Co. Ltd. v. J.A.
  Gregory 136
Regis Property Co. Ltd. v. Dud-
  ley 99
——— v. Redman 118
Reynolds v. Ashby 14
Rogers v. Hosegood 141
Royce's Will Trusts, *Re* 199
Rugby School (Governors) v.
  Tannahill 91

St. Edmundsbury and Ipswich
  Diocesan Board of Finance v.
  Clark (No. 2) 116
Samuel v. Jarrah Timber Corpor-
  ation 152
Saunders v. Vautier 55, 77
Scala House etc. Ltd. v. Forbes .. 91, 92

Schwann *v.* Cotton 118
Shelley's Case 9
Shell-Mex & B.P. Ltd. *v.*
  Manchester Garages Ltd. 84
Shiloh Spinners Ltd. *v.*
  Harding 30, 137, 138, 176
Sikes, *Re* 203
Simmons *v.* Midford 14
Simpson *v.* Foxon 195
Smith, *Re* 50
Smith *v.* Marrable 96
—— *v.* Morrison 186
—— *v.* River Douglas Catch-
  ment Board 138
Sovmots Investments Ltd. *v.*
  Secretary of State for the
  Environment 119
Spencer's Case 134, 135
Standard Chartered Bank Ltd. *v.*
  Walker 156
Steadman *v.* Steadman 81
Strand and Savoy Properties
  Ltd., *Re* 88
Strand Securities Ltd. *v.*
  Caswell 183
Street *v.* Mountford 83, 84
Sugden *v.* St. Leonards 197
Summers *v.* Salford Corpora-
  tion 97
Swiss Bank Corp. *v.* Lloyds Bank
  Ltd. 178
Symons *v.* Leaker 123

Tanner *v.* Tanner 131
Taylor *v.* Twinberrow 174
Taylor Fashions Ltd. *v.*
  Liverpool Victoria Trustees
  Co. Ltd. 178
Tehidy Minerals Ltd. *v.*
  Norman 121
Thatcher *v.* Pearce 90
Thellusson *v.* Woodford 77
Thomas *v.* Brown 81
Thorn *v.* Dickens 201
Tichborne *v.* Weir 173
Tickner *v.* Buzzacott 174
Tiltwood, Sussex, *Re* 142
Timmins *v.* Moreland Street
  Property Ltd. 80
Tito *v.* Waddell (No. 2) 138
Tiverton Estates Ltd. *v.*
  Wearwell Ltd. 80
Tophams Ltd. *v.* Earl of Sefton .. 137
Treloar *v.* Nute 173
Tse Kwong Lam *v.* Wong Chit
  Sen 156

Tulk *v.* Moxhay 136, 139, 140
Twentieth Century Banking
  Corp. Ltd. *v.* Wilkinson 157

Union Lighterage Co. *v.* London
  Graving Dock Co. 117, 120

Villar, *Re* 68, 69

Wakeham *v.* Mackenzie 81
Wakeman, *Re* 50
Wallis's Cayton Bay Holiday
  Camp Ltd. *v.* Shell-Mex &
  B.P. Ltd. 173
Walsh *v.* Lonsdale 85
Warmington *v.* Miller 81
Warren *v.* Keen 98
Webb *v.* Pollmount Ltd. 183
Wellsted's Will Trusts, *Re* 50
Western Bank Ltd. *v.* Schindler . 154
Weston *v.* Henshaw 39, 41
Westminster (Duke of) *v.*
  Johnston 108
Wheeldon *v.* Burrows 118, 119, 125
Wheeler *v.* Mercer 87
White *v.* City of London Brewery
  Co. 154
—— *v.* Williams 119
Wild's Case 205
Williams *v.* Hensman 63
—— *v.* Unit Construction Co.
  Ltd. 136
—— *v.* Williams 59
Williams & Glyn's Bank Ltd. *v.*
  Boland 56, 57, 60, 184
Williams Bros. Direct Supply
  Ltd. *v.* Raftery 173
Wimpey (George) & Co. *v.*
  Sohn 173
Winter Garden Theatre Ltd. *v.*
  Millennium Productions
  Ltd. 130
Wolfe *v.* Hogan 102
Wood *v.* Leadbitter 130
Woodall *v.* Clifton 75
Woodhouse & Co. Ltd. *v.*
  Kirkland Ltd. 120
Woolwich Equitable B.S. *v.*
  Marshall 183
Worthing Corp. *v.* Heather 75
Wright *v.* Dean 177
—— *v.* Macadam 114, 118
Wrotham Park Estate Co. Ltd. *v.*
  Parkside Homes Ltd. 142

Youngmin *v.* Heath 133

Table of Statutes

1285 Statue of Westminster II (13 Edw. 1, c. 1), De Donis Conditionalibus 17
1381 Forcible Entry Act (5 Ric. 2, c. 7) 89
1540 Statute of Wills (32 Hen. 8, c. 1) 193
1623 Forcible Entry Act (21 Ja. 1, c. 15) 89
1730 Landlord and Tenant Act (4 Geo. 2, c. 28) 87
1737 Distress for Rent Act (11 Geo. 2, c. 19) 87
1832 Prescription Act (2 & 3 Will. 4, c. 71) .... 121 *et seq.*
    s. 7 .... 122, 126
    s. 8 .... 122, 126
1833 Fines and Recoveries Act (3 & 4 Will. 4, c. 74) .. 17, 18
    Dower Act (3 & 4 Will. 4, c. 105) 190
1837 Wills Act (7 Will. 4 & 1 Vict. c. 26) .. 16, 193 *et seq.*
    s. 9 .... 193, 194
    s. 11 194
    s. 15 .... 198, 199
    s. 18 .... 196, 199
    s. 18A 199
    s. 20 196
    s. 21 198
    s. 22 197
    s. 24 203
    s. 25 199
    s. 27 204
    s. 28 10
    s. 29 204
    ss. 32, 33 200
1852 Common Law Procedure Act (15 & 16 Vict. c. 76) 90, 93

1881 Conveyancing Act (44 & 45 Vict. c. 41) 9, 10
1882 Settled Land Act (45 & 46 Vict. c. 38) 51
    Conveyancing Act (45 & 46 Vict. c. 39) 204
1918 Wills (Soldiers and Sailors) Act (7 & 8 Geo. 5, c. 58) 194
1922 Law of Property Act (12 & 13 Geo. 5, c. 16) 2, 3, 87–88
1925 Settled Land Act (15 & 16 Geo. 5, c. 18) .... 2, 32 *et seq.*, 129
    s. 1 .... 32, 162
    s. 3 43
    s. 4 .... 34, 42
    s. 5 34
    s. 6 34
    s. 7 .... 44, 45
    s. 8 .... 34, 44, 45
    s. 9 42
    s. 13 42
    s. 17 45
    s. 18 .... 38, 39, 40, 41, 48
    s. 19 .... 34, 54
    s. 20 34
    s. 21 51
    s. 23 35
    s. 24 .... 37, 38
    s. 27 162
    s. 36 .... 33, 54
    s. 41 21
    s. 65 39
    s. 66 .... 21, 29
    s. 67 39
    s. 68 39
    s. 71 36
    ss. 72, 73 .... 40, 58
    s. 104 36
    s. 105 37

1925   Settled Land Act—*cont.*
    s. 106 .... 37, 52
    s. 107 38
    ss. 108, 109 35
    s. 110 .... 41, 42, 46
    s. 117 35
    Sched. I 41
    Sched. II 41
    Sched. III 36
    Law of Property Act (15
      & 16 Geo. 5, c. 20) 2, 10,
        17, 32, 51, 66, 147
    s. 1 ..... 28, 30, 55, 82, 112, 116
    s. 2 .... 27, 40, 48, 50, 58, 155
    s. 5 161
    s. 7 29
    s. 14 58
    s. 19 162
    s. 20 163
    s. 25 .... 33, 46
    ss. 26, 27 .... 47, 48, 58
    s. 28 .... 49, 50, 65
    s. 29 50
    s. 30 .... 49, 57, 59, 65
    s. 34 .... 46, 54, 55
    s. 35 .... 46, 54
    s. 36 .... 46, 54, 63
    s. 40 .... 80, 81
    s. 44 26
    s. 50 44
    s. 52 .. 25, 84, 94, 95, 116, 177,
                  193
    s. 53 .... 84, 94, 95, 148
    s. 54 .... 84, 95
    s. 56 137
    s. 60 10
    s. 62 .... 14, 118, 119, 125
    s. 65 116
    s. 72 17
    s. 77 136
    s. 78 .... 138, 141
    s. 79 .... 133, 137
    s. 84 142
    ss. 85–87 .... 147, 159
    s. 88 .... 155, 157
    s. 89 .... 155, 157
    s. 91 .... 156, 157
    s. 93 149
    s. 94 161
    s. 97 159
    s. 99 158
    s. 101 .... 154, 156
    ss. 104, 105 155
    s. 109 156
    ss. 115, 116 161
    s. 121 144

1925   Law of Property Act—
    cont.
    s. 122 144
    s. 130 11
    s. 131 9
    s. 134 .... 204, 205
    s. 137 160
    s. 141 .... 134, 135
    s. 142 134
    s. 144 99
    s. 146 .... 90, 92, 93
    s. 147 92
    s. 149 .... 30, 87, 88
    s. 153 94
    s. 163 .... 68, 72, 73
    ss. 164–166 77
    s. 175 77
    s. 176 .... 18, 19
    s. 184 201
    s. 191 145
    ss. 198, 199   27, 159, 176, 178
    s. 205 .... 13, 29, 33
    Sched. I 41
    Land Registration Act (15
      & 16 Geo. 5, c.
      21) .... 2, 180 *et seq.*
    ss. 18, 21 185
    ss. 20, 23 185
    s. 59 186
    s. 70 183
    s. 74 184
    ss. 82, 83 187
    s. 86 184
    s. 101 185
    Land Charges Act (15 &
      16 Geo. 5, c. 22) 2, 27,
        31, 40, 175, 179
    Administration of Estates
      Act (15 & 16 Geo. 5,
      c. 23) .... 5, 46, 206 *et seq.*
    s. 22 44
    s. 33 46
    s. 36 .... 47, 193
    s. 51 .... 163, 190
1926   Law of Property (Amend-
      ment) Act (16 & 17
      Geo. 5, c. 11) 43, 64
    Legitimacy Act (16 & 17
      Geo. 5, c. 60) 213
1927   Landlord and Tenant Act
      (17 & 18 Geo. 5, c.
      36) 110
    s. 18 99
    s. 19 99

1929 Law of Property (Amendment) Act (19 & 20
Geo. 5, c. 9) 93
1938 Leasehold Property
(Repairs) Act (1 & 2
Geo. 6, c. 34) 92, 99
Inheritance (Family Pro-
vision) Act (1 & 2
Geo. 6, c. 45) 190
1954 Landlord and Tenant Act
(2 & 3 Eliz. 2, c.
56) 106, 107, 108, 109
1958 Adoption Act (7 & 8 Eliz.
2, c. 5) 212
1959 Rights of Light Act (7 & 8
Eliz. 2, c. 56) 124, 180
1963 Water Resources Act (c.
38) 15
1964 Perpetuities and Accumulations Act (c. 55) 66
                                    et seq.
    s. 1 72
    s. 2 72
    s. 3 .... 73, 78
    s. 4 73
    s. 5 73
    s. 7 71
    s. 9 .... 74, 75
    s. 10 .... 74, 75
    s. 15 76
    Law of Property (Joint
    Tenants) Act (c. 63) .   64
1965 Commons Registration
Act (c. 64) 125, 126
1966 Land Registration Act (c.
39) 181
1967 Matrimonial Homes Act
(c. 75) 132
Leasehold Reform Act (c.
88) 108
1968 Wills Act (c. 28) 198
1969 Family Law Reform Act
(c. 46) 67, 162
    s. 1 162
    s. 12 162
    s. 14 213
    s. 15 202
    Law of Property Act (c.
    59)—
    s. 23 26
    s. 25 178
1970 Administration of Justice
Act (c. 31) 154
Matrimonial Proceedings
and Property Act (c.
45) 56

1971–2 Town and Country
Planning Acts (c.
42) 12
1972 Land Charges Act (c.
61) 2, 27, 40, 85, 132,
        139, 159, 160, 161, 175,
                            184, 185
    s. 4 .... 27, 159, 176, 178
    s. 11 179
    s. 18 27
1973 Administration of Justice
Act (c. 15) 154
Matrimonial Causes Act
(c. 18) 191, 192
    s. 18 212
1974 Consumer Credit Act (c.
39) 153
1975 Inheritance (Provision for
Family and Depen-
dants) Act (c. 63) 190
                                    et seq.
    s. 1 191
    s. 3 191
Sex Discrimination Act
(c. 65)—
    s. 31 100
Children Act (c. 72) 212
Local Land Charges Act
(c. 76) 179
1976 Legitimacy Act (c. 31) 213
Adoption Act (c. 36) 212
Race Relations Act (c.
74)—
    s. 24 100
Rent (Agriculture) Act
(c. 80) 106, 107
1977 Rentcharges Act (c.
30) .... 143 *et seq.*
Rent Act (c. 42) .... 101 *et seq.*
Protection from Eviction
Act (c. 43)—
    s. 1 96
    s. 2 89
    s. 5 86
Criminal Law Act (c.
45)—
    ss. 6, 7 89
1980 Limitation Amendment
Act (c. 24) 169
Housing Act (c. 51) 101
    ss. 51–55 104
    ss. 56–58 106
    s. 69 105
Limitation Act (c. 58) 165
                                    et seq.
    s. 15 .... 165, 166, 167

1980   Limitation Act—*cont.*
       s. 16 170
       s. 17 165
       s. 18 167
       s. 19 168
       s. 20 170
       s. 21 168
       s. 27 19
       s. 28 171
       ss. 29–31 171
       s. 32 172
       s. 38 169
       Sched. 1, paras. 1, 8 166
           para. 4 166
           para. 5 169
           paras. 6, 8 169
           para. 8 .... 173, 174
           para. 9 168
       Highways Act (c. 66) 127
1981   Supreme Court Act (c.
           54)—
       s. 118 163
1982   Forfeiture Act (c. 34) 199
       Administration of Justice
           Act (c. 53) 193
       s. 18 .... 196, 199
       s. 19 200
       s. 20 201
       s. 21 202

1982   Administration of Justice
           Act—*cont.*
       s. 22 202
1983   Matrimonial Homes Act
           (c. 19) 132
       Mental Health Act (c.
           20) 163, 176
1985   Housing Act (c. 68) 105, 106
       Pt. VI 97
       Pt. IX 97
       Landlord and Tenant Act
           (c. 70)—
       s. 8 96
       s. 11 97
1986   Agricultural Holdings Act
           (c. 5) 110
       s. 10 15
       s. 16 169
       Sched. 14, para. 12 158
       Land Registration Act (c.
           26) 180
       Building Societies Act (c.
           53)—
       Sched. 4 156
1987   Landlord   and   Tenant
           Act (c. 31)—
       Pt. I 108
       Family Law Reform Act
           (c. 42)—
       ss. 18–21 213

1. The scope of land law

The law of land, or real property, is concerned with the rights, interests and obligations which can exist over land and buildings; how they are created, enforced, assigned and extinguished. Its undoubted complexity is explained by two main factors.

The first lies in the nature of land itself. Land is permanent property, and thus lends itself to the creation of a diversity of concurrent and consecutive interests. The same plot of land or the same house may at once be "owned"[1] by A, let by A to B, sub-let by B to C, and mortgaged by any of them to secure repayment of a loan; it may also be subject to a right of way in favour of one neighbour, whilst in favour of another it may be subject to a restrictive covenant, preventing A and his successors from building on it. Again, A by his will may direct that the land is to be held on trust for his widow during her life, then for his eldest son during his life, and then for all his grandchildren absolutely in equal shares. The nature and the validity of these diverse interests are determined in accordance with rules and principles established over a long period by the courts and by statute. In contrast, other forms of property, such as goods and company shares, are normally the subject of absolute ownership only, and although goods may be let by the owner under a contract of hire or hire-purchase, and personal property generally may be used as security for a loan or may be included, like land, in a family settlement, the normal transaction with such property is an outright transfer.

The second factor is historical. The foundations of the law of land were laid at a time when land was virtually the sole form of wealth, and formed the basis of the feudal system established after the Norman conquest. The doctrines and rules then developed were appropriate to a feudal society, but they soon acquired a rigidity and formalism which hampered their adaptation to meet the needs of a changing social and economic structure. Although the deficiencies of the common law were in some respects made

---

[1] We shall see that, properly speaking, ownership attaches not to the land itself, but to an estate or interest in the land.

1

good by the system of equity administered by the Court of Chancery, and in others by legislation, the result was seldom to simplify, but almost invariably to complicate, the law.

No serious attempt was made to reduce the complexity and obscurity of the land law until the 19th century, when many statutory reforms were introduced. Finally, sweeping changes were effected by the 1925 property legislation, which came into operation on January 1, 1926. The effect of this legislation, and in particular of the Law of Property Acts 1922 and 1925, the Settled Land Act 1925, the Land Charges Act 1925[2] and the Land Registration Act 1925, will be considered in due course. As a whole it constitutes a watershed in the land law; it is natural, therefore, to speak of the old law and the new law, or the law before 1926 and the law after 1925.

---

[2] Now repealed and largely re-enacted by the Land Charges Act 1972.

2. Tenure and estate

TENURE

At common law[1] the ownership of all the land in the country is vested in the Crown. No one other than the Crown can own land. However, other persons may be *tenants, i.e. holders*, of land and have rights in the land which the law will protect even against the Crown. Originally every such person held his land as tenant of some superior feudal lord (who might be the king himself, or someone holding from the king), to whom he owed certain feudal services. Failure to perform these services would cause a forfeiture of the tenant's rights. There were different *tenures* in the land, *i.e.* different methods of land holding, each of which had its own characteristic services. Thus, if a tenant held by the tenure of knight service he rendered military services to his superior feudal lord, whereas if he held by socage tenure he rendered agricultural services to his lord. By 1925, however, the number of tenures had become so reduced that only two tenures of any importance remained. These were *socage* tenure, otherwise known as freehold, and *copyhold* tenure, formerly known as villeinage. For all practical purposes, by 1925 freehold tenure existed in name only: it had lost its old feudal incidents, and the freehold tenant no longer rendered services to a superior feudal lord. By 1925 freehold tenants almost always held directly of the Crown because it was a rule of the common law that in the absence of evidence of an intermediate lordship (and such evidence was rarely available in 1925) the tenant held directly of the Crown.

Copyhold tenure, on the other hand, remained a living tenure until 1926. The services of this tenure had originally been agricultural, but these services had long since been commuted for annual money payments, known as quit-rents. All copyholds were enfranchised, *i.e.* the tenure was converted into freehold tenure, by the Law of Property Act 1922, as from January 1, 1926. Some of the incidents of this tenure have been permanently preserved,

---

[1] The common law is the basic, judge-made law of the country.

and in particular as a general rule the ownership of any minerals beneath the surface of the land is vested in the former lord or his successor in title—a point that sometimes needs to be watched when buying land even today.

To sum up, there is now only one common law tenure, namely freehold tenure, and this has been shorn of its old feudal incidents, except that former copyhold land is still subject to those few incidents which have been permanently preserved.

ESTATE

The doctrine of estates developed as a corollary of the doctrine of tenure. Since a *tenant* was not regarded as owning the land itself, it was necessary to determine what it was that he did own, *i.e.* the nature and extent of his proprietary interest. His *estate* in the land tells us the answer to that question. This in turn depends upon the terms on which the land was granted to him or to some predecessor in title of his.

The doctrine of estates has two principal features. First, estates are classified according to the length of time for which they are limited to endure; secondly, several persons may simultaneously own distinct and separate estates in the same piece of land.

Before considering these features, we may notice that the word estate is also used in two other senses, *viz.* as referring to a particular plot of land, *e.g.* the Blackacre estate, and as referring to the assets or property of a deceased person. The sense in which the word is used in any particular case will appear from the context.

The estates classified

Broadly there are four estates in land, *viz.* (1) the fee simple, (2) the fee tail, (3) the life estate and (4) the leasehold estate.

1. The fee simple

The word "fee" denotes an estate of inheritance, *i.e.* one that will not necessarily come to an end with the death of the individual tenant, but is capable of being inherited by another. The word "simple" indicates that the fee is the ordinary or normal fee, in contrast to the fee tail. Before 1926 on the death intestate (*i.e.* without leaving a will) of a tenant in fee simple the land devolved upon his heir. The heir was ascertained by applying a series of rules known as the canons of descent. Under these rules the heir might be found among descendants, ancestors, or collateral relatives (*e.g.* brothers). If there was no heir the land passed to the superior feudal lord by a process known as escheat. On a death intestate after 1925 the land will no longer devolve upon the heir, but will be held on trust for the statutory next of kin, under the Administration of Estates Act 1925.[2]

As will be seen later, the fee simple owner has for long been in the position of absolute owner for all practical purposes.

2. The fee tail

A fee tail, or attenuated fee, resembled a fee simple in that on the death of the tenant in tail the land devolved upon his heir, but the fee tail differed from the fee simple in that the heir had to be found amongst descendants of the original tenant in tail; the land could not be inherited by an ancestor or a collateral relative of the original tenant in tail. The position is the same today—this is one of the few cases in which the old canons of descent still apply after 1925.

If upon the death of a tenant in tail it is found that there are no living descendants of the original tenant in tail the fee tail comes to an end. The consequences of this are considered below.

3. The life estate

This explains itself. Land may be granted to a person for his life and his estate then determines with his death. The estate is not one of inheritance. Another form of life estate, known as an estate *pur autre vie*, arises whenever a tenant is entitled to land during the life of another (called the *cestui que vie*). Such an estate determines on the death of the *cestui que vie*, not of the tenant.

4. The leasehold estate

This is the estate enjoyed by a tenant under a lease, *i.e.* a tenant under the modern relationship of landlord and tenant. This relationship is historically distinct from the earlier feudal relationship of lord and tenant, and is based on contract rather than status. Originally leasehold was not recognised as an estate, but today the law recognises it as both an estate and a tenure. It is an estate because it tells us the duration of the tenant's interest in the land. It is a tenure because it is a method of land holding.

---

[2] See Chap. 24.

Reversions and remainders

The law allows the owner of an estate in land to confer a lesser estate upon another person, and a reversion then arises. For example, if S, the fee simple owner of Blackacre, grants the land to A for life, S is said to have a reversion because upon the death of A the land will revert to S or, if S is then dead, to his personal representatives, *i.e.* his executors or administrators.

The law also allows a fee simple owner to create a *succession* of estates in the land, and this is called a settlement. For example, S, the fee simple owner of Blackacre, may grant the land to A for his life and thereafter to B for a fee simple estate. B's estate is then said to be a remainder, because upon the death of A the land will remain away from the grantor instead of reverting to him. If, at the death of A, B is already dead the fee simple estate will vest in B's personal representatives. It will be noticed that, whereas a reversion arises by operation of law, a remainder is created by the express terms of the grant.

As a further illustration, S, the fee simple owner of Blackacre, might grant the land to A for life with remainder to B in tail with remainder to C in fee simple. In this illustration if, at the death of A, B is already dead the fee tail will devolve upon B's heir, found amongst his descendants. If and when the fee tail comes to an end the land will pass to C or, if he is already dead, his personal representatives.

Both remainders and reversions are future interests, or "reversionary interests" (a much wider and looser expression than reversion in the strict sense). A reversionary interest is any interest in property which will fall into possession at some future time.

Reversion has a different meaning in the context of leaseholds: the lessor's reversion on a lease signifies his estate in the land subject to the lease. This, unlike a reversion under a settlement, is an interest in possession,[3] not a future interest.

---

[3] See pp. 28–29.

3. Classification of property

The fee simple, the fee tail and the life estate are known as freehold estates, *i.e.* estates of fixed but uncertain duration—fixed, in that they are limited to endure for the life of a person, or for the lives of a person and his heirs; uncertain, in that the duration of those lives is uncertain. The leasehold estate is a non-freehold estate, *i.e.* an estate of certain duration, being either for a fixed term or (in the case of a periodic tenancy) determinable by notice.[1] The use of the word "freehold" in this sense is not to be confused with its use in connection with the doctrine of tenure. (In practice the word "freehold" is generally used, even by lawyers, in yet another sense, *viz.* as a synonym for the fee simple estate. Thus, if a man is asked whether he owns the freehold of his house, what is meant is whether he owns a fee simple estate, rather than a mere leasehold.)

Most systems of law divide property into immovables (*i.e.* interests in land) and movables, which comprise all other property, including goods and chattels, and stocks and shares. The English classification, however, is into *realty* and *personalty*. Realty comprises those forms of property which in the early days of the common law would support a real action, *i.e.* an action by which, if he were wrongfully dispossessed, the owner of the property could recover the property itself (the *res*). Only the freehold estates in land would support such an action and they alone, therefore, are realty. All other forms of property are personalty[2]. Even the leasehold is personalty, because in the early law a tenant under a lease was not regarded as having an estate at all, his rights being merely contractual and personal; if he was wrongfully dispossessed by anyone except the landlord himself he had no remedy, and even against the landlord his remedy was confined to the personal action of covenant, and was only available if the lease was under seal. Although by the sixteenth century the action of ejectment enabled him to recover the land from anyone

[1] See Chap. 12.
[2] As to "fixtures," see pp. 13–15.

who dispossessed him, and his rights came accordingly to be recognised as constituting an estate in land, the same terminology persists to this day, and leasehold estates are technically still "personalty" (or "chattels real").

This confusion of terminology cannot be regarded with much satisfaction; indeed it constitutes a serious obstacle in the way of understanding English land law. Before 1926 the distinction between realty and personalty had important practical consequences, in relation particularly to devolution on intestacy,[3] but the 1925 legislation assimilated the two forms of property in certain respects: both can now be entailed,[4] both can now be mortgaged by the same method,[5] and both now devolve on intestacy under the same rules.[6] Any remaining problems of classification or definition[7] can and usually will be minimised in practice by avoiding abstract expressions such as "realty" and "personalty" in the drafting of any instrument.

[3] See p. 206.
[4] See p. 18.
[5] See p. 147.
[6] See p. 208.
[7] As to the doctrine of conversion, see pp. 46, 60.

4. Words of limitation

The expression "words of limitation" means the words that are necessary to transfer or create a particular estate in land, such as the fee simple or the fee tail. For example, if the fee simple owner of Blackacre wishes to transfer the fee simple to A by deed,[1] the question arises whether the deed should say that the land is conveyed to A "in fee simple," or "absolutely," or in accordance with some other formal expression.[2]

Grants by deed

Before 1926 in order to transfer a *fee simple* estate in land the grant had to be made to A "and his heirs" or "in fee simple" (the latter expression being first allowed by the Conveyancing Act 1881). No other expressions would suffice, no matter how clear the intention might be, and if the correct expressions were not used then only a life estate passed to the grantee. It is important to note that where a grant was made to A *and his heirs*, the words italicised were words of *limitation*, not words of *purchase*,[3] *i.e.* they operated merely to delimit the estate which A was to take, not to grant any estate to his heirs.[4] Of course if A died without having disposed of his estate the heir or heirs would succeed to the land under the old canons of descent; but until then they had no estate, merely a *spes successionis*.

---

[1] A conveyance (or transfer) of land must generally be made by deed, *i.e.* a written instrument that has been signed and sealed. See p. 25, note 2.

[2] The problem is confined to the fee simple and fee tail estates. No particular form of words has ever been required to create a life estate or a lease.

[3] Anyone is a "purchaser" in this sense who acquires the property otherwise than by operation of law.

[4] Under the rule in *Shelley's Case* (1581) 1 Co. Rep. 93B, this applied even where the grantor's intention plainly was to grant an estate to the heirs, *e.g.* where a grant was made to A for life with remainder to his heirs. This rule was abolished by the LPA 1925, s.131, and the word heirs may now operate as a word of purchase if so intended (see p. 206).

The Law of Property Act 1925, s.60, provides that after 1925 a conveyance of land shall pass the whole estate of the grantor to the grantee unless the deed shows a contrary intention. Thus, assuming that the grantor has the fee simple estate in the land, a simple conveyance of the land to A without any words of limitation will pass the fee simple estate to him, unless the deed shows a different intention.

No words of limitation have ever been necessary in order to transfer a fee simple estate to a corporation aggregate, such as the ordinary limited company, but before 1926 in order to transfer a fee simple estate to a corporation sole, such as a bishop,[5] the words "and his successors" had to be used; otherwise only a life estate passed to whoever was the holder of the office at the date of the grant. The Law of Property Act 1925, s.60, provides that after 1925 the whole estate of the grantor shall pass to the corporation sole, unless the deed shows a contrary intention.

Before 1926 in order to create a *fee tail* the grant had to be made to A "and the heirs of his body" (or some similar expression incorporating the word "heirs" and restricting the heirs to descendants of the grantee) or "in tail," words first allowed by the Conveyancing Act 1881. The same strict rule applies today—it has not been relaxed by the Law of Property Act 1925. The inheritance of a fee tail can be restricted either to male or female descendants of the grantee, *e.g.* where land is granted "to A and the heirs male (or female) of his body" or "to A in tail male (or female)." Further, the inheritance can be restricted to issue of the grantee and a particular spouse, *e.g.* by making the grant "to A and the heirs of his body by his wife B": this is known as a fee tail special.

Gifts by will

The Wills Act 1837, s.28, provided that a testator's whole estate in the land should pass to a devisee[6] unless the will showed a contrary intention. This rule remains today. Thus a simple gift of Blackacre "to A" will prima facie give the *fee simple* to A, if the testator had that estate.

On the death of a testator before 1926 a *fee tail* could be created by the use of any words in the will which sufficiently showed the

[5] Certain institutions, such as the Crown and bishoprics, are regarded as legal persons, distinct from the individual holders of the office. It is a question of construction whether the grantee is intended to take individually or in his corporate capacity.

[6] A *devise* is a gift of *realty* by will; the *devisee* is the donee. A gift of *personalty* by will is called a *legacy* or *bequest*; the donee is called a *legatee*.

intention to do so, *i.e.* the intention to create an estate of inheritance heritable only by descendants of the devisee; for example, "to A and his issue" or "to A and his descendants" would suffice. However, the Law of Property Act 1925, s.130, provides that on the death of a testator after 1925 the same strict, common law or statutory, expressions must be used as are required for a deed, *i.e.* "and the heirs of his body" (or some similar expression which includes the word "heirs") or "in tail."

Failure to use the correct words

Before 1926 if the correct technical expressions required to transfer or create an estate of inheritance were not used in a deed the grantee obtained only a life estate. As has been seen, after 1925 if no words of limitation are used, whether in a deed or a will, the grantee or devisee will prima facie obtain the fee simple estate. But suppose that after 1925, in a deed or a will, words are used which show an *intention* to create a *fee tail*, but fail to do so because they are not the correct technical expressions, what is the result? According to section 130(2) of the Law of Property Act 1925, the effect of such words is to create the same interest as if the property had been *personalty* before 1926. Entails of personalty could not exist before 1926,[7] and it seems that such words would have created an absolute interest. On that assumption, a gift of realty today "to A and his descendants" would pass the fee simple (equivalent to absolute ownership of personalty) to A. Whether A would take the fee simple solely, or jointly with such of his descendants as were *living at the effective date of the gift*, depends on whether the words "and his descendants" are to be regarded merely as ineffectual words of limitation,[8] or on the contrary as words of purchase.[9]

---

[7] They can since 1925; see p. 18.
[8] The better view.
[9] Obviously they could not be so regarded without the qualification indicated in italics, since descendants constitute an open and unidentifiable class.

5. Rights of beneficial owners

The principal rights of a beneficial owner of land are (i) his rights of possession or enjoyment, and (ii) his rights of disposition or alienation. It must be clear that the extent both of (i) and (ii) will vary with the duration of the owner's estate or interest: if it is limited, *e.g.* a life interest or a leasehold estate, the law may restrict his enjoyment of the land to the extent that this might prejudice those subsequently entitled; and, under the principle *nemo dat quod non habet*, his power to dispose of the land will generally be confined to his own particular estate or interest.[1] Accordingly it will be convenient to consider these rights and powers separately in relation to the fee simple, the fee tail, the life estate and the leasehold.

FEE SIMPLE

For all practical purposes a fee simple owner is today the absolute owner of the land. Nevertheless there are restrictions both at common law and by statute upon the right of the fee simple owner to do as he pleases with the land. For example, at common law he is restrained by the law of tort from using his land in such a way as to cause a nuisance to his neighbours.

The main statutory restrictions on a landowner's rights are those imposed by the Town and Country Planning Act 1971 (consolidating earlier legislation). If he wishes to "develop" his land an owner must generally get planning permission from the local planning authority. "Development" is widely defined by the Act and, besides building operations, includes the working of minerals and the making of any material change in the use to which land (including buildings) is put. For example, it would be development, requiring planning permission, to change the use of a building from that of a dwelling house to that of offices, even though no building work was involved. By way of exception, the

---

[1] There are important statutory exceptions to this rule: see particularly Chap. 8.

Act provides that certain things are not "development," *e.g.* change of use of buildings if the change is from one purpose to another purpose in the same class specified in the Town and Country Planning (Use Classes) Order 1987. Further, the need to obtain planning permission may be dispensed with by the provisions of a General Development Order; for example, the General Development Order 1977 permits the carrying out of building work for agricultural purposes on agricultural land.[2]

Subject to what has been said about planning, a fee simple owner's rights over his land are largely governed by common law, and may be considered under the following heads.

Whoever owns the soil . . .

Whoever owns the soil owns the airspace above the surface and everything beneath the surface. *Cujus est solum ejus est usque ad coelum et ad inferos.* However, there are exceptions to this principle both at common law and by statute. Thus, at common law the Crown is the owner of any gold or silver found in a mine, and of treasure trove, *i.e.* any gold or silver coin, plate, or bullion found concealed on land (including any building thereon), the true owner being unknown. By statute, aircraft have the right of passage through the airspace,[3] and various minerals, such as coal, have been vested in the state or state agencies.

Whatever is planted in the soil . . .

Whatever is planted in the soil accedes to the soil, *i.e.* in law it becomes part of the land. *Quicquid plantatur solo solo credit.* It follows both from this and from the preceding principle that any building constructed on land is normally regarded as part of the land itself.[4] Equally, if a chattel is affixed to land, or to a building forming part of the land, it will itself become part of the land, and accordingly cease to be a chattel, if it is regarded in law as a "fixture." In determining whether a chattel has become a fixture two tests are applied:

1. The degree of annexation

Prima facie if a chattel is securely attached to the land it

---

[2] Subject to certain limitations.

[3] See, *e.g. Bernstein* v. *Skyviews and General Ltd.* [1978] Q.B. 479.

[4] LPA 1925, s.205 (definition of "land"). This, however, does not prevent ownership of land being divided, whether horizontally or vertically.

becomes a fixture, whereas if it merely rests upon the land by its own weight it remains a chattel. This, however, is merely the prima facie test and determines the burden of proof. It is the second test that is decisive.

2. The purpose of annexation

If a chattel is brought on or attached to land merely to enable it to be enjoyed as a chattel it does not become a fixture, and this is so even if the chattel is securely attached to the land or a building thereon. Thus in one case[5] tapestry was securely attached to the wall of a house, but it was held to remain a chattel. On the other hand, if a chattel is brought on or attached to land for the purpose of improving that land,[6] or as part of a scheme of design or layout, it becomes a fixture, and this is so even if the chattel rests upon the land merely by its own weight. Thus in one case[7] stone statues and seats were placed in a garden as part of a scheme of design of the garden, and were held to have become fixtures although they rested upon the land merely by their own weight.

Since fixtures are in law part of the land, they pass on any conveyance of the land unless a contrary intention is indicated[8]; and if land is mortgaged, any fixtures form part of the mortgagee's security, and cannot be removed without his consent.[9]

There are, however, important exceptional cases in which fixtures[10] may be removed:

(i) At common law a lessee, before the end of his tenancy, has the right to remove trade, ornamental and domestic fixtures which he has added to the premises. Similarly a tenant for life (or his personal representatives within a reasonable time after his death) has a right to remove similar fixtures as between himself and a remainderman or reversioner. Agriculture, it has been held, is not a trade, so that at common law a lessee or tenant for life has no right to remove agricultural fixtures.

---

[5] *Leigh* v. *Taylor* [1902] A.C. 157.

[6] But not if the purpose is to accommodate *other* land: so where a landowner has the right to lay drains under his neighbour's land, the drains do not become part of the land under which they are laid (*Simmons* v. *Midford* [1969] 2 Ch. 415).

[7] *D'Eyncourt* v. *Gregory* (1866) L.R. 3 Eq. 382. *Cf. Berkley* v. *Poulett* (1976) 120 S.J. 836, C.A.

[8] LPA 1925, s.62.

[9] This applies even to fixtures installed after the mortgage was granted (*Reynolds* v. *Ashby* [1904] A.C. 466).

[10] Chattels which have been so integrated into the land as to lose their individual identity, *e.g.* bricks and timber incorporated into a building, cannot properly be regarded as *mere* fixtures, and accordingly cannot be removed even under the exceptions noted.

(ii) By the Agricultural Holdings Act 1986, s.10 (replacing earlier provisions), a lessee of an agricultural holding has a statutory right to remove agricultural fixtures before the end of his lease or within two months thereafter. This right is subject to certain conditions, and the landlord may elect to purchase the fixtures at a valuation.

Riparian rights

The owner of the bed of non-tidal water has the riparian rights. When a non-tidal stream flows through land belonging to one person that person is prima facie the owner of the bed of the stream to the extent of his frontage. When a non-tidal stream forms the boundary between two plots of land in the ownership of different persons, the presumption is that the owner of each plot is the owner of the bed up to an imaginary middle line.

(The foreshore, *i.e.* the seashore below the ordinary highwater mark, belongs to the Crown or its grantee. Above that mark the presumption is that the shore belongs to the adjoining fee simple owner.)

The riparian rights include the following:

1. Water rights

A riparian owner has the right to take water from the stream for ordinary purposes connected with his tenement even if thereby he exhausts the stream. Domestic purposes and watering cattle are examples of ordinary purposes. He also has the right to take water from the stream for extraordinary purposes connected with his tenement provided that he returns the water to the stream substantially unchanged in quantity and quality. Manufacturing purposes are prima facie extraordinary. A riparian owner has no right to take water from the stream for purposes unconnected with his tenement. If a riparian owner takes water from the stream in breach of these rules, any lower riparian owner who is injured thereby will have an action against him.

These common law rules are to some extent affected by the Water Resources Act 1963, under which, subject to important exceptions, a licence from the local river authority is required before water can be abstracted from a "source of supply" within the Act.

2. Fishing rights

The riparian owners have the exclusive right to fish in non-tidal water, and the public cannot acquire such a right by long user.

The Crown is the owner of the bed of tidal water, and the public have the right to fish in such water unless the Crown has granted the exclusive right to an individual grantee by an ancient grant known as a franchise of free fishery. The Crown does not possess the right to grant such franchises today.

3. Navigation rights

The riparian owners have the exclusive right to navigate non-tidal water except so far as they have dedicated a right of way to the public. Such a dedication may be presumed from user by the public to the knowledge of the riparian owners.

Except so far as the right is restricted by statute the public have the right to navigate tidal water.

Right of alienation

At an early date the law recognised the right of a fee simple owner to alienate (*i.e.* transfer or convey) the land *inter vivos* (during his lifetime). Thus, if land was granted to A and his heirs, A could transfer the land to B and his heirs, thereby passing the fee simple to B, with the result that on the death of B the land would devolve upon B's heir, and not upon A's heir. The ordinary mode of alienation today is by deed of conveyance.[11]

On the other hand, the common law did not recognise the right of a fee simple owner to dispose of the land by will. This rule was evaded by means of trusts, and has long since been abolished by statute; today land can be freely disposed of by will. The formalities of a will are now prescribed by the Wills Act 1837.

The law regards the right of alienation as inviolable, and accordingly a condition purporting to exclude the right, or to impose a forfeiture on alienation, will generally be void.[12]

FEE TAIL

Since the fee tail or entailed interest, like the fee simple, is an estate of inheritance, the owner's rights of enjoyment of the land

[11] See p. 9, note 1.
[12] A *partial* restraint may be valid (*Re Macleay* (1875) L.R. 20 Eq. 186), as also may be a *covenant* not to alienate (which would be enforced, not by forfeiture, but by injunction or damages: see *Caldy Manor Estate Ltd.* v. *Farrell* [1974] 1 W.L.R. 1303).

are generally similar to those of a fee simple owner, and require no further discussion.[13]

Right of alienation

The fee tail was established as an inalienable freehold estate by the Statute De Donis 1285, which provided that land granted to a donee and the heirs of his body should, notwithstanding any alienation by him, descend to his issue on his death, and revert to the donor when the donee and all his issue were dead. The result was that the fee tail, as such, could not be transferred, although, of course, a tenant in tail in possession of land could transfer to another his own personal right to occupy the land during his lifetime.

Before the end of the 15th century, however, methods had been devised for converting a fee tail into a fee simple, and thus barring, or breaking, the entail.[14] Originally this was done by means of collusive actions, but these actions were abolished by the Fines and Recoveries Act 1833. The Act substituted a disentailing assurance (*i.e.* deed of conveyance) as the means of barring an entail. If the tenant in tail wishes to dispose of the land by way of gift or sale he makes the assurance in favour of the donee or purchaser; if he wishes to retain the land he makes the assurance in favour of himself.[15]

The assurance will convert the fee tail into a full fee simple if either (a) it is executed by a tenant in tail in possession, or (b) it is executed by a tenant in tail in remainder with the consent by deed of the "protector of the settlement," *i.e.* the owner of the first subsisting freehold estate created by the settlement.[16] If the assurance is executed by a tenant in tail in remainder without the consent of the protector the fee tail is converted into a base fee, *i.e.* an alienable fee simple which will last only so long as the fee tail would have lasted if it had not been barred (in other words so long as there remain descendants of the original tenant in tail). When the fee tail is converted into a full fee simple any remainder or reversion following the fee tail is extinguished, but when the fee tail is converted into a base fee such interests are unaffected. In neither case are estates preceding the entail affected. A few examples may make the position clearer.

---

[13] As an exception, a tenant in tail after possibility of issue extinct (see p. 19) is impeachable for equitable waste (see pp. 19, 20).

[14] Another word for a fee tail.

[15] Until 1926 it was necessary to convey to a trustee on trust for himself, but by the LPA 1925, s.72(3), a person may now convey land to himself.

[16] Before 1926 a settlor could appoint a "special protector," but this power was abolished by the LPA 1925.

Suppose that land is settled on A for life with remainder to B in tail with remainder to C in fee simple, and that B executes a disentailing assurance with the consent by deed of the protector, A. (A's life estate is a freehold estate and, in the absence of special protectors, he is the protector.) B's fee tail will be converted into a full fee simple. C's fee simple remainder will be extinguished, but A's preceding life estate will be unaffected. Again, assuming the same settlement, if A has died, B without the consent of anyone may execute a disentailing assurance which will convert his fee tail into a full fee simple. Once again C's remainder will be extinguished. But suppose that A is still alive and that B executes a disentailing assurance without the consent of the protector. B's fee tail will be converted into a base fee. This base fee may be transferred from time to time, but whoever has it will have an estate which will come to an end if at any time B's descendants die out. The land will then go over to C or, if C is then dead, C's personal representatives.

The Act of 1833 remains in force, but the Law of Property Act 1925 has made a number of changes, of which the following may be noticed here:

(i) After 1925 an entail can be created in personalty, such as stocks and shares or leaseholds, as well as in realty.

(ii) Fees tail and base fees can subsist only as equitable interests after 1925.

(iii) After 1925 an entail can be barred by will by a simple gift of the property to a devisee or legatee: the donee will then acquire the fee simple or, if the property is personalty, the absolute ownership. But the Act (in section 176) imposes certain conditions. The will must be made or confirmed by codicil after 1925. The testator must be of full age and at the date of his death he must be tenant in tail in possession—hence a barring by will will always create a full fee simple (or absolute ownership), never a base fee. Further, the will must refer specifically to the particular property or to the instrument under which the testator acquired it or to entailed property generally. Hence a gift of "all my property" to X will not bar an entail, and X will not acquire any entailed property to which the testator was entitled.

Enlargement of base fees

A base fee may become enlarged into a full fee simple in any of the following ways:

(i) By the former tenant in tail executing a fresh disentailing assurance with the consent of the protector or after the

protectorship has ceased (*i.e.* after the estates preceding the former entail have come to an end).
(ii) By the owner of the base fee acquiring the fee simple in remainder or reversion.
(iii) By the owner of the base fee remaining in possession of the land for 12 years after the protectorship has ceased.[17] For this reason a base fee will ordinarily come to an end or become enlarged into a full fee simple within a relatively short period of time.
(iv) By a gift of the property by will made by the owner of the base fee if he could have enlarged it during his lifetime without the concurrence of any other person. This power is subject to the conditions laid down by the Law of Property Act 1925, s.176.

Unbarrable entails

The following entails cannot be barred:
(i) an interest in tail after possibility of issue extinct: this arises where the tenant in tail has a fee tail special,[18] and during his lifetime the spouse specified dies without issue;
(ii) entails granted by the Crown (the reversion being in the Crown);
(iii) entails made unbarrable by special Acts of Parliament, such as those granted to the Duke of Marlborough and the Duke of Wellington.

LIFE ESTATE

The doctrine of waste

The law takes the view that a tenant for life has so limited an interest in the land that special restrictions should be imposed upon his right to use the land as he pleases. The rules in question are known as the doctrine of waste. Waste is of three kinds, namely voluntary, permissive and equitable. Voluntary waste is any positive act which alters the land to its detriment, such as felling timber trees, or opening and working a new mine. Permissive waste is allowing the land to deteriorate for want of

[17] Limitation Act 1980, s.27.
[18] See p. 10.

attention, *e.g.* by failure to maintain buildings in repair. Equitable waste is a special kind of voluntary waste and consists of acts of wanton destruction, such as pulling down or defacing the mansion house or felling trees which have been planted for shelter or ornament.

A tenant for life is impeachable for voluntary waste (*i.e.* he is liable in damages to the remainderman or reversioner if he commits it) unless the settlement makes him unimpeachable. He is unimpeachable for permissive waste unless the settlement makes him impeachable, *i.e.* places him under an obligation to repair. (A tenant for life of a leasehold estate is bound to perform any tenant's repairing covenant in the lease, but this liability is not derived from the doctrine of waste, and the liability is not to the remainderman, but to the landlord and the settlor). A tenant for life is impeachable for equitable waste unless the settlement makes him unimpeachable, and for this purpose it is not sufficient that the settlement makes him unimpeachable for ordinary voluntary waste. If the settlement made a tenant for life unimpeachable for voluntary waste the common law courts would not restrain him from committing acts even of wanton destruction, but the Court of Chancery, taking the view that the settlor did not intend the power to commit waste to be abused, would restrain the tenant for life from doing so. This is why waste of this kind is called equitable waste—originally it was restrained only by the Court of Equity.

The expression "impeachable (or unimpeachable) for waste," without specifying the type of waste, by convention refers to voluntary waste.

Timber

Trees may be timber trees or non-timber trees. Timber trees prima facie are oak, ash and elm trees at least 20 years old, but this definition may be varied by local custom, *e.g.* beech trees are timber in Buckinghamshire.

A tenant for life who is unimpeachable for waste may fell timber or non-timber trees and keep all the proceeds for himself, subject to the doctrine of equitable waste. As we have seen, to fell timber trees is voluntary waste, but if a tenant for life is unimpeachable for such waste he is, of course, at liberty to commit it.

A tenant for life who is impeachable for waste may not fell timber trees, subject to the following exceptions:–

   (i) He may take the customary estovers or botes, *i.e.* house-bote (wood required for household purposes), plough-bote (wood required for the repair of agricultural implements) and hay-bote or hedge-bote (wood required for the repair of hedges and fences).

(ii) If the estate is a timber estate (*i.e.* it is used to grow timber commercially) or the custom of the locality permits, he may fell timber in the ordinary course of husbandry and keep all the proceeds for himself. This is not regarded as waste.

(iii) By the Settled Land Act 1925, s.66, he may in any case fell timber trees with the consent of the trustees of the settlement or the court, but if he relies upon this power the tenant for life will take only one-quarter of the proceeds and three-quarters will go to the trustees of the settlement as capital money.[19]

A tenant for life who is impeachable for waste may fell non-timber trees that are ripe and suitable for cutting and keep all the proceeds for himself. This is not regarded as waste.

Minerals

If the tenant for life is unimpeachable for waste he may work the minerals and keep all the proceeds for himself. He may open and work a new mine for the purpose if he wishes: to do so is waste, but as he is unimpeachable for waste he may do it.

A tenant for life who is impeachable for waste may continue to work a mine that is already lawfully open and may keep all the proceeds for himself—he does not thereby commit waste. A mine is lawfully open for this purpose if it was opened before the settlement was created, or it was opened by a previous tenant for life who was unimpeachable for waste. A tenant for life who is impeachable for waste may not open and work a new mine.

By the Settled Land Act 1925, s.41, a tenant for life may grant a mining lease for a period not exceeding 100 years.[20] A lease granted under this statutory power will be binding on the remainderman or reversioner. In general the tenant for life is entitled to three-quarters of the rent which is payable under such a lease and one-quarter goes to the trustees of the settlement as capital money, but if the tenant for life is impeachable for waste and the lessee is authorised to open and work a new mine, the tenant for life takes only one-quarter of the rent and three-quarters go to the trustees.

Apart from this statutory power, a tenant for life at common law may grant a mining lease authorising the lessee to work minerals to

---

[19] See p. 39.
[20] See p. 35.

the extent that the tenant for life himself has the right to do so, but such a lease will not be binding on a remainderman or reversioner.

Right of alienation

As has already been mentioned, the owner of a life estate can at common law dispose of the land only to the extent of his interest, and accordingly can pass only an estate *pur autre vie*; but this is subject to important statutory provisions governing settlements of land, under which extensive powers of disposition are conferred upon a tenant for life.[21]

LEASEHOLD ESTATE

The doctrine of waste, as described above, has a limited application as between a tenant and his landlord under a lease or tenancy agreement,[22] but in practice the rights and obligations of the parties are governed primarily, in this respect as in others, by the express provisions of the lease or tenancy agreement itself.

A tenant or lessee has in general the same right of alienation as any other estate owner, and accordingly can assign his lease (*i.e.* the residue), subject to any contractual restrictions contained in the lease.[23]

---

[21] See Chap. 8.
[22] See p. 97.
[23] See p. 99.

6. The contribution of equity

Trusts

As with the criminal law and the law of contract and tort, the basis of the law of real property is common law, but it is in the sphere of property law that equity[1] has made its most important contribution—notably, but not exclusively, in its enforcement of the trust (formerly known as the use). The common law provided no remedy for breach of trust, so that if S, the fee simple owner of Blackacre, conveyed it to T in fee simple, directing him to hold it upon trust for B in fee simple, T at common law was at liberty to disregard the claims of B and to use the property for his own benefit. The Court of Chancery, however, at the suit of B (the beneficiary) would enforce the trust against T (the trustee) and compel T to apply the property to the use or benefit of B. It should be noticed that the Court of Chancery did not deny T's legal, *i.e.* common law, title to the land, but merely required T to utilise his ownership of the land for the benefit of B on the ground that, having undertaken the trust, he was bound in conscience to do so. It was not long, however, before it was realised that the effect of compelling T to account to B for all the fruits of ownership was to make B for many purposes the real owner of the property.

We are now in a position to understand the meaning of some important terms. The fact that the common law recognises T as the owner of the land is expressed by saying that T is the *legal owner* of the land, or that T has the *legal estate* in the land. The fact that B has the benefits of ownership is expressed by saying that B is the *equitable* (or *beneficial*) *owner*, or that B has the *equitable estate or interest* in the land.

Originally the Court of Chancery would enforce the trust only

[1] Like the common law, "equity" is judge-made law; it has its origin in the activities of the old Court of Chancery. Equity supplemented and corrected the older body of judge-made law known as the common law, which was administered by other courts. Today the same courts administer both, but it remains necessary to distinguish between law (*i.e.* common law) and equity, especially with respect to land.

against the trustee himself, and not against any other person into whose hands the land might come, but in the course of time equity so enlarged the classes of persons that for one reason or another it regarded as bound by the trust that in the end the trust became enforceable, not only against the trustee himself, but against any other person who might acquire the land except a bona fide purchaser for value of the legal estate without notice, actual or constructive, of the trust (or any person claiming through such a purchaser). Equitable rights under a trust, although originally enforceable *in personam* (*i.e.* against the trustee personally), thus became virtually rights *in rem*, or rights of property, enforceable against the whole world—subject to the one important exception mentioned above. The reason for this exception, which distinguishes legal from equitable rights, can be understood if one remembers that the trust, unlike legal ownership, was enforced as a matter of conscience: a purchaser whose conscience was not affected, *i.e.* who had no notice of the trust, would not be regarded as bound in equity.

At first, trusts were of a simple character, *e.g.* a man going on the crusades might convey his land to trustees for the benefit of his family during his absence, but in the course of time it became possible to create a succession of estates under the trust, just as such a succession of estates could be created at common law without a trust. For example, as we have seen, S, the fee simple owner of Blackacre, might convey Blackacre to A for life with remainder to B in fee simple, and A would then have a *legal* life estate and B a *legal* fee simple in remainder. Alternatively, it now became possible for S to convey the land to one or more trustees in fee simple directing them to hold the land upon trust for A for life with remainder to B in fee simple. A would then have an *equitable* life estate and B an *equitable* fee simple in remainder. The trustee or trustees had the legal fee simple; the beneficiaries had equitable estates.

In developing the equitable (or beneficial) interest under the trust in this way, equity borrowed the common law system of estates. In other words equity allowed the settlor to create as equitable estates those estates, and only those estates, that could be created as legal estates at common law without the employment of a trust. Moreover, to these equitable estates equity applied nearly all the common law rules governing the particular estates. For example, on the death of the owner of an equitable fee simple, or fee tail, the equitable estate would devolve in the same way as if it had been a legal estate: it would devolve upon the heir, ascertained by applying the old common law canons of descent. Only in a few instances did equity decline to "follow the law" in this way.

Other equitable interests

Apart from equitable interests arising under a trust, equity also recognised and enforced many other interests to which the common law refused to give effect—usually because due form had not been observed in their creation or transfer. In general any estate or interest in land such as a fee simple, a lease, a mortgage or an easement was (and still is) valid at law only if granted by deed.[2]

Although a *contract* to create such an interest could be enforced at law to the extent of recovering damages for its breach, this would often be an ineffectual remedy, first because it is available only against the other contracting party, not against a third party to whom he may subsequently have transferred the land; secondly because, even as against the other contracting party, monetary compensation is seldom an adequate substitute for the land itself.

The intervention of equity at this point proceeded in two stages: first, the equitable remedy of specific performance could be awarded,[3] compelling the defendant to carry out his promise, *i.e.* to grant the estate or interest which he had contracted to grant; secondly, on the basis that "equity regards as done that which ought to be done," equity would treat any specifically enforceable contract[4] for the disposition of land as *at once* creating an equitable interest in the land, before any order of specific performance was obtained or even sought. Thus, under a contract for the sale of a fee simple, or for the grant of a lease or a mortgage or an easement, the intended purchaser, lessee, mortgagee or grantee of the easement was regarded *in equity* as having an immediate interest equivalent to a fee simple, lease, mortgage or easement respectively. His interest, however, being merely equitable, was subject to the same defect as indicated above in relation to interests under a trust, namely that it was not enforceable against a purchaser without notice (as we may call him for short).

An example will illustrate the significance of this doctrine of equity. V, the fee simple owner of Blackacre, has contracted to sell and convey the land to P. If subsequently, in breach of contract, V fails to execute the conveyance, P can enforce the contract against V *at law* by an action for damages, or in *equity* by seeking an order for specific performance. If V not merely fails to convey the land to P, but (wrongfully) conveys it to Q, P still has his common law remedy of damages against V; alternatively,

---

[2] LPA 1925, s.52. The rule is much earlier in origin.
[3] The remedy is discretionary, unlike the common law remedy of damages: see p. 81.
[4] A purported grant that failed at law because not under seal was treated in the same way, provided it was for value.

however, P can enforce his equitable interest in the land against Q (unless Q is a purchaser without notice), and thereby compel Q to convey the legal estate to him.

Three further species of equitable interest may be briefly mentioned here: first the mortgagor's equity of redemption[5]; secondly, restrictive covenants, the burden of which may in equity (though not at common law) run with the covenantor's land[6]; thirdly a form of interest based upon a principle commonly referred to as equitable or proprietary estoppel.[7]

Legal and equitable interests

We may now compare an equitable interest in land with a legal interest. Every legal right is a right *in rem, i.e.* once it attaches to land it binds that land in the hands of everyone who afterwards acquires it, regardless of notice. For example, if A has a legal lease, or a legal right of way, over the land of B, and B sells the land to C, A may still enforce his lease or his right of way against the land, and it is irrelevant that C may have been unaware that the lease or the right of way existed when he acquired the land. Conversely, if A's lease or right of way is equitable only, or if A has a beneficial interest under a trust affecting B's land, then although A's equitable rights will generally be enforceable against the land itself, not merely *in personam*, they will be unenforceable against C (or anyone claiming through C) if he is a purchaser of the legal estate without notice, actual or constructive.

The expression "constructive notice" requires a few words of explanation. A purchaser of land has constructive notice of any interest in the land which he would have discovered if he had made the customary investigation of his vendor's title for the full statutory period (which is now 15 years[8]). This investigation of title involves an inspection of the documents of title to the land for the period in question. A purchaser also has constructive notice of any interest in the land which he would have discovered if he had made those other inquiries and inspections (such as an inspection of the land itself) which a prudent purchaser customarily makes. Further, if a purchaser employs a solicitor or other agent to act for him in acquiring the land, the purchaser has constructive notice of any interest that his agent discovers in that transaction, or would have discovered if he had made the proper investigation of title,

[5] See p. 148.
[6] See p. 139.
[7] See pp. 130, 131.
[8] Law of Property Act 1969, s.23, replacing the earlier period of 30 years under the LPA 1925, s.44(1).

inquiries and inspections. This form of constructive notice is sometimes called "imputed notice," because the agent's actual or constructive notice is imputed to the purchaser. It follows that if a purchaser fails to inspect the title deeds to the property, and consequently is unaware of a trust imposed by one of the deeds, or if he fails to inspect the land itself, and consequently is unaware of the fact that it is occupied by someone other than the vendor, he will generally be fixed with constructive notice of the rights of the beneficiaries under the trust or of the occupier.[9]

It is still the general rule today that an equitable interest in land is enforceable against everyone except a purchaser without notice, but the 1925 legislation has introduced two far-reaching exceptions. First, beneficial interests under a trust are now for the most part *overreached* on a sale of land, *i.e.* become detached from the land itself and attached to the proceeds of sale in the hands of the trustees, provided that certain statutory conditions are satisfied.[10] Secondly, most other equitable interests such as equitable leases, equitable easements and restrictive covenants are now *registrable* under the Land Charges Act 1972[11]: if the interest is registered, this is deemed to be actual notice of its existence to everyone acquiring the land or any interest in it[12]; conversely, failure to register the interest renders it void against a later "purchaser" of the land, as that word is defined by the Land Charges Act.[13] Whether the interest is overreached, or is void for non-registration, a purchaser of the land takes free from it even if he has actual notice of it.[14]

The doctrine of notice has retained its importance, however, in relation to those equitable interests which can be neither registered nor overreached. These include an interest arising by way of equitable or proprietary estoppel,[15] and an equitable right of re-entry,[16] neither of which is referred to in the Land Charges Act; and they also include interests arising under a trust which, though capable of being overreached, are in the event not overreached (because the statutory conditions are not satisfied).[17]

[9] Occupation by a tenant is constructive notice of his rights (*Hunt* v. *Luck* [1902] 1 Ch. 428): if he had a *legal* lease, this would of course be binding regardless of notice.
[10] See pp. 40, 47–8, 58.
[11] Replacing the LCA 1925. See Chap. 21.
[12] LPA 1925, s.198.
[13] 1972 Act, ss.4, 18.
[14] LPA 1925, ss.2, 199.
[15] See note 7.
[16] See p. 30, note 9.
[17] See pp. 48, 56–7.

7. Legal estates and interests since 1925

Legal estates

It will be evident from what has been said in the previous chapter that until 1926 any of the estates (the fee simple, the fee tail, the life estate and the leasehold) could be created either as legal estates or as equitable estates under a trust. After 1925, however, by section 1(1) of the Law of Property Act 1925 only two estates can subsist as legal estates (*i.e.* without the necessity for a trust), namely (i) the fee simple absolute in possession, and (ii) the term of years absolute. These two estates may also arise as equitable interests[1], but all other estates, such as the life estate and the fee tail, can be created *only* as equitable interests[2] under a trust. Indeed the term "estate" itself is now confined to the two legal estates, all others being properly called "interests," *e.g.* a life interest or an entailed interest.

The policy behind this radical reform was to facilitate conveyancing by confining legal ownership of land[3] to such forms as are appropriate to dispositions of an ordinary commercial kind, namely conveyance of the freehold, and grant of a leasehold. Dispositions of land by way of family settlement, creating successive life or entailed or other limited interests, can accordingly now be effected only by the machinery of a trust which, in combination with the device of overreaching,[4] ensures that legal ownership is both simple in form and effective in operation. The expression "estate owner" means the owner of one of the two legal estates in land; it should also be noted that by section 1(6), a legal estate cannot be held by an infant.

Not every fee simple is capable of subsisting as a legal estate, but

---

[1] *e.g.* under the principle discussed at pp. 25–26.
[2] LPA 1925, s.1(3).
[3] *i.e.* the legal estates.
[4] See p. 27 and Chap. 8.

only a fee simple absolute in possession. As defined by the Act,[5] possession includes receipt of rents and profits of the land, or the right to receive the same, if any. Hence, if the ordinary fee simple owner (or freehold owner, as we generally call him) grants a lease of the land to a lessee, the fee simple remains "in possession" and a legal estate, despite the fact that the lessee acquires the physical possession of the land. But a fee simple which is in remainder or reversion is not "in possession" and cannot, therefore, be a legal estate. For example, if land is settled on A for life with remainder to B in fee simple, B's fee simple remainder is an equitable interest, not a legal estate. Similarly, if the fee simple owner, S, settles land on A for life with remainder to B in tail, S has a fee simple reversion which is merely an equitable interest. The contrast between S's reversion in this case, and the so-called reversion of a landlord who has granted a lease, is so marked that the use of the same word to refer to both can only be regarded as inept. The reversion of a settlor under a family settlement is essentially a *future* interest, entitling him to no present rights whatever of enjoying the property, whether by occupying it or by taking the rents and profits; in contrast, the landlord's reversion on a lease, *i.e.* his legal estate subject to the lease, carries with it all the *present* rights reserved to him by the lease.

An estate is not "absolute" if either its commencement or its duration is made dependent on some contingency which may or may not occur. If an estate is limited to commence on the happening of some future uncertain event, such as the grantee attaining a particular age, it is neither absolute nor in possession: the grantee has merely a conditional interest, and the disposition must be effected by way of trust. Equally, if the grantee has an estate which is limited to *determine* on the happening of some future uncertain event, such as his becoming bankrupt, it is not absolute, but either determinable or (where the provision is expressed as a condition) conditional: the distinction is somewhat technical, but the main difference is that a determinable interest comes to an end automatically in the event stipulated, whereas breach of condition merely gives rise to a right of re-entry whereby the grantor may re-enter the land and forfeit the grantee's estate. In either case, land subject to an interest determinable whether by limitation or by condition is "settled land", and accordingly subject to a trust.[6]

The expression "term of years" is synonymous with leasehold: it is defined[7] as including "a term of less than a year, or for a year or

[5] s.205.
[6] See Chapter 8. There are minor exceptions under the LPA 1925, s.7.
[7] LPA 1925, s.205.

years and a fraction of a year, or from year to year"; and for the purposes of the Act, a term of years is nonetheless absolute even though liable to determination by notice (as in the case of periodic tenancies) or by re-entry (as where the landlord reserves the right to forfeit the lease for breach of the tenant's obligations) or by cesser on redemption (as in the case of a mortgage term). It should be noted that a legal term of years need not be in possession: a lease to commence at some future time[8] may accordingly subsist as a legal estate.

Legal interests

Section 1(2) of the Law of Property Act 1925 reduces to five the number of incumbrances, or rights against the land of another, which can subsist as legal interests. These are—

   (i)   an easement, right or privilege in or over land for an interest equivalent to an estate in fee simple absolute in possession or a term of years absolute;

  (ii)   a rentcharge in possession issuing out of or charged on land being either perpetual or for a term of years absolute;

 (iii)   a charge by way of legal mortgage;

 (iv)   certain statutory charges on land;

  (v)   rights of entry exercisable over or in respect of a legal term of years absolute, or annexed for any purpose to a legal rentcharge.[9]

We shall come across most of these rights in due course.

All other interests which could have been created against the land of another before 1926 can still be created today, but they will be merely equitable, not legal, interests.[10] It is not a question of employing a trust in order to create such an equitable interest—the interest will automatically be equitable if it is not in the list of five given above.

The reason why the Act has reduced the number of possible legal interests will be readily understood if one remembers that, as has been seen, every legal interest gives a right *in rem* which will

---

[8] Not more than 21 years from the grant of the lease (LPA 1925, s.149(3)): see p. 88.

[9] As to equitable rights of entry, see *Shiloh Spinners Ltd.* v. *Harding* [1973] A.C. 691, and p. 138 below. This case affords a valuable insight into the effect of the 1925 legislation in relation to legal and equitable rights in property, and the systems of overreaching and of registration.

[10] LPA 1925, s.1(3).

bind a purchaser of the land affected, whether he has notice of it or not. It is therefore advantageous to a purchaser that the number of such interests should be reduced to the minimum. When it is considered that this reduction in the number of legal interests is coupled with provision for the registration, under the Land Charges Act, of many equitable interests, and that a purchaser will not be bound by such an interest unless it is registered, it will be appreciated that conveyancing is safer from the point of view of a purchaser after 1925 than it was before 1926.

8. Settlements

A settlement of property is a disposition of property which creates a succession of interests in it, *e.g.* where property is settled on A for life with remainder to B in fee simple. Settlements of land are of two kinds, namely (i) the strict settlement,[1] which is governed by the Settled Land Act 1925, and (ii) the trust for sale, which is governed by the Law of Property Act 1925. The principal difference between the two is that under a strict settlement the legal estate (*i.e.* the fee simple where the land settled is freehold, or the term of years where it is leasehold), together with the powers of disposition over it, are and must be vested in the tenant for life (*i.e.* broadly, the person who is for the time being beneficially entitled in possession under the terms of the settlement), whereas under a trust for sale it is the trustees who have both the legal estate and the powers of disposition.

Whichever form of settlement is used, it should be remembered that the interests of those beneficially entitled under the settlement (in the example above, A's life interest in possession and B's fee simple in remainder) can only exist under a *trust*: as we have already seen, the fee simple absolute in possession and the term of years absolute are the only legal estates in land since 1925, and the interests of A and B are therefore both necessarily *equitable*. Furthermore, whatever form the settlement or trust takes, the machinery of the Settled Land Act and of the Law of Property Act enables the land (*i.e.* the legal estate) to be freely disposed of, and the beneficial interests to be overreached, *i.e.* detached from the land and attached instead to the proceeds of sale or capital money in the hands of the trustees. The detailed statutory provisions governing settlements are thus directed towards the twin aims of protecting first a purchaser of the land, secondly the beneficiaries.

The expression "settled land" means land which is subject to a strict settlement, and the broad effect of section 1 of the Settled Land Act is that land is settled land, and accordingly subject to the

---

[1] The expression "settlement" is commonly used as referring to strict settlements only.

Act, wherever it is limited in trust for persons by way of succession or is subject to family charges (*e.g.* an annuity in favour of the settlor's widow).[2] Land which is held upon immediate binding trust for sale, however, is excluded from the operation of the Act. Such a trust for sale will normally be imposed expressly by the settlor, with the specific object of avoiding the provisions of the Settled Land Act; but a trust for sale also arises by statute if two or more persons are entitled in possession to settled land in undivided shares.[3] It will be observed that the settlement will be a strict settlement governed by the Settled Land Act unless there is a trust for sale which is immediate and binding. A trust for sale is "immediate" if it is operative now and not merely in the future. Thus, if land is settled on A for life with remainder upon trust for sale for the benefit of B for life with remainders over (*i.e.* some further remainder or remainders), then during A's lifetime the land will be settled land and subject to the Settled Land Act, because the trust for sale is not immediate. When A dies, however, the trust for sale will become immediate and the land will cease to be settled land, and the Law of Property Act will then apply. The meaning of the word "binding" is a matter of doubt.[4] What is clear, however, is that land will be settled land unless there is a *trust* to sell it (*i.e.* an obligation to sell it), and that if the instrument purports merely to confer a *power* of sale on the trustees this will not take the settlement out of the Settled Land Act.

A trust for sale which otherwise is immediate and binding is not prevented from being so by reason of the fact that the trustees have power to postpone sale, or that they may be required to obtain the consents of specified persons before selling,[5] or that they may be directed to permit a beneficiary to reside on the land.[6] A trust to retain or sell land is to be construed as a trust for sale with power to postpone sale.[7]

STRICT SETTLEMENTS

Vesting instrument and trust instrument

To create a strict settlement *inter vivos* the settlor must employ

---

[2] The Act also applies where land is held in trust for a minor: see p. 162.
[3] SLA 1925, s.36(1). See p. 54, note 5.
[4] See M. & W. pp. 386–389.
[5] LPA 1925, s.205.
[6] *Re Herklots' W. T.* [1964] 1 W.L.R. 583.
[7] LPA 1925, s.25(4).

two documents, namely (i) a *vesting deed*, by which he transfers the land to the tenant for life, and (ii) a *trust instrument*, by which he declares the beneficial interests.[8] If the settlor himself is to be the tenant for life the vesting deed will declare that the land is vested in him.

If a strict settlement is created by will, the will ranks as the trust instrument, and the vesting deed is replaced by a vesting assent by which the testator's personal representatives transfer the land to the tenant for life.[9] (Personal representatives have the power to transfer land by a written instrument, which need not be under seal, called an "assent.")

The trust instrument must:

(i)   declare the trusts affecting the settled land;
(ii) appoint trustees of the settlement;
(iii) contain the power, if any, to appoint new trustees of the settlement;
(iv) set out any powers intended to be conferred by the settlement in extension of those conferred by the Act;
(v)   bear any stamp duty which may be payable in respect of the settlement.[10]

The vesting instrument (whether a deed or an assent) must contain the following statements and particulars:

(i)   a description of the settled land;
(ii) a statement that the settled land is vested in the person or persons to whom it is conveyed, or in whom it is declared to be vested, upon the trusts from time to time affecting the settled land;
(iii) the names of the persons who are the trustees of the settlement;
(iv) any additional or larger powers conferred by the trust instrument;
(v)   the name of any person for the time being entitled to appoint new trustees of the settlement.[11]

Tenant for life

The expression "tenant for life" is defined in detail in the Settled Land Act 1925, ss.19 and 20, and means broadly any person[12] of

---

[8] SLA 1925, s.4.
[9] *Ibid.* ss.6, 8.
[10] *Ibid.* s.4.
[11] *Ibid.* s.5.
[12] If two or more persons are *jointly* so entitled they together constitute the tenant for life.

full age who is for the time being entitled in possession either to the land itself or to the income of the land (*e.g.* when the land is already leased to tenants). The nature of his beneficial interest is irrelevant: whether he has a life interest itself, or an entailed interest, or a conditional or determinable fee, or even a fee simple or term of years absolute subject to family charges, he will be the tenant for life for the purposes of the Act, provided his interest is in possession.

It follows that only in rare cases will it happen that there is no person who satisfies the statutory definition of tenant for life. If, however, there is no such person,[13] or if there is but he is not of full age, the settled land and the statutory powers of disposition will be vested in the "statutory owner." This is defined[14] as the person of full age upon whom the settlement expressly confers the powers of a tenant for life, or, in any other case, the trustees of the settlement.

Powers of tenant for life

The statutory powers of a tenant for life are contained in Part II of the Settled Land Act 1925. They include extensive powers of disposition and management which bind the settled land, *i.e.* the whole legal estate, not merely his own beneficial interest.

These powers may be enlarged by the express terms of the settlement, and any powers which the settlement purports to confer on the trustees or on other persons will be regarded as additional powers of the tenant for life, exercisable by him alone.[15]

The most important of the statutory powers are those of sale, leasing, and raising money on mortgage.

1. Power of sale

The tenant for life may sell the settled land or any part thereof, or any easement, right or privilege of any kind over or in relation to the land.

2. Leasing powers

The tenant for life may grant a building lease or a forestry lease for a term not exceeding 999 years; a mining lease for a term not

---

[13] For examples, see *Re Frewen* [1926] Ch. 580; *Re Gallenga* [1938] 1 All E.R. 106.
[14] SLA 1925, ss.23(1), 117(1) (xxvi). References throughout this chapter to the tenant for life should be taken as referring to one who is of full age, and as including the statutory owner, except where the context indicates the contrary.
[15] *Ibid.* ss.108, 109.

exceeding 100 years[16]; and any other lease for a term not exceeding 50 years.

3. Power to mortgage

The tenant for life may raise money by mortgage of the settled land for a number of purposes specified in section 71 of the Act, and in particular in order to pay for *improvements* authorised by the Act under provisions whch we are now to consider.

4. Improvements

The tenant for life may require capital money, including money raised by mortgage, to be applied in payment for certain improvements, which are specified in the Third Schedule to the Act. This Schedule is divided into three parts. Part I contains a long list of improvements including the construction of drainage, farm roads and farm-houses and other farm buildings. In respect of these the tenant for life cannot be required to repay the cost. Part II contains a much shorter list which includes the building of dwelling-houses generally and the restoration or reconstruction of buildings damaged or destroyed by dry rot. In this case the trustees of the settlement *may* (and shall if so directed by the court) require that the money expended be repaid to them out of the income of the settled land by not more than 50 half-yearly instalments. Part III includes items such as the provision of heating, hydraulic or electric power apparatus for buildings, the installation of artificial light in any building, and the purchase of movable machinery for farming or other purposes. In this case the trustees of the settlement *must* require repayment by such instalments as have been mentioned.

Personal character of statutory powers

The powers conferred by the Act upon a tenant for life are personal to him and they remain with him notwithstanding any assignment of his beneficial interest, whether express or by operation of law, *e.g.* on his bankruptcy (when his beneficial interest would pass to his trustee in bankruptcy for the benefit of his creditors).[17]

An exception to this principle arises when a tenant for life, with intent to extinguish his beneficial interest, assigns it to the person

---

[16] See p. 21.

[17] SLA 1925, s.104, which also provides that any contract not to exercise the statutory powers shall be void.

next entitled in remainder or reversion under the settlement. The remainder is then accelerated and the tenant for life loses his statutory powers.[18] For example, if land is settled on A for life with remainder to B for life, and A assigns his life interest to B (who is of full age) with intent to extinguish it, the remainder is accelerated, B becomes the tenant for life under the Settled Land Act, and A must by vesting deed convey the legal estate to him. Had the remainder to B been in fee simple the remainder again would have been accelerated and the settlement would have come to an end.

If a tenant for life has ceased (by reason of bankruptcy, assignment or otherwise) to have a substantial interest in the settled land, and either he has unreasonably refused to exercise any of his statutory powers, or he consents to an order, the court may make an order authorising the trustees of the settlement to exercise in the name and on behalf of the tenant for life any of the powers conferred upon him by the Act. To this extent the tenant for life is then precluded from exercising his powers.[19]

Protection of statutory powers

The Act invalidates any provision in a settlement which purports to exclude or restrict the powers conferred by the Act on a tenant for life: any provision in the settlement is void to the extent that it would even tend to prevent a tenant for life from exercising the powers.[20] For example, if the settlement provides that the tenant for life's interest shall come to an end if he ceases to reside on the settled land, this provision will be valid, and the tenant for life will lose his beneficial interest, if he ceases to occupy the land for some reason other than the exercise of his statutory powers; but if in exercise of the powers he sells or leases the land and for that reason ceases to reside there, the provision for forfeiture of his beneficial interest will be void, and he will continue to be entitled to the income of the land, either from the proceeds of sale or from the rents under the lease.[21]

The tenant for life as trustee

As we have seen, the legal estate in the land (*i.e.* the fee simple or, if the property settled is leasehold, the term of years) is vested

---

[18] *Ibid.* s.105.
[19] *Ibid.* s.24.
[20] *Ibid.* s.106.
[21] *Re Acklom* [1929] 1 Ch. 195. See also p. 44.

in the tenant for life together with the statutory powers of disposition. The tenant for life is not the beneficial owner of the legal estate—if he were, there could be no settlement because there would be no succession of interests. He holds the legal estate upon trust for all the beneficiaries—including himself—in accordance with the terms of the trust instrument. A tenant for life, therefore, is in a dual position. Under the trust instrument he has whatever beneficial interest is conferred upon him, *e.g.* a life interest or an entailed interest, and of this he is absolute owner. Under the vesting instrument he has the entire legal estate, but this he holds as trustee.

The Act provides generally that a tenant for life shall, in exercising any power under the Act, have regard to the interests of all parties entitled under the settlement, and shall in relation to the exercise thereof by him be deemed to be in the position and to have the duties and liabilities of a trustee for those parties.[22] The effect of this, however, is merely to restrain an improper use of the powers, rather than to afford a means of directing their exercise. Thus, if one of two joint tenants for life wishes to sell the property, and the other wishes to retain it, the court cannot order sale.[23] The same principle would apply if a dispute were to arise between the tenant for life and a remainderman: the latter might have much the more substantial interest in the land, but he could not compel the tenant for life to exercise his statutory powers,[24] however advantageous it might be to dispose of the land; nor, on the other hand, could he challenge the exercise of the powers, except where he could prove fraud.[25] The Act thus ensures the autonomy of the tenant for life, but at the cost of omitting any effective means of protecting the interests of other beneficiaries under a settlement.

The tenant for life is not as such a "trustee of the settlement." The trustees of the settlement must be expressly appointed by the trust instrument, and they have distinct functions under the Act.[26]

The tenant for life can make no disposition of the land except such as the Settled Land Act authorises him to make,[27] and although the Act gives him wide powers of disposition, it attaches conditions which are designed to protect the interests of the other beneficiaries. Thus, in respect of most transactions he is required to give written notice to the trustees of the settlement; exceptionally, he may be required to obtain their consent or an order of

---

[22] SLA 1925, s.107.
[23] *Re 90 Thornhill Road, Tolworth, Surrey* [1970] Ch. 261.
[24] A possible exception arises under SLA 1925, s.24 (see note 19).
[25] See *Cardigan* v. *Curzon-Howe* (1885) 30 Ch. D. 531.
[26] There is nothing to prevent the tenant for life being expressly appointed as a trustee of the settlement.
[27] SLA 1925, s.18.

the court.[28] Again, on a sale or lease of the settled land he must obtain the best consideration in money, or the best rent, that can reasonably be obtained. Above all, any capital money arising on a disposition of the settled land must be paid, not to the tenant for life, but to the trustees of the settlement, who will then hold it upon the same trusts as those affecting the land.

Under the draconian terms of section 18 of the Act, an unauthorised disposition of settled land is *void*[29]: there is, surprisingly, no exception in favour of a purchaser of a legal estate without notice that the land is settled. The unfortunate but inevitable result is that if a tenant for life fraudulently disposes of the land for his own benefit, the purchaser acquires no title even though he acted in good faith and had no means of knowing that the land was subject to a settlement.[30]

Dealings between the tenant for life and the estate

If special provision had not been made by the Act, the fiduciary position of the tenant for life would have precluded any dealing between himself and the estate: for example, it would not have been possible for him to purchase or take a lease of the settled land for his own benefit.

Of course he already holds his life or other interest beneficially, and by virtue of this is entitled to occupy the settled land or receive the rents and profits during his life; but it may happen that he wishes to acquire a more permanent interest, such as the fee simple or a long lease for his own purposes. Equity resolves any possible conflict between duty and interest by prohibiting such dealings altogether, even though shown not to be prejudicial,[31] but by section 68 of the Act they are permitted if a prescribed procedure is followed. The tenant for life must inform the trustees of the settlement of his wish, *e.g.* to purchase all or part of the settled land, and the trustees of the settlement then take over the powers of the tenant for life with regard to that transaction. They will decide whether the transaction should be permitted and, if they agree in principle, will negotiate the terms of the transaction with the tenant for life.

[28] With respect to dispositions of the "principal mansion house" (if the settlement expressly so requires), felling of timber (if he is impeachable for waste: see p. 20), and sale of settled chattels (which requires an order of the court). (SLA 1925, ss.65–67.)
[29] Except to the extent of the tenant for life's own beneficial interest; and of course the purchaser has a remedy against the tenant for life personally.
[30] *Weston* v. *Henshaw* [1950] Ch. 510, in which the tenant for life suppressed the vesting instrument, and produced previous title deeds appearing to show that he was beneficially entitled in fee simple.
[31] *Fox* v. *Mackreth* (1791) 2 Cox Eq. 320.

Overreaching

When the tenant for life sells the land, or any part of it, in exercise of his statutory power of sale, the purchaser must pay his purchase money to the trustees of the settlement and ensure that they are at least two in number or a trust corporation (*i.e.* a corporation authorised by law to undertake trust business).[32] If he does so he will acquire and land free from the interests of the beneficiaries under the settlement, even though he knows of their existence.[33] But the beneficiaries are not prejudiced, because, as we have seen, the proceeds of sale are held by the trustees upon the same trusts as those upon which the land was held by the tenant for life before the sale. The interests of the beneficiaries, therefore, are said to be overreached, because they are taken away from the land and attached instead to the proceeds of sale. Any other disposition which the tenant for life is authorised by the Act to make, such as a mortgage or lease, has a similar overreaching effect.

As an illustration, suppose that land has been settled upon A for life, with remainder to B in fee simple. A is the tenant for life and the legal fee simple will have been vested in him by the vesting instrument. Now suppose that in the exercise of his statutory power of sale A has sold half the settled land. The half that has not been sold remains vested in A and he holds it upon trust for himself for life with remainder to B in fee simple. The proceeds of sale of the other half will have been paid to the trustees of the settlement, and the purchaser accordingly will take the land free from the interests of A and B. The trustees normally will invest the proceeds in authorised trustee securities.[34] These securities will be registered in the names of the trustees of the settlement, who will hold them upon trust for A for life with remainder to B: A will be entitled to the income from the investments during his life, and after A's death B will be entitled absolutely, and may require the trustees to transfer the investments into his own name.

In addition to beneficial interests subsisting or capable of arising under the settlement, a disposition by the tenant for life overreaches certain financial charges, even if created before the settlement and even if registered under the Land Charges Act 1925 or 1972.[35]

---

[32] SLA 1925, s.18. Capital money may alternatively be paid into court.
[33] *Ibid.* s.72; LPA 1925, s.2.
[34] See SLA 1925, s.73, for other authorised modes of applying capital money. These include the purchase of other land (freehold or a leasehold having 60 years or more to run), which will be brought into the settlement and conveyed to the tenant for life by subsidiary vesting deed.
[35] Annuities, limited owners' charges, and general equitable charges, as defined by that Act: see p. 175.

The "curtain" principle

On a sale, lease, mortgage or other disposition of settled land, a purchaser dealing in good faith with the tenant for life is conclusively taken to have given the best price, consideration or rent that could reasonably be obtained, and to have complied with all the requisitions of the Act.[36] The purpose of this provision is to protect the purchaser, not the tenant for life. If, for example, the tenant for life sells at an undervalue, he will be liable for breach of trust to the other beneficiaries under the settlement, but the purchaser will be protected. On the other hand, a purchaser cannot rely on this provision unless he deals with the tenant for life *as such, i.e.* on the faith of the vesting instrument, and pays any capital money to the trustees of the settlement.[37]

The purchaser is neither bound nor even entitled to inspect the trust instrument[38]: this relates to interests which will be overreached by the conveyance to him and he is therefore in no way concerned with it. It is therefore said to be "behind the curtain" as regards the purchaser. On the other hand, he is very much concerned with the vesting instrument, which is designed to give him information that he requires, including the names of the trustees of the settlement, to whom he must pay his purchase money, and he is, in general, required to assume the accuracy of the statements in this instrument.[38] There are certain exceptions to these rules, of which the most important are subsisting settlements created before 1926 and imperfectly constituted post-1925 settlements.

Pre-1926 and imperfect settlements

Until 1926 a strict settlement could be created either by conveying the land to trustees on trust for the beneficiaries in succession, or by conveying it directly to the beneficiaries themselves, *e.g.* to A for life, with remainder to B in fee simple. Neither of these procedures is possible after 1925, and accordingly there are transitional provisions[39] which ensure that in all cases where a pre-1926 settlement was still in existence at the end of 1925 not only the powers of disposition but also the entire legal estate should be vested in the tenant for life, and that a vesting

---

[36] SLA 1925, s.110(1).
[37] See *Weston* v. *Henshaw* (a decision based on s.18), note 30; distinguish *Re Morgan's Lease* [1972] Ch. 1, in which no capital money was involved, and no issue arose on s.18.
[38] SLA 1925, s.110.
[39] SLA 1925, 2nd Sched.; LPA 1925, 1st Sched.

instrument should be executed in his favour. The detail of these elaborate provisions need not concern us: their broad effect is, first, that the legal estate was automatically vested in the tenant for life on January 1, 1926;[40] and, secondly, that the tenant for life could require the trustees of the settlement to execute a vesting deed declaring that the legal estate was vested in him in accordance with the provisions of the Settled Land Act 1925. The old settlement remains in effect, but only as a trust instrument, and this is one of the cases in which the curtain principle does not operate: accordingly a purchaser must examine the trust instrument in order to ensure that the land disposed of is comprised in the settlement and is vested in the appropriate person as tenant for life, and that the trustees are the properly constituted trustees of the settlement.[41]

If after 1925 a settlor attempts to create an *inter vivos* settlement otherwise than by the authorised method, the legal estate does not pass.[42] If, for example, the settlor employs one document only, purporting to deal with both the legal estate and the beneficial interests, or if he purports to convey the legal estate to trustees instead of to the tenant for life, the legal estate will remain with the settlor. The abortive settlement takes effect as a trust instrument only, and the tenant for life can require that the legal estate be vested in him. Although the legal estate is still with the settlor, the Act provides[43] that it is the trustees of the settlement who must execute the vesting deed in favour of the tenant for life; the effect of the deed is then to take the legal estate from the settlor and vest it in the tenant for life. This is another case, however, in which the curtain principle does not apply.[44]

Section 13 (known as the paralysing section) provides that until a vesting instrument has been executed, any purported disposition of settled land shall not take effect except in favour of a purchaser of the legal estate without notice that the tenant for life is entitled to a vesting instrument, but shall operate only as a contract to carry out the transaction once the vesting instrument has been executed. But the section does not prevent a disposition by personal representatives (where the settlement arises by will), nor does it apply where the settlement has come

---

[40] Except where the legal estate was in personal representatives immediately before that date, in which case they held it on trust to convey it to the tenant for life (subject to their powers of administration).
[41] SLA 1925, s.110.
[42] *Ibid.* s.4.
[43] *Ibid.* ss.4, 9.
[44] See note 41.

to an end before a vesting instrument has been executed,[45] or where land is settled only by reason of being subject to family charges.[46]

Duration of settlement

Once a settlement comes into operation the land remains settled land so long as any beneficial interest under the settlement subsists or is capable of arising, or so long as the beneficial owner is an infant.[47] Suppose, for example, that land is settled on A for life with remainder to B in fee simple, but subject to a jointure rentcharge for A's widow (*i.e* subject to a charge upon the land for payment of an annuity to A's widow during her widowhood). Upon the death of A, leaving a widow, the land remains settled land because it is still subject to the charge, and B is the tenant for life. If B, as tenant for life, sells the land under his statutory power of sale, the widow's rentcharge will be overreached. The widow will not be prejudiced, however, because the proceeds of sale will be paid to the trustees of the settlement, who will be responsible for paying the annuity to the widow out of the income from the proceeds. Alternatively, in this particular case, when the land is settled land by reason only that it is subject to such a charge for the payment of money, the Law of Property (Amendment) Act 1926 allows B to sell the land subject to the charge as if it were not settled land and himself receive the proceeds of sale.

The purpose of this curious provision is obscure. Parliament, having in 1925 decided to include land subject to family charges in the definition of settled land and thus enable the overreaching machinery of the Settled Land Act to be used, seems only partly to have changed its mind in 1926 by empowering the beneficial owner (who is also "tenant for life" under the Act) to dispose of the land with the charge still attached. It is difficult to understand how this could be of advantage to anyone—whether the vendor, the purchaser or the annuitant: the most that could be said in its favour is that it avoids the necessity of a vesting instrument and other formalities under the Settled Land Act—though of course, paradoxically, the land in the purchaser's hands is still nominally settled land, and he is the "tenant for life" (with the same power to dispose of it either under the Settled Land Act, or under the 1926 Act). If on the other hand the object of proceeding under the 1926 Act is merely to enable the vendor (as beneficial owner,

---

[45] *Re Alefounder's W.T.* [1927] 1 Ch. 360.
[46] See below.
[47] SLA 1925, s.3.

rather than as tenant for life) to receive the proceeds of sale himself, this could in any event be achieved more effectively by arranging with the annuitant to release her annuity in return for an appropriate share of the proceeds, or by making a payment into court under the Law of Property Act 1925, s.50, whereupon the rentcharge would be discharged (and the land, in whoever's hands it might be, would cease to be settled land).

Death of tenant for life

If on the death of a tenant for life the land remains settled land, the trustees of the settlement are entitled to a grant of probate (if the tenant for life died testate) or letters of administration, limited to the settled land. They then become his special personal representatives with regard to the settled land,[48] and must vest the settled land in the next tenant for life.[49] On the other hand, if when a tenant for life dies the land ceases to be settled land, the land will devolve upon his general (*i.e.* ordinary) personal representatives,[50] who will vest it in the person or persons entitled to it. For example, if land is settled on A for life with remainder to B for life with remainder to C in fee simple, then on the death of A the settled land will devolve upon A's special personal representatives. They will vest the land in B, the next tenant for life, by means of a vesting assent.[51] But when B dies the land will cease to be settled land. It will therefore devolve upon B's general personal representatives and they will vest it in C by a simple written assent (a vesting assent will not be appropriate as the land will have ceased to be settled land).

Premature determination of tenant for life's interest

If the tenant for life has a determinable interest, *e.g.* if land is settled on A for life or until he marries, or until he ceases to reside on the land, with remainders over, the legal estate and statutory powers of disposition will be vested in him. If his interest later determines (on his marriage or on his ceasing to reside, as the case may be) he ceases to be tenant for life and no longer has the statutory powers: but the legal estate remains with him—there is no statutory divesting. He holds the legal estate as a bare trustee, and is bound to convey it to the person next entitled: if the remainderman is entitled absolutely an ordinary conveyance will

---

[48] AEA 1925, s.22.
[49] SLA 1925, s.7.
[50] *Re Bridgett and Hayes' Contract* [1928] Ch. 163.
[51] SLA 1925, s.8.

be appropriate; if not, *i.e.* if the settlement continues and the remainderman is tenant for life, A should convey the legal estate to him by vesting deed.[52]

A difficult question would arise, however, if A in good faith but mistakenly purported as tenant for life to dispose of the land in exercise of the statutory powers after his interest had determined: such a disposition would clearly be in breach of trust, but the question is whether a purchaser from A would get a good title as against the persons entitled under the settlement. The position appears to be as follows: (i) the disposition is not void, and the purchaser acquires the legal estate; (ii) the purchaser is not protected by the overreaching provisions of the Settled Land Act, even though on the faith of the vesting instrument he assumed he was dealing with the tenant for life, and even though he paid the purchase money to the trustees of the settlement; (iii) the beneficial interests under the settlement bind him only if he had notice of them: he necessarily had notice that there was a trust, but it was a trust which he assumed he was overreaching, and which he assumed he was precluded from investigating; it may be doubted whether in these circumstances equity would regard him as bound by the particular interests of those entitled under the settlement, and it seems likely the latter would be confined to their respective interests in the proceeds held by the trustees.

Deed of discharge

If a settlement comes to an end otherwise than on the death of the tenant for life, the trustees of the settlement may be required to execute a deed of discharge, *i.e.* a deed declaring that they are discharged from the trusts of the settlement. In the event of any difficulty the court may be asked to make an order of discharge which will have the same effect. Unless the deed or order of discharge states the contrary (*e.g.* indicates that the land is still settled land under a derivative settlement) a purchaser of the land will be entitled to assume that the land has ceased to be settled land and is not subject to a trust for sale.[53]

Thus, a deed of discharge would be required if the settlement came to an end by reason of some dealing with the beneficial interests, *e.g.* if the tenant for life had an entailed interest and barred the entail. In such case the former tenant for life would now be entitled absolutely, and could call for a deed of discharge to enable him to make title as beneficial owner (rather than as trustee), and in particular to receive any proceeds of sale himself.

---

[52] *Ibid.* ss.7, 8.
[53] *Ibid.* s.17.

A deed of discharge is not necessary, however, if the settlement has come to an end on the death of the tenant for life. In that event, as we have seen, the legal estate will devolve upon his general personal representatives, and they will transfer it by simple assent or ordinary conveyance to the person or persons entitled. A subsequent purchaser upon investigating the title to the land will see that it has been disposed of by this means, and will be bound and entitled to assume that the land in question has ceased to be settled land,[54] and that he is no longer required to pay the purchase money to the trustees of the settlement or into court.

TRUSTS FOR SALE

Trusts for sale are not solely employed as a method of creating settlements of land outside the provisions of the Settled Land Act. They are equally important in two quite different situations where a trust for sale is imposed by statute, namely co-ownership (under the Law of Property Act 1925, ss.34–36) and intestacy (under the Administration of Estates Act 1925, s.33).[55]

Technically a trust for sale of land is not a settlement of land, but of money, by reason of the equitable doctrine of conversion, which in turn is based on the maxim "equity looks upon that as done which ought to be done."[56] As the trustees are under an obligation to sell the land, equity regards the land as having already been sold, and this is so even if the trustees have the usual power to postpone sale (trustees for sale of land always have power to postpone the sale unless the trust instrument otherwise provides).[57] The interests of the beneficiaries under a trust for sale, therefore, are in theory interests in money from the beginning. The doctrine creates problems of definition, and appears to serve no useful purpose today: clearly it cannot of itself deprive a beneficiary under a trust for sale of the right to occupy the land, provided his interest is in possession, not in remainder or reversion.[58]

Procedure

To create a trust for sale *inter vivos* the settlor conveys the land

---

[54] *Ibid.* s.110(5).
[55] See Chaps. 9 and 24 respectively. The general discussion of trusts for sale in the present chapter should be taken as applying equally to statutory trusts for sale.
[56] For another application of this maxim, see p. 25.
[57] LPA 1925, s.25.
[58] See p. 60.

to trustees upon trust to sell it and to hold the net rents and profits pending sale and the proceeds of sale after sale upon trust for certain beneficiaries, *e.g.* on trust for A for life with remainder to B absolutely. The trustees then have the legal estate in the land (*i.e.* the legal fee simple or, if the property is leasehold, the legal term of years) and the beneficiaries have successive equitable interests in the land or (technically) in the proceeds of sale. Thus, in the example given, A has the right to occupy the land or to receive the net rents and profits of the land pending sale and the income from the investments of the proceeds of sale after sale. Upon the death of A, if the land has been sold B will be entitled to require the trustees to transfer to him the investments made with the proceeds of sale; if the land remains unsold the trustees must convey it to B: in either case the trust for sale is at an end.

Both the conveyance of the land to the trustees and the declaration of the trusts can be done in one document; there is no two-document rule as in the case of strict settlements. But except in simple cases it is good conveyancing practice to employ two documents, namely (i) a conveyance upon trust for sale and (ii) a separate trust instrument. If this is done, the conveyance transfers the land and imposes the trust to sell it, but does not set out the beneficial interests: these are set out in the trust instrument. The "curtain" principle then operates, *i.e.* a purchaser of the land from the trustees is not concerned with the trust instrument.

When land is given by will upon trust for sale there normally are two documents. The testator's personal representatives will transfer the land to the trustees by a written assent upon trust for sale. This assent will then correspond to the conveyance upon trust for sale and will not declare the beneficial interests. The will itself operates as the trust instrument: it must be referred to in order to ascertain what the beneficial interests are, but so far as a purchaser is concerned it is "behind the curtain."[59]

Effect of dispositions

Under section 27 of the Law of Property Act 1925, a purchaser from trustees for sale is not concerned with the trusts affecting the land or the proceeds of sale, and this applies even though the trusts might be declared in the instrument which vested the legal estate in the trustees[60]; but the proceeds must not be paid to fewer than two persons as trustees for sale, unless the trustee is a trust corporation.[61] The beneficial interests under the trust are thus

[59] AEA 1925, s.36.
[60] LPA 1925, s.27(1).
[61] *Ibid.* s.27(2).

overreached, in accordance with section 2 of the Law of Property Act 1925, in much the same way as they are on a disposition by a tenant for life of settled land. What the provisions of the Law of Property Act fail to indicate, however, is the effect of a disposition where capital money has not been paid as required by the Act, *e.g.* where the disposition is made by a sole individual trustee. An "unauthorised" disposition of settled land is rendered void by section 18 of the Settled Land Act,[62] but there is no equivalent provision in the Law of Property Act with respect to land held on trust for sale. The result appears to be that a purchaser from a sole individual trustee for sale acquires the legal estate (because the disposition to him is not void), but takes subject to the beneficial interests under the trust unless he has no notice of them—but of course in the case of an express trust for sale he necessarily has notice of them: it is only where a trust for sale arises by statute or by implication that the plea of purchaser without notice might avail him. [63]

Consents to dispositions

Trusts for sale are commonly made subject to a condition that the land shall not be sold without the consent of named persons.[64] Furthermore, the Act provides[65] that trustees for sale shall so far as practicable give effect to the wishes of the persons of full age who are for the time being entitled in possession, and the courts may imply a condition that the consent of any such person must be obtained where a settlor has directed that a beneficiary may occupy the land for life.[66] If the trustees fail to obtain the requisite consents (or an order of the court) they will be in breach of trust, but in favour of a purchaser it is sufficient if two such consents are obtained.[67]

As we have seen, trustees for sale generally have power to postpone sale. However, since there is a trust and therefore an obligation to sell the land, any trustee or any person beneficially entitled can in principle insist upon an immediate sale; and if the

[62] See note 30.

[63] See p. 56.

[64] Such a condition would generally be void in the case of strict settlements (see p. 37, note 20).

[65] LPA 1925, s.26(3). The provision is in terms confined to statutory trusts for sale and those created expressly and indicating an intention that it shall apply: it is difficult to envisage circumstances where trustees could properly ignore it, but in any case a purchaser is not concerned to see that it is complied with.

[66] *Re Herklots' W.T.* [1964] 1 W.L.R. 583, in which the consents of both the beneficiary in possession and the remainderman were held to be required in the special circumstances.

[67] LPA 1925, s.26(1).

co-trustees refuse to join in the sale, or if any requisite consents to sale cannot be obtained, application may be made to the court for an order of sale under the Law of Property Act 1925, s.30. On the other hand, the true purpose of the trust may often be something quite other than sale of the land, as where the settlor indicates an intention that the successive beneficiaries shall have the right to reside there[68]: in such circumstances it is unlikely that a sale would be ordered if this would defeat the manifest purpose of the trust. In a dispute between a beneficiary entitled in possession and a remainderman the wishes of the former are likely to prevail, but in some circumstances an order of sale might be refused if sale would unduly prejudice the interest of the remainderman; and if a person whose consent is expressly required has an interest contingent on the land remaining unsold, it may be doubted whether the court could properly dispense with his consent and order sale, since the effect of doing so would be to defeat his interest altogether.[69] Paradoxically, it thus appears that as a means of retaining land unsold the trust for sale may be more effective than the strict settlement, under which the tenant for life has virtually arbitrary powers of disposition, and a virtually unfettered discretion whether or not to exercise them; and the courts, under the jurisdiction conferred by the Law of Property Act 1925, s.30, are able to exercise over trusts for sale a measure of control which is signally lacking in the case of settlements under the Settled Land Act 1925.[70]

Powers of trustees for sale

The Law of Property Act 1925, s.28, provides that trustees for sale shall, in relation to land and to the proceeds of sale, have all the powers of a tenant for life and the trustees of a settlement under the Settled Land Act 1925. Before exercising any such power, however, the trustees must obtain the same consents, if any, as would have been required on a sale of the land. The trustees, for example, will have the same powers of granting leases of the land as a tenant for life would have had, and the same powers of investment as the trustees of the settlement would have had, if the land had been settled land.

One of the consequences of this provision is that trustees for sale who have sold part of their land may use the proceeds of sale for

---

[68] See note 66.

[69] *Re Inns* [1947] Ch. 576. The effect may be to render the land unsaleable, and even to cast doubt on the "binding" nature of the trust for sale (see p. 33, note 4).

[70] Cf. p. 38.

the purchase of other land, being freehold or a leasehold having at least 60 years to run.[71] Any such land will be conveyed to the trustees and will be held by them upon trust for sale.[72] But it has been held that once trustees for sale have sold all their land they no longer possess this power, and therefore cannot buy land unless such a power is expressly conferred upon them by the terms of the trust.[73]

Another consequence of the provision is that capital money held by trustees for sale may be applied to payment for improvements to land still held by them in the same way that capital money under the Settled Land Act may be used to pay for improvements. Trustees for sale always have power to pay for the cost of repairs out of income. It will sometimes happen that a particular repair is also an improvement within the Settled Land Act, or some other improvement of a permanent nature,[74] in which case the trustees will have a discretion as to whether that repair shall be paid for out of income or out of capital. Subject to this, income from the land, *e.g.* where it is let to tenants, will of course be paid to the person beneficially entitled in possession under the trust.

Trustees for sale may by writing revocably delegate from time to time their powers of leasing, accepting surrenders of leases, and management to any person of full age (not being merely an annuitant) for the time being beneficially entitled in possession to the net rents and profits of the land during his life or for any less period.[75]

SPECIAL (OR AD HOC) TRUSTS FOR SALE AND AD HOC SETTLEMENTS

If the trustees of a trust for sale are either (i) two or more persons approved or appointed by the court, or their successors in office, or (ii) a trust corporation, a conveyance by them to a purchaser has a somewhat wider overreaching effect than would otherwise be the case. Certain equitable interests having priority to the trust for sale can be overreached which could not have been overreached if the trust for sale had not been in this special category.[76] A trust for sale may be specially set up in order that a contemplated sale of the land shall have this wider overreaching

---

[71] See *Re Wellsted's W. T.* [1949] Ch. 296, C.A.
[72] LPA 1925, s.28.
[73] *Re Wakeman* [1945] Ch. 177.
[74] *Re Smith* [1930] 1 Ch. 88.
[75] LPA 1925, s.29.
[76] *Ibid.* s.2.

effect, in which case the trust for sale may be called an ad hoc trust for sale.

Very similarly, an estate owner may set up an ad hoc settlement under the Settled Land Act 1925, for the express purpose of overreaching equitable interests which could not otherwise have been overreached. The trustees of the settlement must then be two or more persons approved or appointed by the court or a trust corporation.[77]

These provisions of the Law of Property Act 1925 and the Settled Land Act 1925 are little used and are relatively unimportant.[78]

SETTLEMENTS OLD AND NEW

Traditionally, the typical settlement was a marriage settlement. If it was desired to keep the land in the family as far as possible, a strict settlement was used, whereas if the land was regarded as an investment a trust for sale was employed (and the settlement was then often known as a trader's settlement).

Assuming that the land was brought into the settlement by the husband and that a strict settlement was used, the husband would settle the land on himself for life with remainder to his first and other sons successively in order of seniority in tail. Subsidiary provision would also be made for the wife, both during the marriage and during the widowhood, and for any younger sons and daughters of the marriage. When the eldest son came of age, his father would induce him to bar the entail with his consent, thereby converting the fee tail into a full fee simple. This fee simple would then be resettled on the son for life with remainder to *his* sons in tail. The result would be that when the father died and the son came into possession of the land he would do so as a mere tenant for life. This process of re-settlement would be repeated generation by generation, and in consequence the tenant in possession of the land at any given time would have only a life estate and no power to dispose of the land in fee simple. So undesirable were the social and economic consequences of this device for keeping the land in the same family that Parliament felt compelled to intervene and finally, by the Settled Land Act 1882, adopted the drastic solution of conferring upon the tenant for life a statutory power to sell the land or any part of it which no provision in the settlement could exclude or restrict. This provision has been

[77] SLA 1925, s.21.
[78] See M. & W. pp. 405–410.

re-enacted by the 1925 Act,[79] and in consequence the use of a strict settlement by no means ensures that the land will be kept in the family even for one generation.

If a marriage settlement was made by the husband by means of a trust for sale, the essential trusts would be for the husband for life with remainder to the wife for life if she survived him, with remainder to the children or remoter issue of the marriage in such shares as the husband and wife should jointly by deed appoint and, in default of such appointment, as the survivor should by deed or will appoint and, in default, for such of the children of the marriage as should attain the age of 21 or being females marry under that age.

Having regard to the historical difference between the strict settlement and the trust for sale, it is odd that today it is possible by means of the trust for sale to ensure that land is kept in the family at least for a time, whereas this is not possible if a strict settlement is employed. When a strict settlement is used no restriction can be imposed upon the statutory power of sale which is given to the tenant for life; but when a trust for sale is employed the trustees can be required to obtain the consents of specified persons before selling, and a sale that would defeat the true purpose of the trust may be restrained.[80]

Settlements in either form may carry a heavy burden of taxation: if property is settled on beneficiaries in succession, tax (formerly estate duty, later replaced by capital transfer tax, now in turn replaced by inheritance tax) is payable on the full capital value of the property each time a beneficiary dies. For this reason trusts of a different kind, namely trusts for accumulation and maintenance, are now more commonly used in order to minimise the tax burden. Nevertheless, strict settlements and trusts for sale as discussed in this Chapter are still likely to be encountered; in particular it must be noted that a strict settlement may arise almost by inadvertence, as where a testator makes a home-made will leaving property to a charity, but indicates that his widow may live in his house if she so wishes for the rest of her life.[81]

---

[79] SLA 1925, s.106 (see p. 37).
[80] See pp. 48–9.
[81] See p. 129, note 2.

9. Co-ownership

Co-ownership subsists when two or more persons have concurrent (not consecutive) interests in the same property. For example, if land is granted to A and B in fee simple, A and B are co-owners, but if land is settled on A for life with remainder to B in fee simple, A and B are not co-owners.

The main forms of co-ownership are joint tenancy and tenancy in common.[1] The principal difference between the two is that the right of survivorship (or *jus accrescendi*) applies to joint tenancy, but not to tenancy in common. Thus, if A, B and C are joint tenants in fee simple and A dies, A's interest survives to B and C, who become owners of the whole. If B then dies his interest likewise survives to C, who becomes sole owner of the land: co-ownership is then at an end. It follows that a joint tenant has nothing that he can leave by his will or that will pass to his statutory next of kin if he dies intestate. The *jus accrescendi* is itself a corollary of the notion that joint tenants are one person holding the whole interest in the property indivisibly: a joint tenant is said to hold *per mie et per tout* (potentially both the least and yet the whole), in the sense that if he predeceases the other joint tenants his ownership dwindles to nothing, whereas if he survives the others he emerges as sole and absolute owner. But if A, B and C are tenants in common in fee simple and A dies, his interest does not survive to the others, but devolves upon his personal representatives and forms part of his estate.

The only other form of co-ownership that can subsist today is coparcenary. This arises when under the old realty canons of descent land devolves upon two or more persons as co-heirs; hence after 1925 coparcenary can only arise in those exceptional cases, such as the devolution of an unbarred entail, in which the old canons of descent still apply.[2] Today for all practical purposes

---

[1] "Tenancy" in this context means simply ownership, whether freehold or leasehold, and should not be confused with the relationship between landlord and tenant under a lease.

[2] See p. 5 and Chap. 24.

coparcenary is indistinguishable from tenancy in common, and it
will not be necessary to refer to it again, except to mention that
the expression "tenancy in undivided shares" embraces both
tenancy in common and coparcenary; this expression may be
used therefore when it is desired to refer to those forms of co-
ownership to which the right of survivorship does not apply.

Statutory trust for sale

After 1925, with one exception, whenever a disposition of
land (by deed or by will) creates beneficial co-ownership in
possession, whether it be joint tenancy or tenancy in common,
the land is held upon statutory trust for sale.[3] The trustees are
then said to hold the land upon the "statutory trusts," *i.e.* upon
trust to sell it and to hold the net rents and profits pending sale,
and the proceeds of sale after sale, upon trust for the beneficial
co-owners according to their interests. It will be observed that
the statutory trust for sale does not apply to the land unless the
co-owners are entitled in possession. If, therefore, land is settled
on A for life, with remainder to B and C in fee simple, the land
will be settled land under the Settled Land Act 1925, so long as
A is alive; upon the death of A, however, B and C will be
entitled in possession and a statutory trust for sale will then
apply to the land.

The one exception to the general rule is that if land is settled
on two or more *joint* tenants for life (and no express trust for
sale is imposed) the land will be settled land under the Settled
Land Act 1925, and the joint tenants for life will together
constitute the "tenant for life" for the purposes of that Act.[4] If,
on the other hand, they are entitled as tenants in common the
general rule applies, and the land will be held on statutory trust
for sale.[5]

The trustees

The trustees of the statutory trust for sale are normally the
beneficial co-owners themselves or, if there are more than four,
the first four named. There is an apparent exception, however,
where co-ownership arises by will: in this case the testator's

[3] The main provisions are in LPA 1925, ss.34–36.
[4] SLA 1925, s.19(2).
[5] *Ibid.* s.36(1). The trustees of the settlement hold the legal estate on the
statutory trusts.

personal representatives will normally constitute the trustees for sale.[6]

Trustees always hold as joint tenants. It follows that, even if the deed or will creates beneficial tenancy in common, the *legal estate* will be held jointly. Indeed, section 1(6) of the Law of Property Act 1925 expressly provides that after 1925 a legal estate cannot be held in undivided shares, and section 34 provides that a conveyance of land to persons as tenants in common operates to vest the legal estate in them *jointly* on the statutory trusts on trust for themselves as beneficial tenants in common. The purpose of these provisions, as may be said generally of the 1925 legislation, is to facilitate conveyancing. If before 1926 a legal estate in land was held by A, B and C as tenants in common, it might be disposed of without difficulty so long as all of them were alive; but if in turn each died leaving his share to (say) his four children, the land would now belong equally to twelve persons, all of whom would have to join in a conveyance to a purchaser if the land was to be sold. Such difficulties cannot now arise, since a legal estate can only be held *jointly*, by not more than four trustees, and remains vested in the surviving trustees upon the death of any of them. A sale by the trustees will overreach[7] the beneficial interests subsisting under the trust, whether they are held jointly or in common, and however diverse they may be.

Some examples will show how these provisions operate in practice.

(i) Land is conveyed to A, B and C as tenants in common in fee simple. The legal estate vests in A, B and C as joint tenants in fee simple upon the statutory trusts for the benefit of themselves as tenants in common in equity (*i.e.* as beneficiaries under the trust for sale). If A then dies, the right of survivorship will operate with regard to the joint tenancy of the legal estate and the legal fee simple will remain vested in B and C, the surviving trustees of the trust for sale, but A's beneficial (or equitable) interest as tenant in common will pass to his personal representatives and will form part of his estate.

(ii) If land is conveyed to A, B and C as joint tenants in fee simple, and A and B are of full age, but C is an infant, the legal estate will vest in A and B as joint tenants upon the statutory trusts for the benefit of themselves and C as joint tenants in equity (*i.e.* as beneficiaries under the trust for sale). If A then dies, B will remain the sole surviving trustee (and a further trustee should be appointed to act with him before a sale of the land is made).

---

[6] The exception is unaccountable: beneficiaries of full age and absolutely entitled can in any event require the legal estate to be vested in themselves (*Saunders* v. *Vautier* (1841) 4 Beav. 115).

[7] See pp. 27 and 58.

56   *Co-ownership*

(iii) If land is conveyed by deed to A and B as joint tenants in fee simple, the legal estate will vest in A and B as joint tenants upon the statutory trusts for the benefit of themselves as joint tenants in equity. If A dies, B will remain the sole owner at law and in equity. The trust for sale will then be at an end and B will be entitled to sell the land without the necessity of appointing an additional trustee to act with him.[8]

Implied co-ownership

The statutory provisions referred to above apply to dispositions made *expressly* in favour of beneficial co-owners; they do not purport to apply where co-ownership arises by implication, *e.g.* where land has been conveyed into the name of one person (A) alone, but another (X) has contributed substantially either to its purchase or to its subsequent improvement. In such cases, unless it appears that X's intention was to make a gift (or a loan) to A, a resulting trust may arise in favour of X to the extent of his contribution,[9] and the land will then be held by A on trust for himself and X as tenants in common. This principle has acquired particular importance in recent years, mainly in cases concerning the matrimonial or quasi-matrimonial home, and the following rules have emerged:

(i) The land is held by A on trust for sale.[10]

(ii) As beneficial co-owner, X is entitled equally with A to possession of the land, and is entitled to be consulted before any disposition of the land is made.[11]

(iii) As sole trustee, A is unable to pass a good title, *i.e.* on a sale, mortgage or other disposition of the land he cannot overreach X's beneficial interest; but a third party acquiring a legal estate from A will not be bound by X's interest (which of course is merely equitable) if X has consented expressly or impliedly to the disposition,[12] or if the third party had no notice of X's interest.

What constitutes notice for this purpose is problematical. If X is in occupation of the land, this of itself may amount to constructive

---

[8] See pp. 64–5.
[9] *Dyer* v. *Dyer* (1788) 2 Cox. Eq. 92, *Gissing* v. *Gissing* [1971] A.C. 886. *Cf.* proprietary estoppel, discussed at pp. 130–1 and see *Grant* v. *Edwards* [1986] Ch. 638. As to improvements to matrimonial property, see Matrimonial Proceedings and Property Act 1970, s.37.
[10] By a somewhat strained interpretation of SLA 1925, s.36(4). See *Bull* v. *Bull* [1955] 1 Q.B. 234, *Williams & Glyn's Bank Ltd* v. *Boland* [1981] A.C. 487.
[11] *Bull* v. *Bull*; *Williams & Glyn's Bank Ltd.* v. *Boland* (see note 10).
[12] In any event, X's interest cannot have priority over a mortgage entered into at the time when A and X acquired the land (*Bristol & West Building Society* v. *Henning* [1985] 1 W.L.R. 778).

notice of his interest; but here it is necessary to distinguish between two different questions, namely (a) whether a purchaser has notice that some person other than (or as well as) the vendor is in occupation, (b) whether the fact that such person is in occupation is of itself notice that he has, or may have, a beneficial interest. Since a purchaser investigating his vendor's title is bound to make proper enquiries and inspections, he will almost inevitably have constructive notice of the fact of occupation[13]: the question remains whether this necessarily points to the conclusion that the occupier has a beneficial interest in the land. Occupation which is inconsistent with the vendor's title may well amount to constructive notice of the occupier's interest: thus if A is purporting to sell with vacant possession, occupation by a tenant will be constructive notice of his rights under the lease.[14] Joint occupation by a member of A's family or household, however, is not inconsistent with his title, and should not necessarily put a purchaser on notice that A is not the sole beneficial owner.[15]

Nevertheless it has become the invariable practice to make full enquiries, not only as to who is occupying the property, but also as to who, apart from the vendor, has or may have a beneficial interest. It is on the latter point that serious doubts may arise: the question whether someone whose name does not appear on the legal title has acquired a beneficial interest under a resulting trust is a difficult one of mixed fact and law, which may require a decision of the court. In practice, therefore, persons who are occupying the property, and who *might* be held to have a beneficial interest, are usually asked for their formal consent to the transaction, or for an undertaking to release their interest.

One final point needs to be made: where land is held on trust for sale, and a dispute arises as to sale, any person interested may apply to the court, and in most cases an order for sale and a division of the proceeds between those beneficially entitled will be the almost inevitable result. It follows that any protection afforded to an occupier who has a beneficial interest in the land is unlikely to prevent the land being sold if an application is made under the Law of Property Act 1925, s.30.

[13] See p. 27, note 9.
[14] *Hunt* v. *Luck* [1902] 1 Ch. 428.
[15] *Caunce* v. *Caunce* [1969] 1 W.L.R. 286 (joint occupation of wife held not to constitute constructive notice of her interest). The decision was criticised in *Williams & Glyn's Bank Ltd.* v. *Boland,* (a case concerning registered land): see note 10.

Overreaching

If in the example discussed above the land had originally been conveyed into the names of A *and* B as joint owners and trustees for sale of the legal estate, but A, B and X had all contributed to the purchase, a conveyance on sale or a mortgage by A and B would comply with the statutory requirement as to payment of capital money,[16] and accordingly would overreach all beneficial interests under the trust, including that of X. At this point it is necessary to consider more fully what is meant by "overreach."

The expression is not defined by statute, nor does it occur in the specific provisions protecting purchasers (including lessees and mortgagees) from either a tenant for life of settled land or trustees for sale[17]: but section 2 of the Law of Property Act 1925 refers to "conveyances overreaching certain equitable interests," and in this context the term has generally been equated with *detaching* beneficial interests from the land in the hands of the purchaser and *attaching* them to the proceeds in the hands of the trustees.

If the land is sold, the notion that the purchaser's estate is unencumbered with any beneficial interests under a trust affecting the land, and that those beneficial interests themselves attach to the proceeds of sale, is intelligible. But if the land is merely mortgaged to secure a loan representing only a fraction of the land's value, it makes little sense to regard the interests of the beneficiaries as attaching only to the sum loaned. For this reason it might be more apt to define overreaching simply as "gaining priority over." Alternatively, the effect of overreaching in the case of a mortgage can be expressed in terms of detaching the beneficial interests from the land as security in the hands of the mortgagee, and attaching them (a) to the sum loaned, (b) to the equity of redemption, *i.e.* the mortgagor's interest in the land subject to the mortgage.[18] *Vis-à-vis* either a purchaser or a mortgagee the result is the same—he gains priority over the beneficial interests: his estate or mortgage accordingly is not subject to them, and the beneficiaries under the trust, whether or not they were in actual occupation of the land at the date of the disposition,[18] are relegated to their rights against the trustees personally.

---

[16] " ... proceeds of sale or other capital money shall not be paid to ... fewer than two persons as trustees for sale, except where the trustee is a corporation ... " (LPA 1925, ss.2(1)(ii), 27(2)).

[17] SLA 1925, s.72 (see p. 40); LPA 1925, s.27(1) (see pp. 47–48).

[18] *City of London B.S.* v. *Flegg* [1987] 2 W.L.R. 1266 (H.L.), reversing a decision of the Court of Appeal which had raised serious doubts as to the efficacy of the whole overreaching process. It appears that the LPA 1925, s.14, on which the Court of Appeal's decision was partly based, can be regarded as nugatory.

Rights of beneficial owners under trusts for sale

The trust for sale imposed by statute whenever beneficial co-ownership in possession arises is evidently intended to achieve two purposes: first, to facilitate conveyancing[19]; secondly, to establish a procedure for resolving disputes between co-owners.[20] In connection with the latter purpose, a distinction should be drawn between three quite different situations in which a trust for sale may operate: first, where it is employed merely as a means of avoiding the application of the Settled Land Act in the case of settlements; secondly, where it is employed with the positive intention that the property should in fact be sold at once, and that the beneficiaries should be entitled only to their respective shares or interests in the proceeds, not to the land itself; thirdly, where it is imposed by statute, regardless of the parties' intention, in the case of beneficial co-ownership in possession.

Of these three situations, the third is by far the most important, applying as it does to most private houses as well as to very many commercial partnership properties. It has little in common with the other two situations, which in turn differ totally from one another. Nevertheless, the same statutory provisions respecting the trust for sale machinery apply in principle to all three; and, in particular, all three are governed alike by section 30 of the Law of Property Act 1925, under which if trustees for sale refuse to sell or to exercise their powers, or if any requisite consent cannot be obtained, any person interested may apply to the court for an order giving effect to the proposed transaction, and the court may make such order as it thinks fit.

In the first situation, where a settlement is made by way of express trust for sale, it has already been noted that an order for sale is likely to be refused if the court holds that sale would defeat the underlying purpose of the trust.[21] In the second situation, however, where the terms of a disposition make it clear that the beneficiaries are intended to take the proceeds, not the land itself, an order for sale will be virtually mandatory if a dispute arises between them.[22]

It is in the third situation, where beneficial co-owners are entitled in possession, that most disputes occur, particularly with respect to the matrimonial[23] or quasi-matrimonial home, when the

---

[19] By overreaching.

[20] Under LPA 1925, s.30.

[21] See p. 49.

[22] See *Barclay* v. *Barclay* [1970] 2 Q.B. 677.

[23] In disputes between husband and wife the courts may proceed under their matrimonial rather than their property jurisdiction (*Williams* v. *Williams* [1976] Ch. 278).

relationship between the co-owners breaks up. Little purpose would be served by attempting to review here the vast body of case law on this vexed and important topic: what should be remembered, however, is that the inherent problems of co-ownership, if the parties cannot agree either to continue living together, or to dispose of the property and divided the proceeds, can in the last resort be resolved only by applying to the court, and the court may then have little choice but to order a sale of the property. Indeed it is of the essence of a trust for sale, at least in principle, that the property must be sold, unless all the owners concur in postponing sale, or unless it appears that sale would defeat the true purpose of the trust[24]: manifestly if the parties are in dispute there is no such concurrence, nor does the original purpose of the trust continue, if that purpose was joint occupation.

What is now clear, however, is that the equitable doctrine of conversion, by which in theory an interest in land held on trust for sale is regarded from the outset as an interest in money,[25] is of no relevance in deciding questions of substance: beneficial co-owners under the statutory trust for sale have an interest in land, and are entitled to possession of the land[26]; if a dispute arises, and the court is constrained to order sale, this is not because it regards the parties as interested in the proceeds only, but because sale may be the only fair or practicable solution. On the other hand, the doctrine may govern questions of definition: thus, the expression "personalty" has been held to include an interest in land held on trust for sale.[27]

Joint tenancy or tenancy in common

Since 1925, as we have seen, a legal estate cannot be held in undivided shares; the equitable interest of the beneficial co-owners under the trust for sale, on the other hand, may be held either jointly or in common. Which it is will usually be indicated by the terms of the grant. A conveyance on sale is drafted by the purchaser, not the vendor, and it is for co-purchasers to decide

---

[24] *Re Mayo* [1943] Ch. 302, *Jones* v. *Challenger* [1961] 1 Q.B. 176; distinguish *Re Buchanan-Wollaston* [1939] Ch. 738. See also *Jones* v. *Jones* [1977] 1 W.L.R. 438 (co-owner out of occupation not entitled to rent from other in occupation); distinguish *Dennis* v. *McDonald* [1982] Fam. 63 (co-owner wrongfully excluded by other).

[25] See p. 46.

[26] *Bull* v. *Bull*; *Williams & Glyn's Bank Ltd.* v. *Boland*, (see note 10). The absurd implications of the contrary view need hardly be stated.

[27] *Re Kempthorne* [1930] 1 Ch. 268, *Irani Finance Ltd.* v. *Singh* [1971] Ch. 59, *Cf. Cooper* v. *Critchley* [1955] Ch. 431.

whether they wish to hold jointly, or to have shares, and to word the conveyance accordingly: the normal practice is to include in the conveyance an express declaration of trust as to how the beneficial interest is to be held, and this will be conclusive in any subsequent dispute between the parties.[28] Thus, if land is conveyed to A and B "jointly at law and in equity,"[29] both the legal estate and the beneficial interest will be held by A and B as joint tenants. Conversely, if land is conveyed to A and B as tenants in common, or if *words of severance* are used, such as "equally" or "in equal shares,"[30] or if the grant otherwise shows an intention that each co-owner shall have a distinct share, then A and B will hold the beneficial interest as tenants in common (although of course the legal estate will be held jointly).

It is only where the terms of the grant are silent or ambiguous on the point that it becomes necessary to invoke certain rules in order to determine the nature of the beneficial interest of co-owners. Here the general rule is that a grant to two or more persons without words of severance creates a beneficial joint tenancy. Thus, if land is conveyed simply to A and B, they will be entitled jointly both at law and in equity. But this rule is subject to two qualifications.

First, there are certain circumstances in which equity may presume that a tenancy in common was intended, unless there is an express indication to the contrary, *viz*:

(i)   When the co-owners have purchased the property and put up the purchase money in unequal proportions: the presumption then is that they intend to have shares in the property proportionate to their contributions.[31]

(ii) When the co-owners are mortgagees, having taken the property as security for a loan which they have made: in this case it is immaterial whether they have advanced the loan money equally or unequally.

(iii) When the co-owners are partners and hold the property as part of their partnership assets.

The second qualification to the general rule concerning beneficial co-ownership is sometimes expressed by saying that joint

---

[28] *Barton* v. *Morris* [1985] 1 W.L.R. 1257, *Goodman* v. *Gallant* [1986] Fam. 106. It will not, however, preclude a resulting trust in favour of a *third party* in circumstances discussed above at pp. 56–7.

[29] "Jointly," on its own, might refer only to the legal estate (although in that sense it is redundant).

[30] *A fortiori* if the shares are unequal.

[31] Conclusively rebuttable by an express declaration of trust: see *Barton* v. *Morris*, above (property conveyed to A and B jointly, though B contributed only £900 of £40,000 purchase price: B held solely entitled on A's death).

tenancy cannot exist without the presence of the *four unities, viz.* the unities of possession, interest, title and time. Unity of *possession* means that each co-owner has possession of the whole, and none can lay claim to separate ownership of any particular part of the property: this is essential to any form of co-ownership, not merely to joint tenancy. Unity of *interest* means that each co-owner has the same interest both in quantum and in duration: thus if one co-owner has a three-quarters interest and the other a one-quarter interest, or if one has a life interest and the other a fee simple concurrently, this unity is lacking and they hold as tenants in common. Unity of *time* means that the interest of each co-owner has vested at the same time: thus if property is given to all the children of A who attain 21, this unity will ordinarily be lacking. Unity of *title* means that each co-owner derives title from the same instrument: it follows that if a joint owner assigns his beneficial interest the assignee becomes tenant in common since he holds, not under the original grant, but under the assignment.

As a touchstone for joint tenancy the four unities appear to add nothing to the basic criteria outlined above. The first unity (possession) is irrelevant, since it applies to all forms of co-ownership; the second (interest) is self-evident—co-owners who have distinct shares or interests, whether equal or unequal, are by definition tenants in common (joint owners are notionally one person owning the whole property: individual ownership of a share or interest necessarily precludes joint tenancy)[32]; the third unity (time) is fallacious, since there is nothing to prevent co-owners in whom a beneficial interest vests at different times from holding jointly if the grant so indicates[33]; and the fourth unity (title) is redundant—assignment by a joint owner creates a tenancy in common, not because unity of title is lacking between the assignee and the other joint owners (a purely formalistic concept), but because in substance the law recognises assignment as a means of severance, *i.e.* converting joint tenancy into tenancy in common.[34] The question of joint tenancy or tenancy in common can be answered quite satisfactorily without recourse to the four unities shibboleth.

Severance

Severance is a process by which joint tenancy is converted into tenancy in common, thereby eliminating the *jus accrescendi*. After

---

[32] See p. 53.
[33] See M. & W. pp. 421–422.
[34] See below.

1925 severance is, of course, only possible with respect to the beneficial interest under the statutory trust for sale, because the legal estate cannot be held in undivided shares.

The *jus accrescendi* precludes severance of a joint tenancy on death (whether by will or by intestate succession), but there is nothing to prevent joint beneficial owners from effecting a severance *inter vivos*. In principle an absolute owner can do what he wishes with his own property, and it follows that joint owners can, simply by agreement among themselves, convert their beneficial joint tenancy into tenancy in common[35]; equally, a course of conduct indicating such an agreement may suffice to sever the beneficial interest.[36] Failing such agreement, any joint tenant can since 1925 sever his interest by giving written notice to the others.[37]

Thus if A, B and C are joint owners at law and in equity, and subsequently agree to hold the beneficial interest as tenants in common, the result is (i) that they still hold the legal estate jointly on trust for sale, but (ii) that the beneficial interest is now held in equal shares. When A and B later die, C will remain sole trustee of the legal estate, holding it on trust for himself (one-third share) and those entitled under the will or intestacy of A (one-third share) and of B (one-third share). Suppose, however, that A and B would not agree to sever, but that C served a notice of severance on them: the result would be (i) that A, B and C would remain joint trustees of the legal estate, but (ii) that they would now hold it on trust for A and B (two-thirds) as joint tenants, and C (one-third) as tenant in common; on A's death the *jus accrescendi* would operate with respect both to the legal estate and to his beneficial interest, and B would then be solely entitled to two-thirds and C to one-third.

Severance also occurs where a joint tenant assigns his beneficial interest—though, once again, this cannot affect the legal estate. Thus if A, B and C are jointly entitled to the beneficial interest and A assigns his interest to X, X will become tenant in common as between himself and the others, who will remain joint tenants *inter se*. Again, if A, B and C are joint tenants for life and A acquires the fee simple in remainder or in reversion, his life interest will merge in the fee simple and he will become tenant in common as between himself and B and C. It must, however, be noticed that if one of several joint tenants acquires the interest of another, so that his interest becomes greater merely in quantum than that of the others, severance occurs with regard only to the interest so

---

[35] *Williams* v. *Hensman* (1861) 30 L.J. Ch. 878.
[36] *Burgess* v. *Rawnsley* [1975] Ch. 429.
[37] LPA 1925, s.36(2) proviso. No severance of the legal estate is permitted.

acquired. For example, if A, B and C are joint tenants in fee simple of the beneficial interest and A acquires the interest of B, A will become tenant in common as between himself and C with regard only to the one-third interest which he has acquired from B; he will remain joint tenant with C in relation to the remaining two-thirds interest.

However a severance of a joint tenancy is effected—whether by agreement, notice or assignment—a notice of severance should be endorsed on the deed by which the property was conveyed to the joint tenants. In the absence of such protection, any beneficial interests arising from severance would be overridden on a sale by a sole surviving joint owner conveying "as beneficial owner."[38]

Determination of co-ownership

Co–ownership may come to an end by partition or by union.

1. By union

One co-owner may become solely entitled to the whole beneficial interest, *e.g.* by operation of the *jus accrescendi.* In that event the beneficial co-ownership will be at an end; the statutory trust for sale will cease to apply,[39] and by the Law of Property (Amendment) Act 1926 nothing in the Law of Property Act 1925 affects the right of a survivor of joint tenants, who is solely and beneficially interested, to deal with his legal estate as if it were not held on trust for sale. In order to facilitate proof of title where a purchaser might otherwise be concerned to ensure that there had been no previous severance of the beneficial interest (in which case the trust for sale would continue, and the appointment of another trustee would be necessary if the resulting beneficial interests were to be overreached), the Law of Property (Joint Tenants) Act 1964[40] provides that the survivor of joint tenants[41] shall in favour of a purchaser of the legal estate be *deemed* to be solely and beneficially interested if he conveys as "beneficial owner." The

---

[38] Law of Property (Joint Tenants) Act 1964. But it may be doubted whether a purchaser who had *actual* notice of a severance would be permitted to rely on the Act.

[39] *Re Cook* [1948] Ch. 212.

[40] Applying to unregistered land only.

[41] This must mean joint *beneficial* owners: thus the Act would not apply if, although the conveyance to the joint tenants contained no words of severance, the case was one in which there was an unrebutted equitable presumption of tenancy in common (see p. 61).

Act does not apply, however, if a memorandum of severance has been endorsed on the conveyance which vested the legal estate in the joint tenants.[42]

2. By partition

Partition is a division of the land amongst the beneficial co-owners. This can be effected by the trustees with the consent of the beneficiaries, and the court may on application order partition if it thinks fit.[43]

---

[42] Nor if a bankruptcy petition or receiving order has been registered in respect of any of the joint tenants.
[43] LPA 1925, ss.28, 30.

10. The perpetuity rule

The courts have always striven to prevent property owners, and in particular land owners, from tying up their property by means of settlements for an excessive length of time. To a considerable extent this is now governed by legislation, such as the Settled Land Act 1925, which as we have seen greatly facilitates dispositions of the legal estate in land that is subject to a settlement. Equally, however, it is the policy of the law to limit the extent to which equitable or beneficial interests in land or its proceeds or income may be tied up. Two weapons which the judges invented for this purpose were known as the old and the modern perpetuity rules, both of which existed until 1926. The Law of Property Act 1925 abolished the old rule, leaving us with only the modern rule to consider. It is called the modern rule in order to distinguish it from the other rule, but in fact it is a rule of some antiquity.[1]

The operation of the rule has been substantially modified by the Perpetuities and Accumulations Act 1964, but it is necessary to consider it first without reference to the Act. As is explained below, the Act does not replace the common law rule, and if a disposition complies with that rule the Act does not apply.

The first point to notice about the rule is that it applies only to contingent interests in property.[2] An interest is contingent for this purpose so long as the identity of the beneficiary in question is unknown and so long as any condition which has been attached to the grant of his interest remains unfulfilled. Thus, if property is given to the first son of A, and when the gift comes into operation A has no son, the interest given to the son is contingent; the identity of the first son is unknown, and of course A might never have a son. Again, if property is given to B if and when he attains the age of 21, and he has not already attained 21 when the gift comes into operation, B's interest is

---

[1] In its present form the rule was finally settled in *Cadell* v. *Palmer* (1833) 1 Cl. & Fin. 372.

[2] Including both realty and personalty.

contingent; a condition has been attached to his interest which has not yet been fulfilled, and which might never be fulfilled.

The law allows a certain period for the vesting of a contingent interest and this period is known as the "perpetuity period." The perpetuity period is the lives of any persons referred to (expressly or by implication) in the gift who are living or conceived when the gift comes into operation, plus a further period of 21 years. The underlying principle is to allow only those gifts which cannot vest beyond a period comprising the lives of the present generation plus a further 21 years (to enable the next generation to attain its majority).[3] The lives of any persons—not necessarily beneficiaries—may be relevant for this purpose, provided that they are referred to expressly or by implication in the gift, that they are living or conceived when the gift comes into operation, and that they exclusively have some causal connection with the vesting of the interest. The expression "lives in being" may conveniently be used to denote the lives that are relevant in defining the perpetuity period in a particular case.

Under the perpetuity rule, *a contingent interest is void if it might possibly vest after the end of the perpetuity period*; in other words an interest is void unless when the gift comes into operation it is certain that the interest will vest, *i.e.* that the identity of the beneficiary will be known and any condition attached to the gift will be fulfilled, before the end of that period—if indeed the interest ever *does* vest: it is in the nature of any contingent interest that it might *never* vest, but for the purposes of the perpetuity rule that is irrelevant; the rule is designed merely to avoid late vesting, and to ensure that the destination of property cannot remain in doubt beyond the prescribed period. (If a gift fails for perpetuity there will normally be a resulting trust to the donor, and in the case of a gift by will the property will normally go to the residuary devisee or legatee or to the person entitled on intestacy.)

It is important to note that the rule is applied, and the perpetuity period starts to run, at the date when the gift comes into operation: there is no "wait and see," and a contingent interest is therefore to be judged valid or void *ab initio*,[4] in the light of the facts as they are at that date (in particular with respect to lives *then* in being). The operative date is (a) the date on which the deed was executed, in the case of a gift *inter vivos,* (b) the date of the testator's death, in the case of a gift by will.

We may now consider some examples:

---

[3] The Family Law Reform Act 1969 reduced the age of majority from 21 to 18 years, but the perpetuity period has remained unaltered.

[4] It is here that the 1964 Act makes the most important of its changes: see p. 73.

(i) Property is given to A for life with remainder absolutely to his first son to attain 21. Unless when the gift comes into operation a son of A has already attained 21 the remainder is contingent. The question therefore is whether this interest might possibly vest after the end of the perpetuity period. As the source of potential beneficiaries, A is the only relevant life in being, and since any son of his who attains 21 is bound to do so (if at all) within 21 years after A's death the interest is valid.[5] Note that, unless A himself is already dead, the lives of any of his sons living when the gift comes into operation cannot be regarded as relevant in defining the perpetuity period: it is possible that no such son might himself attain 21, but that A might have a further son (born after the gift came into operation, and therefore not a life in being), who might attain 21, and do so more than 21 years after his brothers' deaths (though not, of course, more than 21 years after his father A's death).

(ii) T by his will leaves property to his first grandson to attain 21. Unless at T's death a grandson has already attained 21 the gift is contingent. If any of T's children survive him, they (as the source of potential beneficiaries) will constitute the relevant lives in being, and the gift is clearly valid since no grandchild of T can possibly attain 21 years more than 21 years after the death of the survivor of T's children. The gift would be even more obviously valid if no child of T survived him, since any grandchildren living at T's death would themselves be the relevant lives in being.

The same gift would be void, however, if made *inter vivos*. Whether or not children or grandchildren of T were living at the date of the gift, he himself (as the ultimate source of potential beneficiaries) would be the only relevant life in being. He might subsequently have a child[6] (who of course would not be a life in being), who in turn might have a child who might be the first grandson of T to attain 21: this might happen more than 21 years after T's death (or, for that matter, after the deaths of any of T's children who were living at the date of the gift).

(iii) In the above examples, the lives in being by reference to which the perpetuity period was defined were not specified by the donor, but were to be inferred from their connection with the vesting of the gift. Exceptionally, the gift itself may define the period within which it is to vest, by specifying the relevant lives in being. In one case,[7] a testator directed that property should be

---

[5] If an interest is conditional on attaining an age *greater* than 21, and would be void for that reason alone, the age of 21 is substituted (LPA 1925, s.163, a provision now repealed and replaced by the 1964 Act: see p. 73).

[6] At common law no evidence is admissible to prove that a person is beyond the age of child bearing or begetting (but see p. 72).

[7] *Re Villar* [1929] 1 Ch. 243.

divided amongst such of his descendants as should be living 20 years after the death of the survivor of the descendants of Queen Victoria living at the testator's death. Clearly the gift did not infringe the perpetuity rule, since it was expressly limited to vest within the perpetuity period. Nevertheless such a gift would fail[8] if the specified lives in being were so numerous or so obscure as to be untraceable.

(iv) The converse of the above example occurs where an interest is made contingent on the happening of some event unconnected with the life of any particular person. Thus if property is given "to A when the House of Lords is abolished," the identity of the sole beneficiary is known (as it was not in the previous examples), but the interest is contingent upon an event that may or may not happen, and unless it is certain that the event will happen (if it ever does) within the perpetuity period the interest is void *ab initio*. In this case the perpetuity period is a bare 21 years: although the beneficiary A is alive, his life has no causal connection with the contingency specified, and the interest might therefore vest (in his personal representatives) after his death.[9] The result would of course be different if the property were given "to A if the House of Lords is abolished during his life."

(v) Similarly, an interest limited to vest at the expiry of a stated interval after the date of the gift will generally be void if the interval exceeds 21 years, *e.g.* where a testator leaves property to all his descendants (born whether before or after his death) who shall be living 30 years after his death.[10] Such an interest would, however, be valid if it were confined to living and identified beneficiaries, such as the testator's children: here the interest would be conditional merely on survival to the vesting date (rather than on having been born by that date), and for this purpose the children themselves are, of course, relevant lives in being.

Class gifts

A class gift is a gift to a class of persons by description, the members of which are not immediately ascertainable when the gift comes into operation.[11] For the purposes of the perpetuity rule a class gift is wholly contingent until the identity of every possible member of the class is known. Such a gift, therefore, is wholly void if when the gift comes into operation there is any possibility that

---

[8] For uncertainty, not for perpetuity: see *Re Moore* [1901] 1 Ch. 936.

[9] See *Re Engels* [1943] 1 All E.R. 506.

[10] As to whether such a gift would now be valid *ab initio* under the 1964 Act, see p. 72.

[11] *e.g. Re Villar* (note 7).

the identity of every possible member of the class might not be known within the permitted period. For example, if a testator gives property to be divided amongst all A's grandchildren (whether living at the testator's death or born thereafter),[12] and A is alive when the will comes into operation, the gift is wholly void. Even grandchildren of A who are living at the date of the testator's death will take nothing. Under the perpetuity rule a class gift is either wholly valid or wholly void.[13]

Subsequent interests

If an interest infringes the perpetuity rule, a subsequent interest will not thereby be invalidated unless it is made dependent upon the same contingency. For example, if property is given for life to the first son of A to become a barrister with remainder to B absolutely, the gift to the son is void unless either A is dead or a son of his has already become a barrister by the time that the gift comes into operation; there is no certainty that the identity of the first son to become a barrister will be known within the life of A plus a further period of 21 years. But the remainder to B is vested when the gift comes into operation (his identity is known and no condition has been attached to the gift) and it is valid. It will be observed that the perpetuity rule is in no way concerned with the question how long it may be before an interest falls into possession; it is solely concerned with the question how long it may be before a contingent interest vests (in the sense of ceasing to be contingent).

Had the gift been to the first son of A to become a barrister, but if no son of A becomes a barrister then to B, the gift to B would have been void; it would have been made dependent upon the same contingency which invalidated the prior gift.[14]

Powers of appointment

The owner of property may transfer it to trustees directing them to hold it upon trust for such persons, or such members of a specified class or persons, as D may appoint. D is then said to have a power of appointment; he has the power to nominate the persons who are to take the property. D is called the donee of the power. A power of appointment is normally exercisable either by deed or

---

[12] Rules of construction as to class gifts are discussed at pp. 203–4.
[13] *Pearks* v. *Moseley* (1880) 5 App. Cas. 714 (but see p. 73).
[14] See *Proctor* v. *Bishop of Bath and Wells* (1794) 2 Hy. Bl. 358.

by will, unless the instrument creating it otherwise indicates. If D is at liberty to appoint the property to anyone he pleases, including himself, the power is said to be a general power of appointment, but if D may appoint the property only amongst members of a specified class of persons, such as his own children, the power is said to be a special power.[15] The significance of the distinction is that property subject to a general power can virtually be treated by the donee as his own, whereas a special power has the effect of preventing him from so doing.

For the purposes of the perpetuity rule the grant of a power of appointment is treated as the grant of an interest in property, so that the grant of the power is invalid unless when the grant comes into operation it is certain that the power will vest, if it vests at all, in an ascertainable person within the perpetuity period. Moreover, with one exception, the grant of a power is also void if any appointment under it could be made after the end of the perpetuity period. For example, if property is settled on A (a bachelor at the date of the grant) for life with remainder to A's first son for life, with remainder to such of that son's children as he by deed or will may appoint, the power given to A's son is void. The perpetuity period in this case is the life of A together with a further period of 21 years, and A's son might make an appointment which came into operation after the end of this period. This second rule, however, has no application to a general power of appointment exercisable by the donee at any time without obtaining the consent of any other person.

Given the validity of the power, it may next become necessary to consider the validity of any appointment which the donee of the power makes in exercising it (unless, of course, the interest created by the appointment is itself vested). If the power is a general power, the appointment is treated in the same way as a gift of the donee's own property, and accordingly the perpetuity period for any contingent interest created by the appointment will start to run only when the appointment takes effect, *i.e.* when the power is *exercised*; if the power is a special power, however, the perpetuity period is regarded as having started to run when the power was *granted*. It follows that the lives in being with respect to appointments made under a special power are confined to those in being when the power was granted, whereas in the case of a general power they will include those in being when the power is exercised.

An example will illustrate the difference. Suppose that A holds a power of appointment over certain property, that he appoints by will to such of his children as may attain the age of 30, and that at

---

[15] A power is also to be treated as a special power if exercisable only with the concurrence or consent of another person (1964 Act, s.7, confirming the common law rule: see *Re Earl of Coventry's Indentures* [1974] Ch. 77).

his death he has two children, S aged 6 and D aged 3. The interest created by the appointment is contingent, and will remain so until both S and D attain 30 (or die previously). If the power were a *general* one, the perpetuity period would not start to run until the power was exercised, *i.e.* when the appointment took effect on A's death; S and D would themselves be the relevant lives in being, and the interest would be valid as it stands. If the power were a *special* one (*e.g.* to appoint amongst A's issue), however, the perpetuity period would be regarded as having started to run when the power was granted, at which time the only relevant life in being was A himself; it is evident that neither S nor D will attain 30 within the perpetuity period, *i.e.* within 21 years after A's death, and the interest would accordingly fail at common law; but by section 163 of the Law of Property Act 1925[16] it would be validated by substituting 21 for the stipulated age of 30.

The Perpetuities and Accumulations Act 1964

This Act makes important changes in the rule against perpetuities. It came into force on July 16, 1964, and (subject to minor exceptions) applies only to instruments taking effect after that date.[17] Its main provisions are of a *relieving* character, *i.e.* they are designed to save an interest from invalidity if it *infringes* the perpetuity rule as the rule stands apart from the Act; they have no application if the interest is valid without recourse to the Act. It is still necessary, therefore, to know the rule as it was before the Act. The following, in outline, are some of the main provisions of the Act:

Section 1

A period of years not exceeding 80 may be specified by the grantor as the perpetuity period applicable to any disposition, instead of the normal period of lives in being plus 21 years.[18]

Section 2

For the purposes of the perpetuity rule, males under 14 years of age and females under 12 or over 55 years of age are presumed to

---

[16] See note 5.
[17] With respect to appointments made under a special power of appointment, the Act applies only where the instrument creating the power takes effect after that date.
[18] It is doubtful whether this would apply to the gift mentioned at p. 69, note 10, unless the instrument expressly provided that the period stipulated should be the perpetuity period (see *Re Green's W.T.* [1985] 3 All E.R. 455).

be incapable of having children; but evidence is also admissible to show that a living person will or will not be able to have a child.[19]

Section 3

This, the most radical of the Act's provisions, abolishes the "no wait and see" rule.[20] It provides that an interest is not to be treated as void on the ground merely that it *might* vest after the end of the perpetuity period, but shall on the contrary be treated as though it were not subject to the perpetuity rule until such time as it becomes established that it *will* vest after the end of the period.

Furthermore, for this purpose, (*i.e.* for the purpose of "waiting and seeing" whether an interest does in fact vest within the period allowed) the perpetuity period is defined by reference to the lives of persons specified in the section, and these include persons such as potential beneficiaries who, under the stricter rule of common law, would often have been discounted.

Section 4

This—(a) repeals and replaces section 163 of the Law of Property Act 1925,[21] and provides for age reduction, not to 21, but to the nearest age (of 21 or over) that will prevent infringement of the perpetuity rule; (b) abolishes the rule that a class gift is either wholly valid or wholly void, by providing for exclusion of those members of the class whose inclusion would render the gift void.[22] It should be noted that recourse will be had to these provisions only where the disposition has not already been validated either by section 2 (eliminating the possibility of a child being born) or by section 3 (allowing "wait and see" during the perpetuity period).

Section 5

This validates, where necessary,[23] a gift limited to vest on the death of the survivor of a named person and any spouse of that person. Before the Act, a gift "to all the children of A who shall be living at the death of the survivor of A and any wife he may marry" was void, because A was the only relevant life in being, and any wife he married might survive him for more than 21 years, at which

---

[19] See note 6. The possibility of adoption is also excluded by the presumption as to females over 55.
[20] See note 4.
[21] See note 5.
[22] See pp. 69–70.
[23] *i.e.* having "waited and seen" whether the gift in fact vests within the perpetuity period.

time the gift to the children would still not have vested. By section 5, however, such a gift is to be treated as if it were limited to vest (at the latest) immediately before the end of the perpetuity period: it follows that if a wife of A does survive him for 21 years, the gift to the children will vest in such of A's children as are living *at that time* (regardless of whether subsequently they survive A's wife).

Section 9

This, subject to certain conditions, exempts from the perpetuity rule options granted to a lessee to purchase the reversion, and provides that as regards other options to acquire for valuable consideration any interest in land the perpetuity period (when applicable) shall be 21 years. By *section 10,* however, when the perpetuity rule does apply, no contractual remedy is to be available after the end of the perpetuity period against the grantor of an interest created *inter vivos*.[24]

Exceptions to the perpetuity rule

1. Contractual obligations

Before the Act of 1964 the rule did not apply to an action, whether for damages or for specific performance, to enforce an obligation by which the defendant was contractually bound. For example, if a lease for 99 years conferred upon the tenant for the time being an option to purchase the reversion, and an action was brought against the original landlord upon his covenant to sell the reversion, the perpetuity rule had no application, since the landlord's obligation, though contingent (in the sense that the option when granted might or might not be exercised), was merely contractual.[25] It was otherwise if an action was brought against a subsequent owner of the reversion; the perpetuity rule then applied because the action was based, not on a contractual obligation, but on the ground that the grant of the option created an immediate (but contingent) equitable interest in the reversion which would be enforceable by a decree of specific performance.[26] It followed that if the option might be exercised beyond the perpetuity period the contingent interest to which it gave rise was void and a subsequent owner of the reversion was not bound by it, although an action for breach of contract would lie against the

---

[24] See note 25.
[25] *Hutton* v. *Watling* [1948] Ch. 26.
[26] In accordance with the principle discussed at pp. 25–6.

original grantor.[27] Similar principles applied to any other option to purchase land: the original grantor (or his estate) could always be sued, but the perpetuity rule applied to an action against a successor in title of the grantor (other than his personal representative). The Act of 1964[28] has made important changes in these rules which we have just considered, but it must be remembered that the Act applies only to instruments taking effect after its commencement.

2. Leases and mortgages

The perpetuity rule has no application to provisions in a lease, such as a covenant for renewal, which are designed to regulate the relationship of landlord and tenant, and are not concerned with merely collateral matters. A similar exception applies to most provisions in mortgages.

3. Interests following a fee tail

The perpetuity rule does not apply to a remainder which is to take effect during the continuance of a fee tail or at the moment of its determination. For example, if Blackacre is settled on A in tail with a proviso that if at any time the tenant in tail of Blackacre should become entitled to Whiteacre in fee simple, Blackacre is to go over to B in tail, the remainder to B will be valid. This exception is somewhat specious because the barring of the entail at any time would defeat the remainder.

4. Charities

A gift over upon a certain event from one charity to another charity is valid even if that event might occur after the end of the permitted perpetuity period.

OTHER RULES

The perpetuity rule is one of several evolved originally by the courts, and later modified by statute, with the object of ensuring that property, including both capital (in the form of land, or a fund) and income (in the form of rents, or interest or dividends), shall be freely disposable within a reasonable time by someone

---

[27] *Woodall* v. *Clifton* [1905] 2 Ch. 257, *Worthing Corpn.* v. *Heather* [1906] 2 Ch. 532.
[28] ss.9 and 10.

who is absolutely entitled. The perpetuity rule itself is primarily concerned with contingent interests arising out of settlements of capital; certain other rules, which are outlined below, are concerned with directions as to the income of property. Their main application is to personal property such as trust funds and stocks and shares: accordingly they merit only brief mention in a book on real property.

The rule against perpetual trusts

If property is given to trustees on trust to apply the income to a certain purpose, *e.g.* the maintenance of a tomb in a churchyard, the interest created is already vested, and therefore no question arises on the perpetuity rule itself. Such dispositions nevertheless are objectionable on a number of grounds, of which the most relevant in the present context is that they tie up indefinitely the *corpus* or capital of the trust. Accordingly such trusts, commonly referred to as purpose trusts, are generally held void, although it seems they may be valid if expressly confined to the perpetuity period. This rule, which may be regarded as a particular aspect of the more general rule against inalienability,[29] is not established with the same clarity as the perpetuity rule itself. Its operation is not affected by the Perpetuities and Accumulations Act 1964.[30]

The rule is of little practical importance: it does not apply to charitable trusts, and private trusts on the other hand will usually be void, regardless of any question of perpetuity, if the objects are not ascertainable human beneficiaries.

The rule against accumulations

Property is sometimes given to trustees on trust to accumulate the income, *i.e.* use it to purchase additional similar property,[31] for a stated period, and then hold the property and the accumulation on trust for specified beneficiaries.[32]

If the beneficiaries are of full age and, apart from the direction to accumulate, absolutely entitled in possession to the property, they can set aside the direction and demand that the property itself

[29] See p. 16.
[30] See s.15(4).
[31] The instrument may also direct that the income from the additional property be similarly applied.
[32] Accumulations may also be directed for specific purposes, such as paying debts or raising portions. Such accumulations are in general exempt from the rule discussed here.

be transferred to them by the trustees.[33] For example, if a testator leaves property on trust for A absolutely, but directs that until A reaches the age of 30 the income shall be accumulated, A can put an end to the accumulation at any time (provided he is of full age) and require the trustees to transfer the property to him. It follows in general that accumulation can effectively be directed only when beneficiaries of full age are *not* absolutely entitled in possession, *i.e.* when they have either a contingent interest only, or a future interest in the property. Thus, if in the above example the gift to A had been conditional on his attaining 30, A could require neither the property itself nor the income to be paid to him unless and until he attained 30.[34]

Such a contingent interest would, of course, be valid if it complied with the perpetuity rule, and at common law any direction to accumulate that was confined to the perpetuity period would equally be valid. As a result of *Thellusson* v. *Woodford*,[35] however, Parliament resolved to subject accumulations to a more stringent rule, and accordingly passed the Accumulations Act 1800.

The rule today is to be found in the Law of Property Act 1925, ss.164–166, as amended by the Perpetuities and Accumulations Act 1964 (for instruments taking effect after the commencement of that Act). Today a direction to accumulate income if it is to be valid must be for one only of the following periods:

(i) The life of the grantor or settlor.

(ii) 21 years from the death of the grantor, settlor or testator.

(iii) The minority or respective minorities of any person or persons living or conceived at the death of the grantor, settlor or testator.

(iv) The minority or respective minorities of any person or persons who under the terms of the instrument directing accumulation would, for the time being, if of full age, be entitled to the income directed to be accumulated.

To these the 1964 Act has added:

(v) 21 years from the date of the making of the disposition.

(vi) The minority or minorities of any person or persons living or conceived at that date.

In general a settlor may choose whichever of the periods he prefers, but where the direction is that income shall be wholly or partially accumulated for the purchase of land, only the fourth period may be chosen.

---

[33] Under the rule in *Saunders* v. *Vautier* (1841) 4 Beav. 115. The rule is equally applicable where the beneficiary is a charity.

[34] An express direction to accumulate excludes the operation of LPA 1925, s.175 (under which contingent gifts carry intermediate income).

[35] (1805) 11 Ves. 112.

It will be observed that the only life period mentioned in the rule is the life of the settlor. It follows that a *testator* cannot validly direct accumulation of income during the lifetime of any person.

The term "minority," which is used in the third, fourth and sixth periods, refers to the infancy of a given person, *i.e.* the period from the moment when that person is born until he attains full age. If the settlor decides to make use of the third or sixth period he must limit himself to the minorities of persons who are living or conceived at his death or the date of the settlement. But he may direct accumulation of income during the minorities of any such persons: those persons need not be beneficiaries. If the settlor decides to employ the fourth period he is not limited to the minorities of persons living or conceived at his own death or the date of the settlement, but on the other hand he can direct accumulation of income only during the minorities of certain beneficiaries, *i.e.* the beneficiaries who would for the time being if of full age be entitled to the income directed to be accumulated. For example, property may be settled on A (a bachelor at the date of the grant) for life with remainder to such of A's children as are living at A's death, with a direction that if at A's death any such child is an infant the income from his share of the property shall be accumulated for him during his minority. This direction is valid under the fourth period, although it does not fall within the terms of the third or sixth periods as the direction is not to accumulate during the minorities of persons who are living or conceived at the death of the settlor or the date of the settlement.

Breach of the rule

If a direction to accumulate income is for a period exceeding that permitted by the perpetuity rule, the direction is wholly void.[36] If the direction does not infringe the perpetuity rule but infringes the accumulations rule, the direction is not wholly void: it is good for whichever of the permitted periods is most appropriate to the particular case, and is void only for the excess over that period. This means that the court will select whichever of the permitted periods it considers to be most appropriate in the particular case, and the direction to accumulate will then take effect for this period or for the period directed in the instrument, whichever turns out to be the shorter. For example, if a testator directs that the income of certain property shall be accumulated during the life of A and that the property with its accumulations

---

[36] It is doubtful whether the "wait and see" provisions of the 1964 Act (s.3) apply: see M. & W. pp. 304–305.

shall then be divided equally among all A's children living at A's death, this direction does not infringe the perpetuity rule, but it does infringe the accumulations rule. In this case the court will select the period of 21 years from the death of the testator as being the most appropriate period. Accumulation of income will then take place during this 21 year period or the period of the life of A, whichever turns out to be the shorter. If A is still living at the end of the 21 year period accumulation of income must then cease, but distribution of the property cannot take place until the death of A: until A dies it cannot be ascertained who are the beneficiaries entitled to the property. The income accruing from the property between the end of the 21 year period and the death of A is to "go to and be received by the person or persons who would have been entitled thereto if such accumulation had not been directed"; this will usually be the person or persons entitled to the testator's residuary estate.[37]

---

[37] Or entitled on intestacy: see *Re Green's W.T.* [1985] 3 All E.R. 455.

11. Contracts for the disposition of land

The same substantive requirements apply to contracts to sell or otherwise dispose of land as to other contracts, but the Law of Property Act 1925, s.40(1), provides that "no action may be brought upon any contract for the sale or other disposition of land or any interest in land, unless the agreement upon which such action is brought, or some memorandum or note thereof, is in writing and signed by the party to be charged [*i.e.* the party sued] or by some other person thereunto by him lawfully authorised."

It is not necessary that the agreement itself should be in writing: all that is required is that before any action is brought to enforce it there shall be in existence some written document which is signed by the defendant and which sufficiently describes the subject-matter, identifies the parties, and states the consideration and other material terms of the agreement. No particular form is required, and it may be possible to spell out a sufficient memorandum from several documents (*e.g.* letters), one only of which is signed by the defendant, so long as on the face of them they are connected.[1] Even a document denying liability under the alleged contract will suffice, provided that it acknowledges that the contract exists; but it seems a document purporting to set out the terms of an agreement "subject to contract" (*i.e.* one which is not intended to be legally binding) cannot constitute a sufficient memorandum of an oral contract previously concluded in similar terms.[2]

If there is insufficient written evidence to satisfy the requirements of section 40(1), neither party can enforce the contract by an action for damages. The contract is not void, however, and may be relied on, *e.g.* as a *defence* to an action by a defaulting

---

[1] *Cf. Timmins* v. *Moreland Street Property Co. Ltd.* [1958] Ch. 110, *Elias* v. *George Sahely & Co. (Barbados) Ltd.* [1983] A.C. 646.

[2] *Tiverton Estates Ltd.* v. *Wearwell Ltd.* [1974] Ch. 146, not following *Law* v. *Jones* [1974] Ch. 112, and doubting *Griffiths* v. *Young* [1970] 1 Ch. 675.

purchaser to recover his deposit.[3] More important, it may be enforced in equity by an action for specific performance, despite the lack of written evidence, provided that there are sufficient acts of part performance by the plaintiff. The equitable doctrine of part performance[4] is designed to prevent unfair advantage being taken of the absence of written evidence, where one party has allowed the other to act upon the faith of an agreement between them. The conditions for its application include the following:

First, the parties must have made a definite binding contract: this condition is not satisfied if, for example, they have merely entered into an agreement "subject to contract," or into a family arrangement not intended to have legal effect.[5] Secondly, the contract must be specifically enforceable: the equitable remedy of specific performance is discretionary, and may be refused on a number of grounds, *e.g.* mistake, misrepresentation, undue delay, or breach of covenant.[6] Thirdly, the acts relied upon must be those of the plaintiff and must be referable to some contract of the kind alleged[7]: in most cases a change of possession is regarded as sufficient evidence of a contract of sale or of an agreement for a lease, *i.e.* entering into possession is generally a sufficient act of part performance by the purchaser or tenant, and giving up possession is generally sufficient on the part of the vendor or landlord. This third condition, however, has given rise to many difficulties and it seems now that the evidentiary aspect of the doctrine of part performance should be regarded as secondary to the more general principle of detrimental reliance.[8]

As has already been seen, the effect of a contract for the disposition of land, provided that it is evidenced by sufficient writing to comply with section 40(1) of the Law of Property Act 1925, or by sufficient acts of part performance, is that not only can it be enforced by an action for damages or for specific perform-ance, but also it is regarded in equity as at once giving rise to an equitable interest in the land.[9] The *legal* estate or interest does not vest in the transferee, however, until the formal conveyance, lease or other instrument has been executed.

---

[3] *Thomas* v. *Brown* (1876) 1 Q.B.D. 714.

[4] The doctrine is recognised in LPA 1925, s.40(2).

[5] *Re Gonin* [1979] Ch. 16 (which appears otherwise to be inconsistent with *Steadman* v. *Steadman* [1976] A.C. 536) may be regarded as having been decided on this ground. *Cf. Maddison* v. *Alderson* (1883) 8 App. Cas. 467, *Wakeham* v. *Mackenzie* [1968] 1 W.L.R. 1175.

[6] See, *e.g.*, *Warmington* v. *Miller* [1973] Q.B. 877.

[7] *Kingswood Estate Co. Ltd.* v. *Anderson* [1963] 2 Q.B. 169.

[8] *Steadman* v. *Steadman*, above, from which it also appears that a mere payment of money may in certain circumstances amount to part performance.

[9] See p. 25.

12. Leases and tenancies

As we have already seen, the leasehold gained recognition as an estate in land at a relatively late stage in the development of the land law.[1] Over the centuries its importance has gradually increased, and now the term of years or leasehold estate is established, alongside the fee simple or freehold estate, as one of only two possible forms of legal ownership of land.[2] Nevertheless, it retains features which distinguish it from all other estates and interests.

The main distinguishing feature of the leasehold is that it constitutes both an estate in land, and a contract between lessor and lessee, imposing numerous obligations which continue throughout the term of the lease; and although these obligations are enforceable, as we shall see,[3] not only between the original parties but also between their respective successors in title, the basis on which they are enforceable is that of a continuing relationship between landlord and tenant,[4] rather than a purely proprietary basis. The law of landlord and tenant, which regulates the rights and obligations of the parties *inter se,* can be regarded as ancillary to the law of property, which determines the rights of ownership (*i.e.* the estate) that each holds *vis-à-vis* a third party.

Because of its social and economic importance, the law of landlord and tenant, in the sense referred to above, is now subject to extensive statutory controls, which are aimed at securing a fair balance between the parties, and which to that extent override the common law of contract. So far as they relate to security of tenure and rent restriction, these statutory provisions will be dealt with in the following chapter.

---

[1] See pp. 5, 7–8.
[2] LPA 1925, s.1(1) (see Chapter 7).
[3] At p. 133 *et seq.*
[4] Analogous with but distinct from the historical relationship between feudal lord and tenant under the doctrine of tenure.

ESSENTIALS OF A LEASE

Many different transactions may have as their object the occupation by one party of land belonging to another, but a transaction will constitute a lease, as distinct from something else, only if it has certain characteristics. The importance of the distinction between a lease on the one hand, and some other transaction such as a licence on the other, is twofold: first, a lease as an estate in land is binding not merely between the parties (*in personam*) but also in relation to the land itself (*in rem*), whereas in principle a licence creates no estate or interest in the land and is binding, if at all, only between the original parties[5]; secondly, a tenant under a lease may have the protection of the extensive statutory provisions referred to above, whereas in general an occupier under a mere licence has no such protection.

The essential requirements of a lease are as follows:

Exclusive possession

Unless the occupier is entitled to exclusive possession, *i.e.* unless he has the right to exclude all other persons from the premises, any agreement under which he occupies another's property is a mere licence, not a lease. Thus in the case of a lodging agreement, under which the householder normally remains in general control of the premises, and retains virtually unlimited rights of access for the purposes of providing board and other services, the lodger is a licensee, not a tenant.[6]

Estate in land

Even where there is a right to exclusive possession, the transaction is not a lease unless it appears from the circumstances of the case that the intention or the effect of the agreement between the parties is to create the relationship of landlord and tenant, *i.e.* not merely to create legal relations (indicating a contract, and giving rise to personal rights and obligations) but to create an estate or interest in the land (giving rise to property rights enforceable by and against non-parties).[7] It follows that there will be no lease where the circumstances point merely to a

---

[5] See Chap. 15.

[6] *Marchant* v. *Charters* [1977] 1 W.L.R. 1181. But see *Street* v. *Mountford* [1985] A.C. 809.

[7] *Barnes* v. *Barratt* [1970] 2 Q.B. 657.

family arrangement of some kind,[8] or where an employee occupies premises of his employer merely for the purposes of his employment.

The distinction between lease and licence is one of substance not form: however worded, an agreement will create a lease if in fact it gives the occupier exclusive possession and there is nothing in the circumstances of the case to negative the relationship of landlord and tenant.[9] Reviewing the considerable body of case law on the matter, the House of Lords, in *Street* v. *Mountford*,[10] has deprecated attempts to disguise tenancy agreements as licences by the use of sham devices designed (on the landlord's part) merely to avoid the provisions of the Rent Acts or similar legislation: however clearly the parties may have expressed their intention, it is the *effect* of the transaction that is decisive.

Certainty of term

Both the commencement date and the duration of the term must be certain: a lease which fails to satisfy this condition is void.[11]

The duration of a periodic tenancy is initially indefinite, but may be regarded as sufficiently certain for this purpose in that it can be determined by notice; alternatively, it has been suggested, periodic tenancies may be treated as exempt from the requirement of certainty of term.[12]

LEGAL AND EQUITABLE LEASES

In general, if a lease is to be a legal lease (*i.e.* if the lessee is to obtain a legal estate), it must be granted by deed. As an exception, a lease for three years or less taking effect in possession at the best rent reasonably obtainable without taking a fine (premium) will be a valid legal lease however granted—even if it is granted merely by word of mouth.[13] The exception includes periodic tenancies, such as monthly or yearly tenancies, provided that the basic term does not exceed three years. A lease that is not within the exception given above and not granted by deed is void at law, except that if

[8] *Errington* v. *Errington and Woods* [1952] 1 K.B. 290.
[9] *Addiscombe Garden Estates Ltd.* v. *Crabbe* [1958] 1 Q.B. 583, *Facchini* v. *Bryson* [1952] 1 T.L.R. 1386; contrast *Shell-Mex B.P. Ltd.* v. *Manchester Garages Ltd.* [1971] 1 W.L.R. 612.
[10] See note 6.
[11] *Lace* v. *Chantler* [1944] K.B. 368, *Harvey* v. *Pratt* [1965] 1 W.L.R. 1025.
[12] *Re Midland Railway Co.'s Agreement* [1971] Ch. 725.
[13] LPA 1925, ss.52–54.

the tenant goes into possession with the landlord's consent a tenancy at will arises, which will become a periodic tenancy if the landlord accepts rent.[14] In equity, however, an informal lease that would be void at law may, provided that it is for value, be treated as an agreement to grant a lease and thus, on the basis that equity looks upon that as done which ought to be done, as a valid equitable lease.[15] An express agreement for a lease is treated in the same way. As between landlord and tenant, an equitable lease has the same effect as a legal lease, *i.e.* all the obligations created by the agreement or by the informal lease can be enforced by the same means and to the same extent as if they were set out in a properly executed lease. In some respects, however, an equitable lease is not as good as a properly executed legal lease: in particular it requires registration under the Land Charges Act 1972, failing which it will be void against a subsequent purchaser from the landlord.[16]

DIFFERENT KINDS OF LEASES

1. Leases for a fixed term

In general, such leases come to an end automatically at the end of the agreed term and no notice to quit is required. There are important statutory exceptions, which are considered in Chapter 13.

2. Yearly tenancies

A yearly tenancy is otherwise known as a tenancy from year to year: the tenancy continues from year to year until one side or the other brings it to an end by serving the requisite notice to quit. Such a tenancy may be created expressly or it may arise by implication of law. It arises by implication of law when the parties to a tenancy do not expressly agree what the nature of the tenancy shall be and the tenant tenders, and the landlord accepts, some payment of an annual rent. For example, if the parties have agreed on the payment of a yearly rent by four equal quarterly instalments, the payment of a quarter's rent will give rise to a yearly tenancy. A particular case in which a yearly tenancy may arise by implication of law occurs when a tenant under a lease for a fixed term holds over after the end of the term (*i.e* remains in

---

[14] See below.

[15] This principle is discussed at pp. 25–6. In its application to leases it is known as the doctrine of *Walsh* v. *Lonsdale* (1882) 21 Ch.D. 9.

[16] For further disadvantages, see pp. 94, 119.

possession) and then makes some payment of an annual rent which the landlord accepts. In this case the terms of the old lease continue to apply to the new yearly tenancy so far as they are not inconsistent with the nature of such a tenancy.

At common law, in the absence of contrary agreement, in order to determine a yearly tenancy one party must give to the other at least half a year's previous notice expiring at the end of one of the years of the tenancy, *i.e.* expiring on an anniversary of its commencement. But the parties can make what bargain they like unless precluded from doing so by statute. Half a year's notice means 182 days' notice unless the tenancy began on a customary quarter day (Lady Day, Midsummer, Michaelmas, or Christmas), in which case it means the two previous quarters.

3. Other periodic tenancies

These too may be created expressly or may arise by implication of law, as in the case of yearly tenancies; for example, if the parties have not agreed upon the precise nature of the tenancy, but have agreed that a quarterly rent shall be paid, the payment of a quarter's rent will give rise to a quarterly tenancy.

At common law, subject to contrary agreement, such a tenancy can be brought to an end only at the end of one of the periods of the tenancy, and the length of notice required is the same as that of the period upon which the tenancy is based; for example, if a monthly tenancy began on the 15th of a month it can be brought to an end on the 15th of any month, and for this purpose notice to quit must have been given at least one month before that date. Although in general the parties can vary the common law rule by special agreement, the Protection from Eviction Act 1977, s.5, provides that where the letting is of a dwelling, notice[17] must be given at least four weeks before the date on which the tenancy is to determine, and this provision applies notwithstanding any contrary agreement. It should be understood that the Act does not *reduce* the length of notice required where under the common law rule a longer period of notice is necessary. Furthermore it is open to the parties to agree in what circumstances, as well as for what period, notice may be given.[18]

4. Tenancies at will and at sufferance

A tenancy at will arises whenever a person occupies as tenant

---

[17] The notice must be in writing, and contain such information as may be prescribed.
[18] *Re Midland Railway Co.'s Agreement*, note 12.

the land of another with that other's consent, on terms that either party may determine the tenancy at any time. It may be created expressly or by implication, as where a tenant whose lease has expired holds over with the landlord's consent, or where a tenant takes possession under an agreement for a lease. The relationship between the parties to a tenancy at will is essentially personal,[19] and accordingly terminates if either party dies, or if either party assigns his interest in the land.[20] The tenant is liable to pay any rent that has been agreed; otherwise, unless the parties have agreed that no rent is payable, the tenant must pay a reasonable sum for use and occupation of the land. Once the tenant has tendered and the landlord has accepted a periodic rent, the tenancy will be converted into a periodic tenancy, on the basis discussed above.

A tenancy at sufferance (which is not perhaps a true tenancy) arises when a tenant without the landlord's consent holds over after a previous tenancy has come to an end. A tenant at sufferance is bound to pay compensation to the landlord for his occupation of the land. Moreover tenants who hold over after notice to quit has been given are liable to certain statutory penalties, payable to the landlord.[21]

5. Leases for lives, etc.

A lease for a life or lives or for a term of years determinable with a life or lives or on the marriage of the lessee (*e.g.* a lease for 50 years which, the lease provides, shall come to an end automatically on the death of a specified person or on the lessee's marriage) is converted by the Law of Property Act 1925, s.149, into a lease for 90 years. After the end of the life or lives or the marriage of the lessee either party may determine this lease by giving at least one month's notice expiring on any quarter day which is applicable to the tenancy or, if there is no such quarter day, any customary quarter day. This provision applies only to leases at a rent or in consideration of a fine. If no rent is payable the result may be to create a settlement, the lessee being tenant for life: it follows that in order to avoid this consequence a nominal rent must be imposed.[22]

6. Perpetually renewable leases

Another curious provision, this time in the Law of Property Act

[19] *Wheeler* v. *Mercer* [1957] A.C. 416.
[20] Or if the tenant commits voluntary waste (as to waste generally, see p. 22).
[21] Landlord and Tenant Act 1730, Distress for Rent Act 1737.
[22] See *Griffiths* v. *Williams* (1977) 248 E.G. 947 (p. 129, below).

1922, applies to perpetually renewable leases, *i.e.* leases which give to the tenant a perpetual right of renewal. For example, a lease for seven years may provide that the tenant shall have the right, not less than one month before the end of the term, to require the landlord to grant a new lease for seven years upon the same terms, including the provision for renewal, as the original lease. The Act converts such leases into terms of 2,000 years, determinable by the *lessee* by the giving of at least 10 days' notice expiring on any date on which, but for the Act, the lease would have come to an end if it had not been renewed, *i.e.* in the example given above, the end of any seven-year term. If the lease provides for payment of a fine on renewal, then (a) if the lease was granted before 1926, the fine is commuted into additional rent, but (b) if the lease was granted after 1925, the provision for payment of the fine is void.

The 1922 Act also renders void any contract to renew an existing lease for more than 60 years after its termination.

7. Reversionary leases

The Law of Property Act 1925, s.149, renders void the grant after 1925 of a lease which is to take effect more than 21 years after the date of the grant.[23] The same section invalidates a contract to grant such a lease, *i.e.* a lease which is to commence more than 21 years from the grant of the lease; but this does not invalidate a contract to grant a lease which is to start more than 21 years from the date of the *contract*.[24]

TERMINATION OF LEASES

We have already seen that a lease may come to an end by effluxion of time or may be determined by the service of notice to quit in certain cases. We must now consider some other ways in which a lease may come to an end.

FORFEITURE[25]

A landlord is said to forfeit a lease when he exacts a forfeiture of

---

[23] See p. 30.

[24] *Re Strand and Savoy Properties Ltd.* [1960] Ch. 582.

[25] Law Commission Report No. 142 of 1985 makes radical proposals to replace the entire regime of re-entry, waiver, notice and relief by a procedure whereby either the landlord or the tenant can apply to the court for a "termination order" on the ground of breaches by the other party.

it by reason of the tenant's breach of some obligation under the lease. In general, if a landlord wishes to have this right of forfeiture he must stipulate for it in the lease; the law does not confer such a right upon the landlord even if the tenant fails to pay the rent. The landlord may stipulate for the right either by providing in the lease that the tenant's performance of his obligations is a condition of the lease, or by inserting into the lease an express right of re-entry, *i.e.* a provision that the landlord may re-enter and determine the lease upon breach by the tenant of his obligations. A right of re-entry may in general be exercised by physically entering the land, but if in so doing the landlord uses force he may be guilty of a criminal offence,[26] and it is for this reason that forfeiture is normally enforced by an action for possession.[27] Service of the writ operates in law as a re-entry, but the lease is not extinguished until the landlord obtains judgment for possession; until then the tenant is accountable to the landlord for mesne profits[28] during the period of his continued occupation.

Waiver

A landlord may lose his right of forfeiture in respect of a particular breach of the tenant's obligations by waiving the right. Waiver may be express or implied. There is usually an implied waiver if the landlord with knowledge of a breach does any act showing that he has elected to treat the lease as still in existence, *e.g.* by claiming rent accruing due after the breach,[29] or by distraining for rent accruing due whether before or after the breach (the act of distraining shows an election to treat the lease as still in existence, because the remedy of distress[30] can be used by a landlord only so long as the relationship of landlord and tenant subsists). But a landlord's claim for possession on the ground of breaches of covenant is not inconsistent with an alternative claim for an injunction restraining further breaches, and the two may properly be joined in the same action.[31] Furthermore, if the landlord assigns the reversion, *i.e.* conveys his estate expressly subject to the lease, this does not of itself constitute a waiver of

---

[26] Criminal Law Act 1977, ss.6 and 7, replacing the Forcible Entry Acts 1381–1623.
[27] This is the *only* lawful method where premises are let as a dwelling and any person is lawfully residing there (Protection from Eviction Act 1977, s.2).
[28] Or for rent, if he successfully resists the landlord's claim for possession.
[29] See *Central Estates (Belgravia) Ltd.* v. *Woolgar (No. 2)* [1972] 1 W.L.R. 1048.
[30] This consists in seizing and selling the tenant's chattels for the purpose of recovering arrears of rent.
[31] *Calabar Properties Ltd.* v. *Seagull Autos Ltd.* [1969] 1 Ch. 451.

previous breaches by the tenant, and the assignee accordingly acquires the assignor's right to forfeit the lease.[32]

Restrictions on right of forfeiture

Even where a landlord has expressly reserved a right of forfeiture for breach of a tenant's obligation, and has not waived the right, the law imposes certain restrictions upon its exercise.

1. Forfeiture for non-payment of rent

At common law a landlord cannot exercise a right of re-entry for non-payment of rent unless he has made a formal demand for the rent upon the premises before sunset on the last day on which the rent has to be paid in order to avoid forfeiture; and this demand must continue until sunset. However, the terms of the lease may exempt the landlord from the need to make this formal demand, and the Common Law Procedure Act 1852 exempts him from doing so if half a year's rent is in arrears and unpaid and there are no sufficient chattels upon the premises to enable the landlord to recover the rent by distress.

A tenant may ask the court to grant him relief against a forfeiture which he has incurred for non-payment of rent, *i.e.* may ask that his lease be restored to him. The court has a discretionary power to grant such relief; the power is equitable in origin but is now regulated by the Common Law Procedure Act 1852. Under this Act the tenant must make his application for relief within six months of ejectment.[33]

The power to grant relief is based on the principle that the landlord's right of re-entry is merely a security for due performance of the tenant's obligations. Accordingly the court may relieve the tenant from forfeiture of the lease if he is now prepared to discharge his obligations, *i.e.* to pay the rent together with any costs incurred by the landlord, provided always that the court is satisfied that it would be just and equitable to grant relief.

2. Forfeiture for breach of other obligations

The Law of Property Act 1925, s.146, contains certain general provisions which apply to forfeiture for breach of a tenant's

---

[32] *London & County (A. & D.) Ltd.* v. *Wilfred Sportsman Ltd.* [1971] Ch. 764.
[33] It seems this limit does not apply where forfeiture is enforced by peaceable re-entry, not by court proceedings (*Thatcher* v. *C. H. Pearce & Sons (Contractors) Ltd.* [1968] 1 W.L.R. 748).

obligations other than to pay rent and other than certain obligations which are specially mentioned below. Under these provisions the landlord is required to serve a statutory notice upon the tenant and to give him a reasonable time within which to comply with it; if the tenant does comply he avoids forfeiture. Moreover, under the same section, the court may grant relief against forfeiture if the tenant applies before the landlord obtains possession of the premises. The landlord generally sues for possession, and the tenant applies for relief in the landlord's action. Relief may be granted or refused as the court thinks fit, "having regard to the proceedings and conduct of the parties . . . and to all the other circumstances."

The statutory notice must:

(i) specify the breach complained of,
(ii) require the tenant to remedy it, if it is capable of remedy, and
(iii) require the tenant to make compensation in money (if the landlord desires that).

In determining whether a statutory notice is valid, it may not always be clear whether the breach complained of is "capable of remedy." Where for instance premises have been used for an immoral purpose in breach of covenant, the breach may be held incapable of remedy, even though the immoral user has ceased, if it appears that a continuing stigma or devaluation has resulted.[34] Another example occurs where the tenant has assigned or sub-let in breach of covenant: such a breach, it has been held, is never capable of remedy, and it follows that the landlord need allow the tenant only a short time, such as a fortnight, before proceeding to enforce the forfeiture.[35] But, according to a later decision,[36] it does not follow that a "once and for all" breach of a positive covenant is incapable of remedy: if for instance the tenant has failed to perform a covenant within the time stipulated, the court may consider that the breach could be sufficiently "remedied" by the payment of compensation (which of course might also apply to an assignment or sub-letting in breach of covenant). There is some confusion here, arising from the ambiguity of the expression "capable of remedy": a possible solution would be to regard the second and third statutory requirements, in some circumstances at least, as alternatives, and if there is any doubt as to whether the breach can be remedied, in the sense of being undone or rectified, the landlord should require compensation.

---

[34] *Rugby School (Governors)* v. *Tannahill* [1935] 1 K.B. 87.
[35] *Scala House and District Property Co. Ltd.* v. *Forbes* [1974] Q.B. 575.
[36] *Expert Clothing Service & Sales* v. *Hillgate House* [1986] Ch. 340.

In any event, technical questions concerning the validity of the landlord's notice are distinct from the substantive issue whether his claim to forfeit the lease should succeed. Thus it by no means follows from the fact that the breach complained of cannot be remedied that the tenant will be refused relief.[35]

There are special provisions where the notice relates to breach of a repairing covenant. In particular, by the Leasehold Property (Repairs) Act 1938, if a lease is for seven years or more, of which at least three remain unexpired, the notice must inform the tenant of his right to serve a counter notice under the Act, and if the tenant does this within 28 days the landlord cannot proceed further in a claim either for possession or for damages without the leave of the county court. Under section 147 of the Law of Property Act 1925 the court in its discretion may relieve a tenant from liability under a covenant for internal decorative repair.

3. Forfeiture for breach of inspection covenant in mining lease

The rent payable under a mining lease is usually in the form of a royalty which varies with the amount of the mineral got by the tenant under the lease. The lease generally contains detailed provisions requiring the tenant to keep proper accounts and giving to the landlord a right of inspection of the accounts and of the working of the mine. Parliament has recognised the vital importance of such provisions to the landlord by enacting that the Law of Property Act 1925, s.146, shall have no application to a breach by the tenant of such inspection covenants. In the event of a breach by the tenant of such provisions, therefore, the landlord may forfeit the lease without serving the usual statutory notice, and the court has no power to grant relief to the tenant.

4. Forfeiture on the bankruptcy, etc., of the tenant

The lease may contain provisions which allow the landlord to re-enter if the tenant becomes bankrupt or suffers the lease to be taken in execution. (A lease may be a valuable asset, and a creditor of the tenant who obtains judgment against him may by means of the appropriate writ of execution sell the tenant's interest in the lease for what it will fetch. This is what is meant by the tenant's suffering the lease to be taken in execution.) Section 146 provides that in the case of certain types of property the section shall have no application to the exercise by a landlord of his right of re-entry on these grounds, *i.e.* the landlord can forfeit the lease without having served notice, and the tenant cannot be granted

---

[35] *Scala House and District Property Co. Ltd.* v. *Forbes* [1974] Q.B. 575.

relief. These cases are where the lease is of (i) agricultural or pastoral land, (ii) mines or minerals, (iii) a public-house, (iv) a furnished house, or (v) property with respect to which the personal qualifications of the tenant are of special importance to the landlord. In any other case the section applies for one year after the bankruptcy or taking in execution, and it applies indefinitely after the end of the year if during the year the lease has been sold by the tenant's trustee in bankruptcy or execution creditor.

5. Relief for sub-lessees

If a head lease is forfeited any sub-lease automatically falls with it. However, the Law of Property Act 1925, s.146, as amended by the Law of Property (Amendment) Act 1929, gives to a sub-lessee the right to apply to the court for relief against the forfeiture of the head lease, whatever the ground may be on which the head lease has been forfeited (*i.e.* even if the head lessee himself could not have applied for relief against the forfeiture). The court has a similar jurisdiction in equity, which may be exercised even after forfeiture of the head lease.[37] If relief is granted, the court will make an order vesting in the sub-lessee the property comprised in the head lease for a term not longer that the residue of the sub-lease, and on such conditions as the court thinks fit. In general, relief will only be granted to a sub-lessee if he complies with the tenant's obligations under the head lease, and makes good any subsisting breaches; it follows that he may have to pay arrears of rent due under the head lease.[38]

When a head lease is forfeited for non-payment of rent a sub-lessee has a separate right to apply for relief against the forfeiture under the Common Law Procedure Act 1852.

OTHER MODES OF DETERMINATION

A lease will also come to an end if the tenant surrenders it to his landlord and the landlord accepts the surrender. Surrender may be express, in which case it should be by deed, or it may be implied by law, *e.g.* if the tenant gives up possession of the premises to the landlord and the landlord accepts that possession. If a lessee who has granted a sub-lease surrenders his lease to his landlord, the sub-lease will not be extinguished and the superior landlord will take subject to it.

---

[37] *Abbey National B.S.* v. *Maybeech* [1985] Ch. 190.
[38] He would have a right of indemnity against the head lessee.

A lease may also come to an end by merger. Merger occurs when the owner of the lease acquires the reversion, in which case the lease is said to merge in the reversion, and the lease ceases to exist.

Finally, it may be mentioned that the Law of Property Act 1925, s.153, allows a lessee to execute a deed of enlargement enlarging his lease into the fee simple. The principal conditions are that the lease should have been granted for at least 300 years, of which 200 years or more remain unexpired, that no rent of any money value should be payable, and that no trust or right of redemption should exist in favour of the reversioner.[39]

ASSIGNMENTS AND SUB-LEASES

Assignment of a lease

A lessee has an estate in land of which, like any other estate or interest, he can dispose, or which on his death will devolve under his will or intestacy. If it is a legal term of years (including, it will be recalled, various forms of periodic tenancy which may be validly created even by word of mouth),[40] any assignment must be made by deed if it is to be effective at law,[41] but an informal assignment[42] or a specifically enforceable agreement to assign may be treated in equity as transferring to the assignee the beneficial or equitable interest in the lease.

If the lessee holds only an equitable lease, he can assign[43] his rights thereunder, including his right to claim specific performance against the lessor, but in other respects the position of an assignee of an equitable lease *vis-à-vis* the lessor is less clear.[44]

Two further aspects of the assignment of a lease will be discussed later: first, the effect of an express provision in the lease prohibiting or restricting assignment[45]; secondly, the basis on which covenants in a lease are enforceable between the original parties, and between their assigns.[46]

---

[39] For the possible implications of this provision, see M. & W. pp. 687–688.
[40] See p. 84.
[41] LPA 1925, s.52.
[42] Provided it is for value (see p. 25).
[43] By written instrument (LPA 1925, s.53); but an informal assignment might be effective in equity.
[44] See *Purchase* v. *Lichfield Brewery Co.* [1915] 1 K.B. 184, *Boyer* v. *Warbey* [1953] 1 Q.B. 234.
[45] p. 99.
[46] p. 133 *et seq.*

Sub-lease

A lessee who does not wish to part with his whole interest in the land may, instead of assigning the lease, create a sub-lease: this must be for a term at least one day less than the head-lease, otherwise the transaction will constitute an assignment, not a sub-lease. The sub-lessee will hold a legal term of years,[47] and the same incidents of the landlord-tenant relationship will attach to the sub-lease as attach to the head lease, subject, of course, to any variations in their express terms. A further underlease may be created by the sub-lessee, and so on.

IMPLIED OBLIGATIONS OF LANDLORD AND TENANT

Certain obligations are imposed upon the landlord or the tenant by implication of law. In general, these implied obligations may be varied by express provisions in the lease, but in some instances variation is prohibited by statute.

Landlord's obligations

1. Implied covenant for quiet enjoyment

The landlord impliedly covenants that the tenant shall have quiet enjoyment of the premises free from any interference by the landlord himself, or by anyone lawfully claiming through the landlord.[48] It will be observed that the covenant is in a restricted form. If, for example, the lease in question is a sub-lease and the sub-lessor loses his own lease by the exercise by the superior landlord of a right of re-entry, the sub-lessee will not be able to sue the sub-lessor (his own landlord) for damages for breach of the sub-lessor's implied covenant for quiet enjoyment. The sub-lessee has not been disturbed in his possession of the premises by any act of his landlord or anyone claiming lawfully through his landlord— the superior landlord does not claim through his own tenant (the sub-lessor), but by title paramount. (As we have seen,[49] the sub-lessee's remedy in this case is to apply to the court for relief against forfeiture of the head lease.)

---

[47] Provided that the sub-lease complies with LPA 1925, ss.52–54; if not, it may be valid as an equitable sub-lease (see p. 85).
[48] *Cf. Celsteel Ltd.* v. *Alton House Holdings Ltd.* (*No.* 2) [1987] 1 W.L.R. 291.
[49] p. 93.

Breach of the covenant will usually consist in some act of physical interference with the tenant's possession of the land,[50] but persistent threats intended to drive him out have also been held to constitute a breach.[51]

2. Derogation from grant

Like any other grantor, a landlord is not at liberty to derogate (*i.e.* detract) from his grant. Accordingly he must not do, or suffer to be done, anything which would render the premises unfit for the purposes for which they have been let. For example, a landlord can be restrained from so using adjoining land as to prejudice the tenant's use of the demised premises.[52]

3. Condition of the premises

In general no obligation is implied on the landlord's part that the premises are fit for occupation, or that he will maintain them in repair.[53] There are, however, some exceptions:

(i) *Furnished houses.* On the letting of a house furnished there is (unless otherwise agreed) an implied condition that the premises are reasonably fit for human habitation at the commencement of the lease (but the landlord does not undertake to keep them so). This common law rule is known as the rule in *Smith* v. *Marrable*.[54]

(ii) *Landlord and Tenant Act 1985, s.8.* When a house is let at a rent which does not exceed £80 a year in London or £52 a year elsewhere (half these amounts if the tenancy was granted before July 6, 1957) there is an implied condition that the premises are fit for human habitation at the commencement of the tenancy, and the landlord impliedly agrees to keep them so. The parties cannot generally contract out of these provisions. Quite a small defect may amount to a breach of the landlord's obligation where, as in the case of a broken sash-cord, it

---

[50] *Markham* v. *Paget* [1908] 1 Ch. 697 (undermining), *Owen* v. *Gadd* [1956] 2 Q.B. 99 (scaffolding obstructing access); contrast *Browne* v. *Flower* [1911] 1 Ch. 219 (mere intrusion on privacy).
[51] *Kenny* v. *Preen* [1963] 1 Q.B. 499. It is a criminal offence unlawfully to evict or harass the occupier of residential premises (Protection from Eviction Act 1977, s.1).
[52] *Harmer* v. *Jumbil (Nigeria) Tin Areas Ltd.* [1921] 1 Ch. 200.
[53] As to the landlord's implied obligations with respect to premises retained by him, where these constitute the tenant's only means of access, see *Liverpool City Council* v. *Irwin* [1977] A.C. 239.
[54] (1843) 11 M. & W. 5 (premises bug-ridden).

is such as to render the premises dangerous.[55] But a landlord incurs no liability in respect of a defect unless he had notice of it, and this rule applies even where the defect was latent so that the tenant could not have notified the landlord of it (the same rule applies when a landlord expressly covenants to keep the premises in repair).[56]

(iii) *Landlord and Tenant Act 1985 s.11.* If a lease of a dwelling house is granted after October 24, 1961, for less than seven years (or the landlord can determine the lease within seven years) there is an implied covenant by the landlord to keep the structure and exterior of the premises, including the drains, in repair, and to maintain the installations for the supply of gas, water, and electricity, for sanitation and for space and water heating. When this provision applies any liability in respect of these matters which would otherwise have rested on the tenant is excluded. The parties cannot contract out of these provisions without the leave of the county court.

It should also be noted that local authorities have wide statutory powers[57] under which they may compel the owner of a house to maintain it in reasonable condition, so that a tenant by complaining to the local authority may sometimes be able to compel his landlord to do work which as between himself and the tenant he is not contractually bound to do.

Tenant's obligations

A tenant is bound to pay the rent, to pay tenants' rates and taxes (*i.e.* all ordinary rates and taxes), and if the landlord is liable to repair the premises to allow the landlord to enter and view the state of repair.

Tenants generally are impeachable for voluntary waste.[58] A tenant for a fixed term is also impeachable for permissive waste, so that he is under a general obligation to maintain the premises in repair. Periodic tenants are not impeachable for permissive waste, but are bound to use the premises in a tenant-like manner (*e.g.* to

---

[55] *Summers* v. *Salford Corporation* [1943] A.C. 283.
[56] *McCarrick* v. *Liverpool Corporation* [1947] A.C. 219.
[57] Now contained in the Housing Act 1985, Parts VI and IX.
[58] See p. 22.

keep the drain pipes clear), and a yearly tenant may perhaps be bound to keep the premises wind and water tight.[59]

THE "USUAL COVENANTS"

The grant of a lease is sometimes preceded by the signing of an agreement to grant the lease. Such an agreement may expressly provide that the lease shall contain the usual covenants, and if the agreement is silent as to what covenants the lease shall contain it is an implied term of the agreement that the lease shall contain the usual covenants. What covenants are usual is then a matter of evidence and depends upon the practice of conveyancers in the locality, but the following covenants are usual by the general custom of conveyancers[60]:

  (i) On the part of the landlord, a covenant for quiet enjoyment, restricted to the acts of the landlord and those lawfully claiming through him.
 (ii) On the part of the tenant, covenants to pay the rent and to pay tenants' rates and taxes, to keep the premises in repair, and to permit the landlord to enter and view the state of repair.
(iii) A condition of re-entry for non-payment of rent.

If the parties have expressly or impliedly agreed that the lease shall contain the usual covenants, then when the lease comes to be drawn up either party may insist upon the inclusion of the usual covenants and may prevent the insertion of any other covenant.

EXPRESS COVENANTS

Mention may be made here of two covenants that are most commonly found in leases.

Covenant to repair

The main principle which applies to the interpretation of such a covenant is that it is a covenant to repair, not to re-build, the premises. The covenantor is bound by timely repair to maintain the premises in as good a condition as possible, regard being had

---

[59] See *Warren* v. *Keen* [1954] 1 Q.B. 15, C.A.
[60] *Hampshire* v. *Wickens* (1878) 7 Ch.D. 555; *Hodgkinson* v. *Crowe* (1875) 10 Ch. App. 622.

to the age and condition of the premises at the commencement of the tenancy; but he is not bound to rebuild main parts of the structure which have become beyond ordinary repair. The covenant may, however, extend to the replacement of subsidiary parts of the premises if they are beyond ordinary repair.

The addition to the word "repair" of such expressions as "tenantable" or "good and substantial" seems to have little, if any, effect.

Sometimes a covenant to repair is qualified by the addition of some such words as "fair wear and tear excepted." Such excepting words are restrictively construed by the courts, and although they will exempt the tenant from liability for the immediate consequences of the excepted cause they will not exclude liability for consequential damage. For example, if a slate blows off the roof, the tenant is not immediately liable to replace it, but if he does not prevent the entry of rain, and this causes the roof timbers to rot, he will be liable for the damage to the timbers.[61]

By the Landlord and Tenant Act 1927, s.18, the damages recoverable by a landlord may not exceed the injury to the reversion. Hence if at the end of the tenancy the landlord intends to pull down the premises he can recover nothing.[62]

Covenant against assigning, etc.[63]

The lessee often covenants not to assign or under-let the premises. If the covenant is in this simple form, only an *inter vivos* disposition of the whole of the premises will amount to a breach; an underletting of part of the premises will not, therefore, be a breach. It is rare, however, to find a covenant in this simple form, and it often requires the tenant not to assign or under-let or part with possession of the premises or any part thereof.

If the covenant is qualified, *i.e.* if it prohibits assignment or subletting *without the landlord's consent,* two statutory provisions come into operation. First, by the Law of Property Act 1925, s.144, subject to contrary agreement, the landlord may not demand payment for his consent.[64] Secondly, by the Landlord and Tenant Act 1927, s.19, notwithstanding any contrary agreement, the landlord may not unreasonably withhold his consent; and in the case of building leases for more than 40 years, of which more

---

[61] *Regis Property Co. Ltd.* v. *Dudley* [1959] A.C. 370.

[62] For a further restriction on the landlord's rights, see the Leasehold Property (Repairs) Act 1938 (p. 92).

[63] Radical proposals for reform are made by Law Commission Reports No. 141 (1985) and Nos. 161 and 162 (1987).

[64] Other than a reasonable sum for legal or other expenses.

than seven remain unexpired, the landlord's consent is not required for an assignment or sub-letting. There is no hard and fast rule as to the matters which a landlord may properly consider in deciding whether or not to grant his consent, but the personality of the proposed tenant and the nature of the proposed user of the premises are clearly relevant considerations.[65] As a general rule the landlord need consider only his own relevant interests, but there may be circumstances in which it would be unreasonable to withhold consent if the resulting detriment to the tenant far outweighed any benefit to the landlord.[66]

If consent is requested, and is unreasonably refused, the tenant will incur no liability by assigning without consent; but he will be in breach if he assigns without having sought consent, even though the assignment is one to which consent could not reasonably have been refused. An assignment made in breach of covenant is not void, and accordingly the assignee acquires the lease.[67] But if the lease contains a condition of re-entry, the landlord will be able to forfeit the lease in the hands of the assignee: relief against forfeiture might be granted in the case of breach of a qualified covenant, if the assignment was not one to which the landlord could reasonably have objected, though presumably not if the covenant was absolute.

[65] It is generally unlawful to withhold consent on grounds of sex (Sex Discrimination Act 1975, s.31) or race (Race Relations Act 1976, s.24).
[66] *International Drilling Fluids Ltd.* v. *Louisville Investments (Uxbridge) Ltd.* [1986] Ch. 513.
[67] *Old Grovesbury Manor Farm Ltd.* v. *W. Seymour Plant Sales & Hire Ltd. (No. 2)* [1979] 1 W.L.R. 1391.

13. Security of tenure and rent restriction

In Chapter 12, the nature of a lease or tenancy was considered purely in terms of contract and property, but note was taken that this is pre-eminently a field in which for social, economic and political reasons the legislature has intervened to increasing effect in recent years. All legislation of this kind has two main objects—first to give security of tenure to the tenant, secondly to restrict the amount of the rent that the landlord may lawfully charge. Statutory protection has been extended separately to residential, business and agricultural tenancies.

DWELLINGS

Protection has for many years been conferred on tenants of residential property by a long series of statutes, commonly known as the Rent Acts, beginning with an Act passed in 1915. Since then varying social and economic conditions, and varying political dispensations, during wartime, between the wars, and after the Second World War, have given rise to different systems and degrees of control. The principal statute presently in force is the Rent Act 1977, but important changes were made by the Housing Act 1980, and it will be necessary even in the short account which follows to deal both with the basic system, and with modified versions. This aspect of land law is of undeniable practical importance, and cannot be neglected even in an introductory book; what is to be regretted is that the statutory provisions in question are excessively elaborate, and subject to continual change.

Regulated tenancies: Rent Act 1977

The main provisions of the Act apply to any tenancy under which a dwelling-house (which may be part of a house) is let as a separate dwelling, provided in most cases that the dwelling-house has a rateable value not exceeding £1,500 in London or £750 elsewhere.[1]

The Act does not apply where premises have been let solely for business purposes[2]; furthermore (for reasons concerned with user rather than purpose) the majority of mixed business-residential lettings, *e.g.* a small shop with rooms above, also fall outside the Act.[3] The requirement that the dwelling should be separate prima facie excludes shared accommodation, but a distinction is drawn between the tenant obliged to share with his landlord and the tenant obliged to share with others: the former has the more limited protection afforded to restricted contracts, whereas the latter enjoys the main benefits of the Act with only minor modifications.

The Act is excluded (a) where no rent is payable or where the rent is less than two-thirds of the rateable value of the property, (b) where the rent bona fide includes payments in respect of board or attendance, provided as regards attendance that the amount of the rent fairly attributable thereto forms a substantial portion of the whole rent, (c) in general where the tenancy is created by a "resident landlord," *i.e.* a landlord who resides in part of the same building (other than a purpose-built block of flats),[4] (d) where the tenancy is a holiday letting or a letting to students by specified educational institutions, (e) where the tenancy is an "assured tenancy," (f) in general where the tenancy relates to an agricultural holding or a public house. In cases (b) and (c), however, the tenant may have the limited protection afforded by the restricted contract provisions, which are discussed below.

The Act is also excluded where the landlord is the Crown or a government department or a local authority, development corporation, housing trust or similar body.

For the purpose of security of tenure under the Act, regulated tenancies are classified as either "protected tenancies" or "statutory tenancies." So long as the ordinary contractual tenancy continues it is a protected tenancy in the sense merely that the tenant is protected by the provisions of the Act with respect to rent; his security of tenure, *i.e.* his protection against eviction, is conferred by the general law, not by the Act. But once that contractual, protected tenancy comes to an end, the tenant must rely on the provisions of the Act for his security, and it is then that a "statutory tenancy" arises.

---

[1] Lower rateable values apply where a dwelling was first rated before April 1, 1973.
[2] Nor where the purpose is to provide more than one dwelling (*Horford Investments Ltd.* v. *Lambert* [1976] Ch. 39).
[3] *Wolfe* v. *Hogan* [1949] 2 K.B. 194.
[4] Except for limited periods following sale or death, the landlord or his successor must *continue* to reside in the same building.

A statutory tenancy is based on the tenant's statutory right to remain in possession, despite termination of his contractual tenancy by notice, effluxion of time, forfeiture or otherwise, unless and until the court makes an order against him on specified grounds. Such a tenancy is subject to all such terms of the contractual tenancy as are not inconsistent with the Act.

This statutory tenancy, however, is a legal anomaly because the right to remain in possession is personal to the tenant, and he cannot dispose of it *inter vivos* or by his will (although there is provision whereby the tenant has a limited power with the landlord's consent to substitute another tenant in his place). On the tenant's death, his right is transmitted to his widow residing with him at his death, or if there is no widow so residing then to some other member of his family who had resided with him for six months before his death. Only two such transmissions are possible, and a statutory tenancy subsists only so long as the tenant or his successor resides on the premises.

Once the tenant has become a statutory tenant, there are certain grounds upon which the landlord may obtain an order for possession upon application to the court, namely, either on the ground that suitable alternative accommodation is available, or in certain specified "cases," *e.g.* where the tenant has broken certain of his obligations; or where the tenancy was a service tenancy (*i.e.* the premises were let to the tenant in consequence of his former employment by the landlord) and the premises are reasonably required as a residence for another employee of the landlord; or where the landlord[5] reasonably requires the premises as a residence for himself, his son or daughter over 18, or his father or mother, or his father-in-law or mother-in-law, provided that the tenant is unable to satisfy the court that in all the circumstances greater hardship would be caused by making the order for possession than by refusing it. In general the court must be satisfied that in all the circumstances it is reasonable to make an order for possession. There are, however, certain cases in which the court is bound to make an order for possession without the landlord having to establish reasonableness.[6]

The provisions of the Act with respect to rent apply to all regulated tenancies, whether protected or statutory. The maximum rent recoverable is that *registered* for the dwelling-house in accordance with the provisions of the Act, or, if no such rent is registered, the rent payable under the present tenancy. Applica-

---

[5] Other than a "landlord by purchase."

[6] The "mandatory grounds," *e.g.* when a former owner-occupier wishes to resume occupation. Another such ground ("case 19") relates to protected shorthold tenancies (below).

tions for registration of a rent may be made to the rent officer by the landlord or by the tenant or jointly by both. There is nothing to prevent a tenant from agreeing to a rent on one day and applying to the rent officer on the next. The rent officer registers the rent if he thinks it fair; if not, he determines and registers a *fair rent*.[7] If either party objects, the matter is referred to a rent assessment committee. In determining a fair rent, regard must be had to all the circumstances (other than personal circumstances) and in particular to the age, character and locality of the dwelling-house and to its state of repair. Registered rents tend to be substantially lower than free market rents, because rent officers are required to exclude scarcity of accommodation from consideration.

Protected shorthold tenancies

The Housing Act 1980, ss.51–55, introduced this limited form of protection in order to encourage owners to let dwellings, where otherwise they might be reluctant to do so because of the security of tenure provisions of the Rent Act 1977. Accordingly, a protected shorthold tenant under the Housing Act is given the same protection with respect to rent as an ordinary protected tenant, but no security of tenure once the protected tenancy has expired.

To qualify as a protected shorthold tenancy, a tenancy must be granted for a term not less than one year nor more than five years, and the landlord must formally notify the tenant that it is to be a protected shorthold tenancy.

The tenant may determine the tenancy by one month's notice or, if it is for a term exceeding two years, three months' notice. The distinctive feature of this form of protected tenancy is that on or after its expiry the landlord has a mandatory ground[8] for possession on giving written notice to the tenant in accordance with the statutory provisions.

Restricted contracts

As we have seen, a tenancy to which the "resident landlord" exception applies, or under which the rent includes any payment for board or a substantial payment for attendance, or under which the tenant shares living accommodation with the landlord, is not a

---

[7] Subject to certain exceptions, no application to register a different rent may be made within two years.

[8] "Case 19" (see note 6).

protected tenancy within the main provisions of the 1977 Act. In these cases, however, a limited protection is given by Parts V and VII of the Act.[9]

These provisions apply only to dwellings of which the rateable value is within the limits set by the Act, and they are excluded if any substantial payment is made for board, or if occupation is for the purposes of a holiday. Subject to these limitations, protection is given not only to a tenant under a lease, but also to a lodger or paying guest provided he has exclusive occupation[10] of some part of the premises.

The protection given is twofold. First, the contract of tenancy may be referred (by either party or by the local authority) to the local rent tribunal to determine a reasonable rent. The tribunal may confirm, reduce or increase the rent to the amount that it considers reasonable. Rents so determined are registered, and the landlord may not thereafter charge any greater rent than the registered rent unless the rent tribunal authorises an increase on the ground of a subsequent change of circumstances.[11] Secondly, although even such limited security of tenure as was afforded by the 1977 Act has been abolished for contracts made after 27 November 1980, a court making an order for possession against an occupier with a restricted contract now has power to stay or suspend the order, or postpone the date for possession, for up to three months, subject to terms as to payment for occupation.

Secure tenancies

The Rent Act does not apply when the landlord is a public body such as a local authority.[12] The Housing Act 1980,[13] recognising the substantial increase in public housing in recent times and the need to protect occupiers of such housing, created a new form of "secure tenancy" applying[14] where a dwelling-house is let[15] as a separate dwelling by a local authority, development corporation, housing association or similar body to an individual who occupies it as his only or principal house.

A secure tenancy can be terminated only by an order of the court on one of the grounds specified in the Act, and the landlord

---

[9] As amended by the Housing Act 1980, s.69.
[10] Not "exclusive possession" in the technical sense (*Luganda* v. *Service Hotels Ltd.* [1969] 2 Ch. 209).
[11] The two year rule applies (note 7 above).
[12] Above, p. 102.
[13] In provisions now replaced by the Housing Act 1985.
[14] Subject to exceptions, most of which correspond to Rent Act exceptions.
[15] These provisions apply also to a licence.

must first have served a notice in prescribed form. Some of the grounds for possession are similar to those applying to regulated tenancies; in general the court cannot make an order unless it considers it reasonable to do so, and in some cases suitable alternative accommodation must be available. There is provision for one succession to a secure tenancy on the death of the tenant.

There is no system of rent control under these provisions of the Housing Act, but under the Rent Act 1977 provision is made for the registration of fair rents in respect of dwellings let by a housing association or housing trust or the Housing Corporation.

Perhaps the most important of the rights conferred by the 1980 Act on secure tenants is the right to buy at a discounted price the freehold or a long lease of the dwelling, and to obtain a mortgage loan for some or all of the price, repayable over twenty-five years.

Assured tenancies

These constitute a further innovation under the Housing Act 1980.[16] Although the tenancies concerned are those of dwellings, they are to be governed by modified provisions of Part II of the Landlord and Tenant Act 1954, rather than by the Rent Act. A tenancy is an assured tenancy only if it (i) relates to a building, construction work on which began after 8 August 1980; (ii) is granted by an approved body specified by the Secretary of State; (iii) is not the subject of a notice by the landlord stating that it is to be a protected or housing association tenancy, rather than an assured tenancy.

Dwellings occupied by farm workers

The Rent Acts have never applied to most so-called "tied cottages," *i.e.* residential accommodation supplied to farm workers under their terms of employment. Two main reasons explain why the Acts do not apply: first, the arrangements under which the accommodation is provided are usually such as to create a mere licence, rather than a lease; secondly, in most such cases either no rent is payable, or the rent is less than two-thirds of the rateable value. The Rent (Agriculture) Act 1976 is designed to bridge this gap.

The Act confers security of tenure (either as a protected occupier or, where his initial licence or lease is determined, as a

---

[16] Sections 56–58. These provisions are unaffected by the Housing Act 1985.

statutory tenant) on a qualifying worker who under a relevant licence or tenancy occupies a dwelling-house belonging to his employer.

In broad terms, (i) a worker "qualifies" for this purpose if he has been employed in agriculture for not less than 91 out of the past 104 weeks, (ii) the licence or tenancy is "relevant" notwithstanding that it *is* a mere licence, or that little or no rent is payable, provided that it gives exclusive occupation of a separate dwelling. Subject to this, however, much the same limitations apply as have already been mentioned in relation to the Rent Act: for example, farm workers employed and housed by resident landlords or by government departments fall outside the 1976 Act.

A statutory tenancy arising under the 1976 Act is similar in most respects to its counterpart under the Rent Acts, but only one transmission can take place in favour of the tenant's family. The grounds on which a landlord may be entitled to recover possession are also similar, but with one important variation. If possession is sought solely on the ground that the house is needed for another worker, the landlord must apply to the local housing authority for suitable alternative accommodation for the statutory tenant. If satisfied that vacant possession of the house is required for the other worker and his family, that the landlord himself cannot reasonably provide suitable accommodation, and that the interests of efficient agriculture so require, the authority must then use its best endeavours to provide the accommodation.

The provisions of the 1976 Act with respect to rent come into play only when a statutory tenancy has arisen. Thereafter, no rent is payable until either the parties have agreed a rent, or the landlord has served a notice of increase on the tenant. The rent then payable must not exceed any rent registered for the premises under the Rent Act or (if no such rent is registered) a weekly rent based on an annual amount equal to one and a half times the current rateable value of the premises. There is provision for the registration of rents in accordance with a procedure similar to that set out in the Rent Act 1977.

Long tenancies of dwelling-houses

The old Rent Acts did not apply to tenancies for a term exceeding 21 years, but a limited security was given by Part I of the Landlord and Tenant Act 1954. Such tenancies, however, if not at a low rent (*i.e.* a rent less than two-thirds of the rateable value of the property) are now governed by the Rent Act 1977. In determining whether a *long tenancy* is at a low rent, such part of the rent (if any) as is expressed to be payable in respect of rates, services, repairs, maintenance or insurance is to be disregarded, unless it could not have been regarded by the parties as so payable.

If the tenancy is at a low rent it is outside the Rent Act, but remains subject to the Landlord and Tenant Act 1954 provided that the *only* reason why the Rent Act does not apply is the low rent. Under the 1954 Act, the tenancy is automatically continued after the end of the term if the tenant so desires, and the landlord may terminate it in only two ways. First, after service of notice he may apply to the court for possession on grounds similar to those under the Rent Act. Secondly, he may serve a notice proposing a statutory tenancy, in which case the terms of the tenancy will be settled by agreement between the parties or by the court. After commencement of the statutory tenancy, the rent will be governed by the provisions of the Rent Act.

If the lease is of a house to which the Leasehold Reform Act 1967 applies, the tenant may wish, alternatively, to take advantage of the provisions of that Act, as described below.

Leasehold enfranchisement

Leases for a very long term such as 99 years or 999 years are frequently granted at a low, or "ground," rent in consideration either of the tenant building on the land or (where there is already a building on the land) of his paying a "fine" or premium virtually equivalent to the capital or freehold value of the land. The tenant (including of course his successors in title) at the end of such a lease had no security of tenure, because the tenancy, being at a low rent, was excluded from the operation of the Rent Acts. The Leasehold Reform Act 1967[17] meets this case by giving to the tenant of a leasehold house[18] within certain rateable value limits held for a term exceeding 21 years at a rent less than two-thirds of the rateable value a right to acquire on fair terms the freehold or an extended lease (of 50 years), provided that when he seeks to exercise the right he has occupied the house, or some part of it[19], as his only or main residence for the last three years or for periods amounting to three years in the last ten years.[20]

---

[17] As to the dubious principle of "equity" on which the Act was said to be based, see M. & W., pp. 1127–1128, and note *Duke of Westminster* v. *Johnston* (1987) 53 P. & C.R. 36, H.L.

[18] For this purpose a flat is not a house. The Landlord and Tenant Act 1987, Part I, contains detailed provisions under which "qualifying" tenants of flats have rights with respect to the acquisition of the landlord's reversion.

[19] See *Harris* v. *Swick Securities Ltd.* [1969] 1 W.L.R. 1604.

[20] See *Poland* v. *Earl Cadogan* [1980] 3 All E.R. 544.

If the tenant elects to purchase the freehold, the price is based broadly[21] on the market value of the house, but on the assumption that the tenancy would be extended under the Act, or that the tenant would remain in possession as statutory tenant under the Landlord and Tenant Act 1954, Part I. If he claims a new lease, the rent is to be the current letting value of the site without the buildings, and may be revised after 25 years. In default of agreement as to price or rent, terms will be settled by the Leasehold Valuation Tribunal or, on appeal, by the Lands Tribunal. The county court has general jurisdiction over claims.

In certain cases the landlord may oppose the tenant's claim (*e.g.* if the landlord proposes to demolish or reconstruct the house, or if he reasonably requires the house as a residence for himself or a member of his family), but only at the cost of compensating the tenant for the loss of his rights under the Act.

BUSINESS PREMISES

Most tenancies of business premises (including mixed business-residential premises)[22] are protected by Part II of the Landlord and Tenant Act 1954. The broad effect of the Act is to continue the existing tenancy indefinitely unless and until terminated in accordance with the provisions of the Act. These require service by the landlord of a statutory notice to terminate the tenancy, which in turn gives the tenant the right to claim a new lease.

In default of agreement between the parties a tenant who is served with such a notice will have to apply to the court for a new tenancy. Unless the landlord can establish one of certain statutory grounds set out in his notice, the court is bound to grant a new tenancy for a period not exceeding 14 years on such terms as it thinks fit having regard to certain matters specified in the Act. The rent is fixed in accordance with current market values; in respect of other terms, the burden is on the party who seeks to depart from those of the existing tenancy.[23] In principle there is no limit to the number of renewals.

The grounds on which a landlord may oppose a new tenancy include breach by the tenant of certain of his obligations, that the landlord intends to demolish or reconstruct the premises, and that the landlord intends to occupy the premises himself (provided that the landlord's interest has not been purchased or created less than five years before the termination of the tenancy). If a new tenancy

---

[21] The method of calculation is complex, and outside the scope of this book.
[22] See p. 102.
[23] *O'May* v. *City of London Real Property Co. Ltd.* [1983] 2 A.C. 726.

is refused on certain of these grounds, notably the last two that have been mentioned, the tenant is entitled to compensation from the landlord. This compensation amounts to three times the rateable value of the premises, unless the tenant and his predecessors have occupied the premises for business purposes for the last 14 years, in which case the amount is six times the rateable value.

There are certain exceptions to the Act, *e.g.* agricultural holdings, service tenancies, and licensed premises.

Under the Landlord and Tenant Act 1927, a tenant who leaves may recover compensation from his landlord for improvements which he has made to business premises if these have added to their letting value.

AGRICULTURAL HOLDINGS

Agricultural tenancies have since 1875 been regulated by a series of statutes, conferring on agricultural tenants rights to compensation for improvements or disturbance and, more recently and more importantly, rights with respect to security of tenure and the control of rent.

The main provisions for security of tenure are now contained in the Agricultural Holdings Act 1986. Under these provisions, a tenancy for two years or more does not determine automatically at the end of the term, but will continue thereafter as a yearly tenancy unless either party gives written notice of termination not less than one year, nor more than two years, before the end of the original tenancy. Any letting for value for an interest less than a yearly tenancy is, subject to certain exceptions, converted into a yearly tenancy. To determine any tenancy of an agricultural holding, a full twelve months' notice is required, expiring at the end of a year of the tenancy.

Under the Act, a tenant who receives a notice to quit has the right to serve a counter-notice on the landlord, claiming the benefit of the Act, whereupon the notice to quit will become inoperative unless the Agricultural Land Tribunal consents to its taking effect, which it can do only in specified cases, *e.g.* in order to enable the landlord to carry out some purpose which is desirable in the interests of good husbandry. In certain cases, however, the tenant has no right to serve a counter-notice, *e.g.* where the landlord's interest in the holding has been materially prejudiced by an irreparable breach by the tenant of a term of the tenancy. The landlord's notice must indicate the ground relied on, and any question as to whether the tenant has a right to serve a counter-notice is settled by arbitration. Although the death of the tenant is one of the cases in which there is no right to serve a counter-notice, the Act provides in relation to tenancies granted before July 12, 1984 that on the death of the tenant any member of his near family who has recently derived his livelihood from the holding for five years can apply to the Agricultural Land Tribunal for a tenancy, and the application will be granted if the Tribunal is satisfied as to the applicant's suitability. The Act also provides that a tenant who wishes to retire may nominate an eligible successor.

A tenant who is required by his landlord to quit the land is (with some exceptions) entitled to compensation for disturbance. The amount of the compensation is not less than one year's and not more than two years' rent. A tenant who quits his holding may also be entitled to compensation for certain improvements carried out by him. The amount of the compensation is generally the increase in the value of the holding, but where the improvement is of a short term character the amount is the value of the improvement to a new tenant.

Finally, there are provisions under the Act whereby, at intervals of not less than three years, either party may require the amount of the rent to be settled by arbitration.

14. Easements and profits

EASEMENTS

An easement gives the right to use the land of another in a particular way (a positive easement, *e.g.* a right of way) or the right to prevent another from using his own land in a particular way (a negative easement, *e.g.* a right of light, which prevents the neighbour from building on his land in such a way as to obstruct unduly the flow of natural light to the windows of a house or other building). An easement is a right *in rem*, which binds the land over which it is exercisable in the hands of successive owners, and which can be enforced by successive owners of the land for the benefit of which it was granted. It is recognised in section 1(2) of the Law of Property Act 1925 as one of the interests in land which since 1925 are capable of subsisting at law.

The conditions of an easement

No right can be an easement unless it satisfies the following conditions:

(i) There must be a dominant tenement and a servient tenement *i.e.* one tenement to which the right is annexed and another tenement which bears the burden of the right.

(ii) The dominant and the servient tenements must be in different hands, or more precisely the two tenements must not be both owned and occupied by the same person in the same right.[1]

(iii) The right must accommodate the dominant tenement, *i.e.* in some way add to or protect the amenities of the land.

---

[1] *i.e.* the same capacity: thus, if one tenement is owned beneficially and the other as trustee, the two tenements are not owned in the same right.

(iv) The right must lie in grant, *i.e.* it must be capable of being granted by deed.

A right which does not satisfy these conditions will not be an easement. It does not, however, necessarily follow that the law will not recognise the right at all; it may be a perfectly valid right such as a contractual licence, but it will not be an easement.

As an easement is a right against the land of another it is obvious that there must be a servient tenement. The requirement of a dominant tenement is less obvious. It means that the benefit of an easement must be annexed to a definite plot of land, so that only the occupiers of that plot have the benefit of the right. An easement cannot, therefore, be created in favour of a grantee personally, *i.e.* independently of the ownership or occupation by him of adjacent land. In technical language an easement cannot exist in gross.

The requirement that there must be a dominant tenement itself implies the third condition, that the easement must "accommodate" the land, and only rarely will this condition fail to be satisfied. In *Hill* v. *Tupper*,[2] however, a right to hire out boats on a canal (the supposed servient tenement) was held not to constitute an easement, although the boats were stored on land adjoining the canal (the supposed dominant tenement); the right was a mere commercial licence granted by the canal owners to the boat owner personally, not in virtue of his ownership of the adjoining land.

Because the right must lie in grant, *i.e.* be capable of forming the subject-matter of a grant by deed, vague rights such as rights of view or privacy cannot be created as easements.[3] Such rights are essentially negative, operating to prevent a neighbour from using his land in a particular way, *e.g.* by building. To formulate a grant of negative rights presents obvious difficulties,[4] and the only negative easements recognised at law are those of light, air and support,[5] all of which are sufficiently definite to form the subject-matter of a grant: the first two are confined to light or air flowing to particular apertures in the dominant building, and accordingly do not prevent the servient owner from building altogether, but only from materially obstructing that limited access of light or air[6]; the third is confined to the support of one building by another, and prevents the servient owner from removing that support.

---

[2] (1863) 2 H. & C. 121.
[3] *Browne* v. *Flower* [1911] 1 Ch. 219.
[4] Restrictive covenants are the most effective means of creating such rights (see p. 139).
[5] See *Phipps* v. *Pears* [1965] 1 Q.B. 76 (no easement of protection from weather).
[6] Compare *Cable* v. *Bryant* [1908] 1 Ch. 259, *Bryant* v. *Lefever* (1879) 4 C.P.D. 172.

The category of positive easements, on the other hand, is manifestly not closed; there is no difficulty in formulating the grant of a right to use the land of another in a particular way, and the law has recognised as easements a very wide variety of rights, provided always that they comply with the prescribed conditions. Problems have arisen, however, where a right claimed as an easement has been held to be too extensive, amounting virtually to possession rather than mere use: as an example, different decisions have been reached by the courts on the question whether a right of storage can exist as an easement.[7] In the leading case of *Re Ellenborough Park*,[8] the right in question was a right which had been expressly granted as an easement to the purchasers of houses on a new estate to use an adjoining park for recreational purposes: at the end of an exhaustive analysis of the nature of an easement, the Court of Appeal arrived at the perhaps unsurprising conclusion that the right was indeed capable of being an easement. It must however be emphasised that there are good reasons why the category of easements, whether positive or negative, is unlikely to be extended much further. Like any other interest in land an easement must be granted by deed, but unlike the grant of other interests the grant of an easement may be merely implied (where an owner disposes of part of his land) or presumed (where rights in the nature of easements have been exercised for a long period with the apparent acquiescence of the servient owners). Whereas the law is almost bound to recognise as an easement a right which has been expressly granted as such, much greater resistance might be expected where the right is very extensive, encroaching seriously on the servient owner's freedom to enjoy his own property, and is claimed merely on the basis of an implied grant or, even more questionably, a presumed grant.[9]

Easements and natural rights

An easement is an acquired right, *i.e.* it must have been created by a grant of the right made by the owner of the servient tenement. A natural right is one that a landowner has as a necessary incident of his ownership of the land. Most natural rights are rights which a man has with respect to his own land, *e.g.* the right to walk about it.[10] There is, however, a natural right of support which gives to

---

[7] Compare *Copeland* v. *Greenhalf* [1952] Ch. 488, *Grigsby* v. *Melville* [1972] 1 W.L.R. 1355, *Wright* v. *Macadam* [1949] 2 K.B. 744.
[8] [1956] Ch. 131.
[9] As in *Copeland* v. *Greenhalf* (see note 7).
[10] As to riparian rights, see pp. 15–16.

every landowner the right to have his land supported laterally by the land of his neighbour. If this support is withdrawn and in consequence the surface of his land subsides, he will have an action for damages[11] against his neighbour. Any resulting damage to buildings can be recovered unless the weight of the building contributed to the subsidence, in which case *no* action will lie for breach of the natural right. Distinct from the natural right to support is the easement of support, which, like every easement, requires acquisition by grant. An easement of support can be acquired which will give the right to have one's building supported by neighbouring land or a neighbouring building.

Extent of easements

Rights of light and rights of way, which are the commonest easements, both give rise to a question as to the extent to which they may be exercised against the servient land.

There is no natural right of light, and in general a landowner cannot be prevented from obstructing the flow of light to his neighbour's land unless the neighbour has acquired an easement of light, or some other right such as a restrictive covenant against building. An easement of light does not extend to the whole of the light flowing from the servient land, but is confined to the light flowing to particular windows or apertures in a building on the dominant land. It gives the right only to sufficient light for use of the building for ordinary domestic or business purposes.[12] An obstruction of the flow of light which substantially diminishes the amount of light reaching the windows of a building will not necessarily constitute an infringement of an easement of light appurtenant to the building. The question is not how much light has been taken away, but how much light is left; if there is sufficient for ordinary domestic or business purposes no action will lie.[13]

The extent of a right of way, *i.e.* whether it is for all purposes and at all times, or is subject to certain limitations, depends upon how it was acquired. If it was expressly granted the question is one of construction of the terms of the grant, and for this purpose the *contra proferentem* rule applies, *i.e.* any doubt as to the meaning of the terms will be resolved against the grantor and in favour of the grantee: accordingly a right of way granted in general terms will

---

[11] See *Redland Brick Ltd.* v. *Morris* [1970] A.C. 652, in which a mandatory injunction was refused on the ground that the cost of restoring support would greatly exceed the loss caused by subsidence.

[12] Including use as a greenhouse (*Allen* v. *Greenwood* [1980] Ch. 119).

[13] *Colls* v. *Home and Colonial Stores Ltd.* [1915] A.C. 599.

not be confined to the purposes for which the land was used at the time of the grant.[14] (The rules determining the extent of rights of way and other easements acquired by implied grant and by prescription are discussed below.[15]) In the absence of contrary agreement or special circumstances,[16] it is for the grantee of the way, not the grantor, to maintain and repair it.

Acquisition of easements

An easement must have its origin in a grant by deed or by will. The grant may be express, implied or presumed (presumed grant is otherwise known as prescription).

1. Express grant or reservation

If A, the fee simple owner of Blackacre, grants to B, the fee simple owner of Whiteacre, an easement (*e.g.* a right of way) against Blackacre, the easement so created will be a *legal easement* if and only if (a) it is granted for an interest equivalent to an estate in fee simple absolute in possession or a term of years absolute,[17] and (b) it is granted by deed.[18] It follows, first, that an easement granted for the life of some person cannot be a legal easement, though it can exist as an equitable easement; secondly, that an easement created otherwise than by deed is void at law, though if there is a specifically enforceable agreement to grant it this too may give rise to a valid equitable easement. The essential difference between the two, it will be recalled, is that a legal easement is binding on anyone who acquires the servient land, regardless of notice, whereas an equitable easement is enforceable only on the basis of notice or (since 1925) registration.

A legal easement is commonly created by reservation. If a landowner sells part of his land to another person he may expressly reserve for the benefit of the land retained by him an easement (*e.g.* a right of way) against the land sold. The reservation of an easement in a conveyance of land creates a legal easement after 1925.[19]

---

[14] *British Railways Board* v. *Glass* [1965] Ch. 538.

[15] At pp. 117, 120.

[16] See *Liverpool C.C.* v. *Irwin* [1977] A.C. 239.

[17] LPA 1925, s.1(2) (see p. 30).

[18] *Ibid.*, s.52 (see p. 25).

[19] *Ibid.*, s.65. As to the extent of such an easement, see *St. Edmundsbury and Ipswich Diocesan Board of Finance* v. *Clark* (*No.* 2) [1975] 1 W.L.R. 468.

2. Implied reservation or grant

(i) In favour of the grantor of land

If A grants part of his land to B the law is reluctant to imply the reservation of any easement against the land granted to B in favour of that retained by A. A claim by A to any such easement is an attempt by him to derogate (*i.e.* detract) from his grant and it is a general principle of the law that a grantor may not derogate from his grant.[20] In such a case the law is prepared to imply the reservation only of intended easements and of easements of necessity.

An intended easement is one which it appears in the circumstances the parties must mutually have intended to create. For example, on the sale of a terrace house the grant and reservation may be implied of mutual easements of support as between the house sold and an adjoining house retained by the vendor.

An easement of necessity is one "without which the property retained cannot be used at all, and not one merely necessary to the reasonable enjoyment of the property."[21] An easement of light will not be implied in favour of the grantor of land, because a building is not unusable without the benefit of natural light, but the reservation of an easement of way against the land granted will be implied in favour of the grantor if he would have no other means of access to the land retained by him. The law implies the reservation of such an easement grudgingly, however, and accordingly an easement of necessity can be used only to supply the needs of the dominant tenement as they were at the date of the grant. For example, if at the date of the grant the dominant tenement was used for agricultural purposes, a right of way impliedly reserved as an easement of necessity cannot be used to cart building materials across the servient tenement for some non-agricultural purpose.[22]

(ii) In favour of the grantee of land

When a landowner conveys part of his land to another person the law is much readier to imply the grant of an easement against the land retained by the grantor for the benefit of the land conveyed than it is to imply a reservation in favour of the land retained. There will be an implied grant of intended easements and of easements of necessity[23] and, under the doctrine of

---

[20] See p. 96.

[21] *Union Lighterage Co.* v. *London Graving Dock Co.* [1902] 2 Ch. 557.

[22] *Corporation of London* v. *Riggs* (1880) 13 Ch.D. 798.

[23] See, *e.g. Liverpool C.C.* v. *Irwin* [1977] A.C. 239. The grant of a way of necessity will generally be implied on the basis either of public policy or of the presumed intention of the parties, if the property conveyed would otherwise be landlocked (*Nickerson* v. *Barraclough* [1981] Ch. 426).

Wheeldon v. *Burrows*,[24] there will also be an implied grant of all
such continuous and apparent rights ("quasi-easements") as are
capable of becoming easements, as are required for the reasonable
enjoyment of the land conveyed, and as were in fact enjoyed for
the benefit of that land immediately before the grant. For
example, if there is a house upon the land conveyed which before
the conveyance enjoyed the flow of natural light across the land
retained by the grantor, there will be an implied grant of an
easement of light for the benefit of the house. The word
"continuous" means "regularly exercised," rather than strictly
continuous. A right is "apparent" for this purpose if its existence
will be revealed by an inspection of the land: a way, for example, is
apparent if a visible track can be seen.

The doctrine of *Wheeldon* v. *Burrows* is also applicable when a
landowner by contemporaneous grants disposes of parts of his land
to different persons, *e.g.* he makes devises thereof to different
devisees by his will. In such a case the grantee of what we may call
the quasi-dominant plot (*e.g.* the land with the house on it in the
above example) will get the *Wheeldon* v. *Burrows* easements
against the quasi-servient plot.[25] The two plots will then be truly
dominant and servient tenements.

There is some overlap between this common law doctrine and
the Law of Property Act 1925, s.62 (known as the "general words"
section because, with the object of shortening the traditional form
of parcels clause in conveyances of land, it imports into every
conveyance the words generally used by conveyancers, except
where a contrary intention is expressed). By section 62(1), a
conveyance of land shall be deemed to include and shall operate to
convey with the land "all buildings, erections, fixtures... *privileges, easements, rights and advantages whatsoever*, appertaining
or reputed to appertain to the land, or any part thereof, or, at the
time of conveyance ... enjoyed with, or reputed or known as part
or parcel of or appurtenant to the land or any part thereof."

So far as this provision refers to existing easements it is of course
redundant, since it is in the nature of an easement that the benefit
runs automatically with the dominant tenement; what is surprising
is that, as judicially interpreted, it operates to convert a mere
personal "privilege" into an irrevocable right of property."[26] For
example, in *Wright* v. *Macadam*[27] a landlord allowed his tenant to
store his coal in a coal-shed belonging to the landlord, although

---

[24] (1879) 12 Ch.D. 31.
[25] *Schwann* v. *Cotton* [1916] 2 Ch. 120.
[26] Unless the right fails to satisfy the conditions of an easement: see *Phipps* v.
Pears, note 5; *Regis Property Co. Ltd.* v. *Redman* [1956] 2 Q.B. 612; *Green* v.
Ashco Horticulturist Ltd. [1966] 1 W.L.R. 889.
[27] Note 7.

the terms of the lease did not confer such a right upon the tenant. When the lease expired the landlord granted a new lease to the tenant, which again made no mention of the right to store the coal in the landlord's coal-shed. This new lease, however, was a "conveyance"[28] within the terms of section 62, and the court held that the lease had to be read as if it expressly conferred upon the tenant the right to store the coal in the landlord's coal-shed. The privilege which during the earlier lease was merely precarious and could be withdrawn by the landlord at any time had now become an easement.

Although an easement may arise by implied grant both under section 62 and under *Wheeldon* v. *Burrows*, there are important distinctions between the two. In particular, section 62 applies only to a "conveyance" of land, *i.e.* an instrument effective to create a legal estate in the land. *Wheeldon* v. *Burrows* is wider and applies to a disposition which creates only an equitable interest in the land, *e.g.* an informal lease for more than three years.[29] Again, *Wheeldon* v. *Burrows* applies to rights that have been enjoyed *by* the common owner of the quasi-dominant and quasi-servient plots, but it is now clear that section 62 applies only to rights or privileges that have been exercised *against* him, *e.g.* by his tenant.[30] On the other hand section 62 is wider in that it applies to rights generally, not just those that are "continuous and apparent."[31]

In either case, however, it must be remembered that no grant can be implied if the conveyance expresses a contrary intention.[32]

3. Prescription or presumed grant[33]

Long user (enjoyment of a right) may give rise to the presumed grant of an easement. For example, if the owners of Blackacre have been in the habit of using a path across Whiteacre as a convenient means of access to Blackacre, and they have done this for a sufficiently long time, the law may presume that at some time

---

[28] Including a merely written lease for three years or less which is effective at law, even though not under seal (see p. 84).

[29] *Borman* v. *Griffith* [1930] 1 Ch. 493, and see p. 85.

[30] *Sovmots Investments Ltd.* v. *Secretary of State for Environment* [1979] A.C. 144. The easement of light is an exception (*Broomfield* v. *Williams* [1897] 1 Ch. 602).

[31] It accordingly applies to profits, as well as to easements: *White* v. *Williams* [1922] 1 K.B. 727.

[32] A conveyance may be rectified to accord with such an intention (*Clark* v. *Barnes* [1929] 2 Ch. 368).

[33] Radical proposals for reform were made by the Law Reform Committee in its 14th Report (1966).

in the past the fee simple owner of Whiteacre granted an easement of way across Whiteacre for the benefit of Blackacre.

Prescription is based upon the acquiescence of the fee simple owners of the servient tenement in the assertion of a right against that land by the owners of the dominant tenement: the law infers the grant of an easement as the only possible explanation of this long-continued acquiescence. To justify this inference the user must have been as of right (*nec vi nec clam nec precario*[34]), and there must be evidence that the fee simple owners of the servient tenement have acquiesced in it.

Acquiescence must be distinguished from permission: acquiescence by the servient owners in the open and continuous assertion of a right by the dominant owners is the essence of prescription,[35] but permission negatives the existence of any right, and precludes any prescriptive claim.[36] There can be no acquiescence without knowledge of user,[37] and power to prevent it: thus, a prescriptive claim will normally fail if the servient owner was unaware of the user and could not with reasonable diligence have discovered it,[38] or if the period of user was during a time when the servient tenement was leased to a tenant.[39]

The user must have been continuous,[40] but this condition will be satisfied if the right has been exercised from time to time as circumstances require, provided that the intervals are not excessive.[41] An easement acquired by prescription will be confined to user of the kind that has in fact been enjoyed (*e.g.* a right of way for foot passengers only), but a mere increase in user at some later time will not be excluded.[42]

We must now consider the different modes of prescription at common law and by statute.

(i) At common law

The common law has two modes of prescription. Under the

---

[34] Not by force nor by stealth nor by permission.

[35] *Dalton* v. *Angus* (1881) 6 App.Cas. 740.

[36] But user may cease to be *precario*, *i.e.* permissive, if permission is not continually sought: see *Healey* v. *Hawkins* [1968] 1 W.L.R. 1967.

[37] As to knowledge of an agent, see *Diment* v. *N. H. Foot Ltd.* [1974] 1 W.L.R. 1427.

[38] *Union Lighterage Co.* v. *London Graving Dock Co.* [1902] 2 Ch. 557.

[39] See p. 123. Conversely, user by a lessee of the dominant tenement enures for the benefit of the fee simple owner.

[40] See *Davis* v. *Whitby* [1974] Ch. 186, in which an agreed variation of the route of a right of way did not break continuity, nor render user thereafter permissive.

[41] *Hollins* v. *Verney* (1884) 13 Q.B.D. 304.

[42] *British Railways Board* v. *Glass* [1956] Ch. 538, *Woodhouse & Co. Ltd.* v. *Kirkland Ltd.* [1970] 1 W.L.R. 1185. As to the effect of *excessive* user resulting from alterations to the dominant tenement, see note 60.

earlier doctrine an easement is presumed if it appears that there
has been user as of right since the beginning of legal memory
(which by a fiction is fixed at A.D. 1189). Upon proof of user for a
minimum period of 20 years the law presumes that there has been
user since 1189, but this presumption is rebuttable and if it can be
proved that user in fact began later than that date the claim will
fail. In practice it is generally a matter of no great difficulty to
prove that user began at a date later than 1189, *e.g.* when an
easement of light is claimed, to prove that a building was first
erected on that spot at some later date.

The common law has a great reverence for rights, or apparent
rights, which have in fact been long enjoyed, and it therefore
invented a second theory of prescription to supplement the first.
This second mode of prescription at common law is known as the
doctrine of the lost modern grant, whereas the earlier mode is
known, somewhat inappropriately, as common law prescription—
it would more aptly be called the doctrine of the lost ancient grant.
To establish a claim under the doctrine of the lost modern grant
the claimant must show that there has been user as of right for a
minimum period of 20 years. The court may then presume the
grant of an easement at some time before user began which has
since been lost. This mode of prescription has its own disadvan-
tage, *viz.* that of uncertainty. One can say no more than that upon
proof of at least 20 years' user the court may be prepared to infer a
grant. Whether the court will do so depends upon all the
circumstances of the particular case, and upon the likelihood or
otherwise of a grant having been made.[43] Parliament, therefore,
intervened with the Prescription Act 1832, which provides a third
and alternative ground upon which a claim by prescription may be
based.[44]

(ii) The Prescription Act 1832
Easements other than light. The Act provides that a claim to an
easement other than light may be based upon proof of user for
either 20 years or 40 years. In both cases the user must be *as of
right*. Moreover, the user must be for 20 years or 40 years *without
interruption* and *next before* (*i.e.* immediately preceding) some
action in which the right to the easement is brought into question.
It will be seen that user alone does not give rise to an easement
under the provisions of the Act: the right is inchoate until some

[43] It seems, however, that a claim cannot be defeated by proof that no such grant
has in fact been made (*Dalton* v. *Angus* (1881) 6 App.Cas. 740, *Tehidy* v.
Norman [1971] 2 Q.B. 528).
[44] It is normal practice to plead all three modes of prescription. A claim might fail
under the Act yet succeed on the basis of lost modern grant. (See *Hulbert* v. *Dale*
[1909] 2 Ch. 570; *Pugh* v. *Savage* [1970] 2 Q.B. 373).

action is begun in which the claim to the easement is brought into question. The action may be brought by either side. Thus the dominant owner may issue a writ claiming a declaration that he has acquired an easement under the Act; or the right may be brought into question in an action brought by the servient owner, claiming an injunction to restrain the dominant owner from continuing to exercise the right, in answer to which the dominant owner claims that he has acquired an easement under the Act.

User must have been *without interruption*, but the Act provides that nothing ranks as an interruption unless the dominant owner has acquiesced in it for a full year[45] after becoming aware of it and of the person responsible for it. For this reason it is often stated that user for 19 years and one day is as good as user for 20 years. This is a half-truth. It is not possible after user for merely 19 years and a day to issue a writ claiming an easement, because it will not then be possible to prove user for the requisite period of 20 years. What is meant is that after user for 19 years and a day it is too late for the servient owner to interrupt, so long as the dominant owner does not submit to the interruption for more than 364 days: if at the end of that period the latter immediately issues his writ, he will be able to establish user for 20 years for the purposes of the Act, and the interruption, having lasted for less than a full year, will not rank as an interruption for the purposes of the claim.

On these matters then the rules are the same whether the claim is based upon the shorter or the longer period of user. There are differences, however, some of which appear to arise virtually by chance out of the obscure and inept drafting[46] of the Act. The following points must be noticed.

Disabilities. If the claim is based upon the shorter period of user, section 7 of the Act requires that there shall be deducted from the period of user any periods during which the servient owner has been an infant, lunatic, or tenant for life. The claim will not succeed unless there still remains a period of 20 years after these deductions have been made. If the claim is based upon the longer period of user no deduction is to be made under section 7, but section 8 of the Act provides that if the claim is to a right of "way or other convenient watercourse or use of water" there shall be deducted from the period of user any periods when the servient tenement has been held under a tenancy for life or a lease for a term exceeding three years, provided that the claim to the easement is resisted by a reversioner within three years after the

---

[45] If the dominant owner has made strong protests to the servient owner against interference with the exercise of the right, failure for a year to make further protests will not necessarily amount to acquiescence during that period: see *Davies* v. *Du Paver* [1953] 1 Q.B. 184.

[46] Or reproduction: simple printing errors might account for some anomalies.

end of the tenancy for life or lease. Obviously something has gone wrong with the wording of the Act, because a right of way is not a watercourse, whether convenient or inconvenient. It is therefore doubtful whether section 8 applies to all easements other than light, or only to rights of way and water. Even when the section applies, deduction is not to be made unless the claim to the easement is resisted by a reversioner within three years after the determination of the tenancy for life or lease. Moreover the word "reversioner"[47] has been strictly construed and, it has been held, does not include a remainderman.[48] Thus, if Whiteacre is settled on A for life with remainder to B in fee simple and the tenant of an adjoining property, Blackacre, uses a way across Whiteacre for upwards of 40 years, there can be no deduction of A's tenancy for life. B is a remainderman, not a reversioner. But if during the period of user Whiteacre had been held under a lease for more than three years, the period of the lease would have had to be deducted from the period of user, provided that the landlord of Whiteacre had resisted the claim to the easement within three years after the end of the lease. The landlord is a reversioner.

Strange as it may seem, it sometimes pays to base a claim upon the shorter period of user, even if the longer period can be proved, because there is no provision for deduction of leases when the claim is based upon the shorter period, as there is when it is based upon the longer period. If, however, the servient tenement was let when user began, then, even if the claim is based on the shorter period, the period of the lease will generally have to be deducted upon the general principle that prescription is founded upon acquiescence of the fee simple owner of the servient tenement: the fee simple owner was not then in a position to prevent the user. (The position is quite different if the lease was granted *after* user began: the servient owner has then, by his own act, put it out of his power to prevent further user.[49])

Consents. If permission for the exercise of the right has been sought from the servient owners from time to time the claim to an easement will generally fail. The user is not in such a case "as of right," as the Act requires. There is, however, one exception to this rule. If user for the longer period is established, a merely oral consent given *before* the user began will not defeat the claim. This is because the Act provides that a claim based on the longer period of user shall be indefeasible unless the right has been enjoyed by written consent or agreement, and some meaning must be given to the reference to written consent. This, at least, appears to be the

[47] More accurately "person entitled to any reversion."
[48] *Symons* v. *Leaker* (1885) 15 Q.B.D. 629 (*sed quaere*).
[49] *Palk* v. *Shinner* (1852) 18 Q.B. 215; *Pugh* v. *Savage* [1970] 2 Q.B. 373.

position resulting from some ill-drafted and seemingly contradictory provisions of the Act.

The easement of light. The Act provides that a claim to an easement of light may be founded upon proof of actual enjoyment of the light for a period of 20 years without interruption and next before some action in which the right is brought into question. Proof that user was by virtue of written consent given by the servient owner will defeat the claim, but in other respects user need not have been as of right, nor need it have been by or on behalf of one fee simple owner against another: actual user suffices. In consequence a lessee can acquire an easement of light under the Act against land which is occupied by another tenant of his own landlord or which is occupied by the landlord himself: this is possible only in the case of the easement of light and only when the claim is brought under the Act. No provision is made for deduction of periods of disability of the servient owner.[50]

To enable a landowner to prevent his neighbour from acquiring an easement of light without the necessity of erecting a screen to obstruct the flow of light to the neighbour's building, the Rights of Light Act 1959 provides for the registration as a local land charge[51] of a light obstruction notice, specifying the size and position of a notional obstruction. The dominant owner may then sue for a declaration that he has acquired an easement of light as if there had been an actual obstruction, and the Act provides that in such an action the claimant may treat his user as having begun a year earlier than in fact it did.

PROFITS

A profit is similar to an easement in that it also is a right against the land of another, but whereas an easement is said to be a right without profit a profit gives the right to take something from another's land which is either part of the soil itself (*e.g.* a right to take gravel) or part of the produce of the soil (*e.g.* a right to pasture one's cattle on a neighbour's land or to take fish from his stream). A right to take water from another's stream is an easement, not a profit, because the water is not regarded as being part of the soil or of its produce.

A profit may be a several profit or a profit in common (or a common). A several profit gives to the owner the right to take the

---

[50] A further distinction between the provisions of the Act with regard to the easement of light and those relating to other easements is that only the latter bind the Crown.

[51] See Chap. 21.

subject-matter, *e.g.* the fish, from another's land to the exclusion of everyone else, including the servient owner himself. A profit in common gives the right to take the subject-matter in common with others. It depends upon the terms of the grant whether a profit is a several profit or a profit in common, but several profits are comparatively rare: hence the term "common" is often used as a synonym for profits.[52]

Profits may also be divided into profits appurtenant and profits in gross. A profit appurtenant is one the benefit of which is annexed by the grant to a dominant tenement. It, therefore, resembles an easement, and indeed a profit appurtenant must conform to the four conditions of an easement.[53] Hence it is not possible to claim as a profit appurtenant a right to fish in another's stream for commercial purposes; such a right does not accommodate the dominant tenement.[54] A profit in gross is one which is given to the grantee personally, *i.e.* irrespective of his ownership or occupation of land: there is no dominant tenement.

Mention may also be made of the profit *pur cause de vicinage*; this is a right which commoners of adjoining commons[55] may have to allow their cattle to stray on to the neighbouring common.

Modes of acquisition

The modes of acquiring a profit are similar to the modes of acquiring an easement, and it will be simplest to notice the main differences:

(i) An easement can be acquired both under section 62 of the Law of Property Act 1925 and under the doctrine of *Wheeldon* v. *Burrows*, but only the former applies to profits.[56]

(ii) A profit in gross cannot be claimed by prescription under the Act of 1832, although it can be claimed under the other modes of prescription.

(iii) If a profit is claimed under the Act of 1832 the periods of user provided by the Act are 30 years and 60 years, instead of the periods of 20 years and 40 years provided for easements. In the main there are the same differences as for easements between claims founded on the

---

[52] Rights of common are registrable with the appropriate local authority under the Commons Registration Act 1965, and cannot be exercised unless so registered.

[53] See p. 112.

[54] *Harris* v. *Earl of Chesterfield* [1911] A.C. 623.

[55] *i.e.* (in this context) land subject to a right of common.

[56] See note 31.

shorter and those founded on the longer period. For example, if the claim is founded on the shorter period a deduction will have to be made for any periods when the servient owner has been under one of the disabilities mentioned in section 7 of the Act. But section 8 of the Act, which applies to a claim to an easement based on the longer period of user, has no application when a profit is claimed on the ground of user for 60 years. There is, therefore, no provision for deduction of periods of leases of the servient tenement; but such leases may have to be taken into account in deciding whether there has been that acquiescence by the fee simple owners of the servient tenement which is normally essential to prescription.[57] In the case of commons, deductions must also be made of periods of non-user for reasons of animal health or government requisition; but such non-user is not an interruption for the purposes of the 1832 Act.[58]

EXTINGUISHMENT OF EASEMENTS AND PROFITS

An easement or profit may be extinguished by release, which may be either express or implied. To be effective at law an express release must be by deed, but an informal agreement to release may be effective in equity if the servient owner has furnished consideration or has acted to his detriment on the faith of the agreement.

Release may be implied if there is evidence of an intention on the part of the dominant owner to abandon the easement.[59] Non-user of itself does not necessarily show such an intention: thus release of an easement of way cannot be inferred from non-user during a period when the owner of the easement of way temporarily enjoyed a more convenient means of access to his property. Again, if a house enjoys the benefit of an easement of light, knocking down the house will not show an intention to abandon the easement if the owner intends to re-build the house and the house when re-built has windows which enjoy substantially the same light. The question is always whether an intention to

---

[57] *Davies* v. *Du Paver* [1953] 1 Q.B. 184.
[58] Commons Registration Act 1965, s.16.
[59] *Moore* v. *Rawson* (1824) 3 B. & C. 332; distinguish *Cook* v. *Mayor & Corporation of Bath* (1868) L.R. 6 Eq. 177.

abandon can properly be inferred from all the circumstances of the particular case.[60]

An easement or profit will also become extinguished if the same person becomes both owner and possessor of the dominant and the servient tenements, provided that he holds the two tenements in the same capacity.

Approvement and enclosure are means by which the waste land of a manor may become freed from the rights of the commoners. Both procedures are subject to complicated statutory provisions and require ministerial and parliamentary approval, respectively.

PUBLIC RIGHTS OF WAY

Apart from creation by special statutory provision, a public right of way must have its origin in a dedication of the way to the public by the land-owners concerned, coupled with an acceptance of the way by the public. Dedication may be express or it may be presumed from user of the way by the public as of right to the knowledge of the land-owner or land-owners concerned. Dedication may be presumed at common law, in which case no particular period of user is prescribed by the law, or it may be presumed under the Highways Act 1980. Under the Act dedication is to be presumed upon proof of uninterrupted user as of right for 20 years next before the right of user is brought into question unless there is sufficient evidence that there was no intention during the period of user to dedicate a way to the public. Absence of intention to dedicate may be proved in a number of ways provided by the Act, *e.g.* by exhibiting a suitable notice, or it may be proved in any other way, *e.g.* by the land-owner's closing the way to the public for one day in each year (a method commonly adopted.)

It will be observed that under the Act the relevant period of user is that of 20 years next before the right of user is "brought into question." The right can be brought into question in any way, *e.g.* by the land-owner's turning back the public. It is not necessary that an action should be brought on either side (as is necessary for the establishment of an easement under the Prescription Act 1832).

---

[60] An easement may be extinguished if alterations are made to the dominant tenement which would excessively increase the burden on the servient tenement: see *Ankerson* v. *Connelly* [1907] 1 Ch. 678, *Ray* v. *Fairway Motors (Barnstaple) Ltd.* (1968) 20 P. & C.R. 261.

CUSTOMARY AND SIMILAR RIGHTS

A fluctuating body of persons (other than the public at large) may claim a right in the nature of an easement: for example, the inhabitants of a particular village may claim the right to pass across private land in order to reach the parish church (a right known as a church-way).[61] Such a right cannot subsist as a true easement, because, as we have seen,[62] an easement must have its origin in a grant, and a grant cannot be made to such a fluctuating body of persons. A valid foundation for the right may, however, be established under the doctrine of custom. The main requisites of a valid custom are that the right claimed should be limited to a defined locality known to the law, such as a parish or manor, and that the right should have been enjoyed continuously since 1189. Proof of user for 20 years raises a rebuttable presumption that the right has been enjoyed continuously since 1189.[63]

A fluctuating body of persons cannot directly claim a profit, because a profit, like an easement, must have its origin in a grant. Nor is such a body allowed to claim a right in the nature of a profit under the doctrine of custom.[64] But there are two very restricted methods by which the claim may be established. First, if the right has been granted by the Crown, the Crown may have incorporated the fluctuating body of persons,[65] in which case as a corporation it becomes a competent grantee. Moreover, when the right has been granted by the Crown incorporation may sometimes be presumed. Secondly, if it can be established that from time immemorial the right has been claimed by a local corporation, as well as by a fluctuating body of persons, the court may presume the grant of a profit to the corporation upon trust for itself and the fluctuating body.[66]

---

[61] *Brocklebank* v. *Thompson* [1903] 2 Ch. 344.
[62] See p. 113.
[63] Cf. common law prescription (p. 120).
[64] *Alfred F. Beckett* v. *Lyons* [1967] Ch. 449.
[65] The Crown has power to confer the status of corporation upon any body of persons.
[66] *Goodman* v. *Mayor of Saltash* (1882) 7 App.Cas. 633.

15. Licences

In its simplest form, a licence is merely a permission to enter the land of another (such entry otherwise being trespass). In that sense it is distinguished from both a lease and an easement in that it does not amount to an estate or interest in the land, and accordingly cannot be assigned, and is binding (if at all) on the licensor alone[1]: a lease on the other hand is assignable, and the burden of the lease runs with the reversion, just as the benefit and burden of an easement run with the tenements of the dominant and servient owners respectively. A licence is further distinguished (a) from a lease, in that normally a licensee does not have exclusive possession of the land, (b) from an easement, in that a licence may (and generally does) exist in gross, without reference to any dominant tenement. In some cases it may also be necessary to distinguish between a mere licence to reside in property for life and a life interest in the property: if a disposition is held to have created a life interest, the property will be settled land, and the person beneficially entitled for life will have the statutory powers of sale, lease and mortgage under the Settled Land Act 1925.[2]

Another characteristic of a simple licence is that, unlike an interest in property, it can be revoked at any time, whereupon the former licensee becomes a trespasser. Here, however, a distinction must be drawn between a bare or simple licence on the one hand, and on the other a licence arising either under a contract between the parties, or in connection with some legal or equitable interest held by the licensee.

---

[1] *King* v. *David Allen & Sons Billposting Ltd.* [1916] 2 A.C. 54; *Clore* v. *Theatrical Properties Ltd.* [1936] 3 All E.R. 483.
[2] See *Re Carne's Settled Estates* [1899] 1 Ch. 324 (gift by will), *Bannister* v. *Bannister* [1948] 2 All E.R. 133 (resulting trust under disposition *inter vivos*); *cf.* equitable licences, below. For a means of avoiding a result so far from what may have been intended, see *Griffiths* v. *Williams* (1977) 248 E.G. 947 (p. 87 above).

Bare licence

A licence given gratuitously, and not coupled with some interest in the land, is revocable at will.

Contractual licence

A licence for value, such as that implied on the sale of a theatre ticket,[3] was regarded at common law as being revocable at will;[4] and although if it was revoked in breach of contract the licensor would be liable in damages to the licensee, the revocation was nevertheless effective, and the former licensee had no right to remain on the land. As a result of the intervention of equity, however, such a licence is now regarded as irrevocable for so long as the parties must have intended, *i.e.* for any period expressly stipulated, or until terminated by the giving of prescribed notice or (if none is prescribed) reasonable notice.[5]

Licence coupled with an interest

A licence may be coupled with the grant of an interest in land, as where standing timber is sold on terms that the purchaser is to sever the timber; the sale implies a grant to the purchaser of a licence to enter the vendor's land in order to obtain the timber. The interest may be legal, arising for example from the formal grant of a profit, or equitable, where there is a specifically enforceable agreement for a grant. The licence is irrevocable so long as the interest to which it is annexed lasts, and unless otherwise agreed it can be assigned together with the interest.

Equitable licences

A further instance of a licence coupled with an equitable interest in land is one that has acquired increasing importance in recent

---

[3] *Hurst* v. *Picture Theatres Ltd*. [1915] 1 K.B. 1. Lodging agreements are another example, but these may enjoy some security of tenure under the Rent Acts (see pp. 104–5).

[4] *Wood* v. *Leadbitter* (1845) 13 M. & W. 838.

[5] *Winter Garden Theatre (London) Ltd*. v. *Millennium Productions Ltd*. [1948] A.C. 173; *Hounslow L.B.C*. v. *Twickenham Garden Developments Ltd*. [1971] Ch. 233. The basis of equity's intervention is the equitable remedy of injunction (compare the role elsewhere of the equitable remedy of specific performance: see p. 25).

years, during which the courts have developed the doctrine of equitable or proprietary estoppel. Under this doctrine, if a licensee incurs expenditure or some other detriment (*e.g.* by building on the licensor's land)[6] with the acquiescence of the licensor, and in the reasonable expectation that the licence will not be revoked, an equitable estoppel may arise in his favour, the effect of which is that both the licensor himself and persons claiming through him (other than a purchaser without notice)[7] will be estopped from revoking the licence.

The extent of the interest thus created may vary, between at one extreme a determinable life interest,[8] and at the other an interest in fee simple.[9] Alternatively in some cases, where the licensee has adjoining land and the detriment incurred is in relation to that land, the interest acquired may be in the nature of an easement rather than a right to possession over the licensor's land.[10] Interests arising in such widely diverse circumstances do not fall readily under any particular rubric of the law of property. Some cases have been decided on the basis that the licence in question was (in some sense, at least) contractual, others on the basis of constructive trusts,[11] yet others on the basis merely that the licence (whether contractual, or arising by estoppel, or otherwise) was not terminable in the circumstances of the case,[12] and different judges have given different reasons for the same decision in the same case. All that can be said to emerge from a very large and confused body of case-law—mostly concerned with family relationships—is a trend towards conceding a much greater degree of protection to the licensee. It may still be true to say that a licence is not *per se* an interest in land, but it can no longer be said with the same confidence that a licence confers no property rights at all.

Rights in respect of the matrimonial home

Despite attempts to elevate it to the status of an interest in land, the right or licence of a deserted spouse (not being himself or

---

[6] *Dillwyn* v. *Llewelyn* (1862) 4 De G.F. & J. 517; *Inwards* v. *Baker* [1965] 2 Q.B. 29.

[7] *E. R. Ives Investment Ltd.* v. *High* [1967] 2 Q.B. 379.

[8] *Inwards* v. *Baker*, above; *Binions* v. *Evans* [1972] Ch. 359 (from which it appears that the land affected may be settled land: see note 2).

[9] *Dillwyn* v. *Llewelyn*, above; *Errington* v. *Errington and Woods* [1952] 1 K.B. 290; *Pascoe* v. *Turner* [1979] 1 W.L.R. 431.

[10] *E.R. Ives Investment Ltd.* v. *High*, above; *Crabb* v. *Arun D.C.* [1976] Ch. 179.

[11] *Binions* v. *Evans*, above.

[12] *Tanner* v. *Tanner* [1975] 1 W.L.R. 1346; *Hardwick* v. *Johnson* [1978] 1 W.L.R. 683; *Chandler* v. *Kerley* [1978] 1 W.L.R. 693. In other circumstances, beneficial co-ownership may arise (see p. 56).

herself owner or part owner of the house) to remain in the matrimonial home was held in *National Provincial Bank Ltd.* v. *Ainsworth*[13] to be enforceable only as against the other spouse, and to be incapable of binding a third party such as a purchaser or mortgagee. As a result of this decision the Matrimonial Homes Act 1967[14] was passed, under which a spouse who is not the owner or part-owner[15] of the matrimonial home has certain "rights of occupation," which are a charge on the other spouse's estate or interest and registrable as such under the Land Charges Act 1972.

---

[13] [1965] A.C. 1175.
[14] Repealed and replaced by the Matrimonial Homes Act 1983.
[15] Disregarding for this purpose a mere equitable interest.

16. Covenants concerning land

LEASEHOLD COVENANTS

As between original parties

Between the original landlord and the original tenant there is *privity of contract, i.e.* the parties are bound personally to one another upon any covenants into which they have entered in the lease. This contractual liability subsists throughout the whole term of the lease,[1] notwithstanding the death of either party (*i.e.* his personal representatives remain liable on his covenants in the lease),[2] and notwithstanding any assignment of the reversion or of the lease. The covenants are usually so worded that the covenantor undertakes liability not only for his own acts and omissions but also for those of his successors in title and persons deriving title under him. Furthermore, under section 79 of the Law of Property Act 1925 any covenant affecting land of the covenantor is *deemed* to be made in these terms unless a contrary intention is expressed.

As between assignees

Upon an assignment of the reversion the *benefit* of the tenant's covenants can be (and usually is) expressly assigned with the reversion, and the assignee can then sue the original tenant upon the tenant's covenants in the lease; similarly upon an assignment of the lease the benefit of the landlord's covenants can be expressly

---

[1] It is otherwise with the *implied* obligations of landlord and tenant (see p. 95 *et seq.*); the landlord or tenant is liable only for breaches committed while he held the reversion or the lease, respectively.

[2] To the extent of the deceased's assets. The same rule applies to a periodic tenancy: the estate of the deceased tenant remains liable for the rent until the tenancy is validly determined by notice (*Youngmin* v. *Heath* [1974] 1 W.L.R. 135).

assigned with the lease, and the assignee can then sue the original landlord upon the landlord's covenants.[3]

The doctrine of privity of contract prevents the *burden* of a landlord's or tenant's covenants being assigned with the reversion or the lease, however, and accordingly it is in each case the original covenantor who remains liable. The inconvenience of this rule is avoided by the doctrine of *privity of estate*, which treats the relationship of landlord and tenant as subsisting between the owner of the reversion for the time being and the owner of the lease for the time being: accordingly, both the benefit of the tenant's covenants and the burden of the landlord's covenants run with the reversion,[4] and the benefit of the landlord's covenants and the burden of the tenant's covenants run with the lease.[5] In each case the doctrine extends only to such covenants as "touch and concern the land" (or "have reference to the subject matter of the lease").[6] A covenant touches and concerns the land in this sense if it regulates the position of the landlord and the tenant in those capacities, as distinct from merely collateral matters.

All covenants commonly found in leases do touch and concern the land, *e.g.* a landlord's covenant for quiet enjoyment, or to maintain the exterior of the premises in repair, or to renew the lease at the tenant's option[7]; or a tenant's covenant to pay the rent, to pay tenant's rates and taxes, to maintain the premises in repair, or not to use the premises for certain purposes. An example of a provision that does not touch and concern the land is a tenant's option to purchase the reversion on the lease; such a provision does not regulate the relationship of landlord and tenant, but contemplates its determination by the exercise of the option.[8]

There is an important distinction between liability by privity of contract and liability by privity of estate. As we have seen, each of the original parties remains liable by privity of contract upon his covenants *throughout the term of the lease*, but a landlord or tenant who is liable only by privity of estate is liable only for breaches of covenant committed by him while he held the reversion or the lease, as the case may be. An example may make the position

---

[3] The benefit may also pass, even without express assignment, under the principle discussed at pp. 137–8.

[4] LPA 1925, ss.141–2. The rule was first enacted in 1540.

[5] *Spencer's Case* (1583) 5 Co. Rep. 16.

[6] The latter (which is synonymous with the former) is the expression used in LPA 1925, ss.141–2.

[7] The inclusion of this covenant is anomalous (and an option for renewal, is registrable under the Land Charges Act: see *Beesley* v. *Hallwood Estates Ltd.* [1960] 1 W.L.R. 549).

[8] Such options are enforceable on the basis discussed at p. 25.

clearer. Suppose that L is the original landlord and T the original tenant, and that T has assigned the lease to A and A in his turn has assigned the lease to B. Suppose further that the lease contains a tenant's repairing covenant and that B breaks this covenant. L may sue T, who cannot excuse himself by the plea that he had assigned the lease before the breach of covenant occurred. T is liable by privity of contract and remains liable for breach of tenant's covenants committed at any time during the lease. Alternatively, L may sue B, the tenant who in fact committed the breach of covenant: B is liable by privity of estate. But L cannot sue A: A was liable only by privity of estate and ceased to be liable, as to future breaches of tenant's covenants, when he parted with the lease.

There is no privity of contract or estate between an assignee of the reversion and the original tenant if the latter has already parted with the lease before the former acquired the reversion. Nevertheless it has been held that under the Law of Property Act 1925, s.141, the assignee of the reversion acquires *all* the rights of the assignor, including the right to sue the original tenant (whose contractual liability, as we have seen, continues indefinitely) as well as the tenant for the time being (whose liability is based only on privity of estate).[9] Furthermore, it seems the same principle should apply, for instance, where an assignee of the lease seeks to enforce a repairing covenant against the original landlord after the latter has assigned the reversion: there is no privity between the parties, but the original landlord remains liable indefinitely, and the benefit of his covenant would pass to the assignee of the lease either by express assignment or under the principle discussed below.[10]

Indemnities

If the original tenant is sued for breach of a tenant's covenant committed after he had parted with the lease, he may claim indemnity from the assignee of the lease who in fact committed the breach. Thus, in the above illustration, If L sued T in respect of the breach committed by B, T could claim indemnity from B. This is a common law right.[11] It will be observed that T could not claim

[9] Furthermore the assignee can sue for breach of a tenant's covenant committed whether before or after the assignment (*Re King* [1963] Ch. 459; *London and County (A. & D.) Ltd.* v. *Wilfred Sportsman Ltd.* [1971] Ch. 764; *Arlesford Trading Co. Ltd.* v. *Servansingh* [1971] 1 W.L.R. 1080).

[10] At pp. 137–138. The benefit does not pass under *Spencer's Case*, above, which applies only where there is privity of estate.

[11] *Moule* v. *Garrett* (1872) L.R. Ex. 101.

indemnity from A under this common law right; the common law right of indemnity is potentially defective, therefore, in that B may prove to be not worth suing. Hence, it became the practice of conveyancers to insert into an assignment of a lease an express covenant by the assignee to indemnify the assignor against liability for any breach of a tenant's covenant committed after the assignment, whether by the assignee himself or by a later assignee. Such an indemnity covenant is now implied by the Law of Property Act 1925, s.77, in an assignment for value. Thus, in our last illustration, if L sued T and such an indemnity covenant, express or implied, was included in the assignment of the lease by T to A, T could claim indemnity from A in respect of the breach committed by B.

Upon an assignment of the reversion there is no statutory provision implying an indemnity covenant. An express covenant of indemnity should, therefore, be included in the conveyance.

As between lessor and sub-lessee

If L grants a lease to T and T grants a sub-lease to S, there is no privity of contract or estate between L and S, and it follows that L cannot enforce T's covenants in the head-lease directly against S. It should not be supposed, however, that there is no basis on which liability can arise between L and S. Thus, if S's use of the land is inconsistent with a restrictive covenant in the head-lease, he may be liable directly to L under the doctrine of *Tulk* v. *Moxhay*[12]; and if the head-lease contains a right of re-entry in the event of breach of T's covenants, L may be able to forfeit the head-lease, whereupon the sub-lease will also fall.[13] By the same token, if the head-lease contains a landlord's repairing covenant, it seems that S may be able to enforce this directly against L.[14]

OTHER COVENANTS

Covenants other than those between landlord and tenant are commonly referred to as vendor and purchaser covenants, because they are commonly entered into upon the sale by a vendor of part

---

[12] See pp. 139 *et seq.* It is immaterial whether the covenants were taken for the benefit of other land owned by the landlord: his reversion on the lease is a sufficient "dominant tenement" for this purpose (*Regent Oil Co. Ltd.* v. *J. A. Gregory (Hatch End) Ltd.* [1966] Ch. 402).

[13] See p. 93.

[14] See *Williams* v. *Unit Construction Co. Ltd.* (1951) 19 Conv. (N.S.) 262, and note 20.

of his land: the purchaser may then enter into a covenant with the vendor (*e.g.* to use the land bought for the purposes of a private dwelling-house only), and the vendor may perhaps enter into a similar covenant with the purchaser. Such covenants are sometimes also referred to as freehold covenants (to distinguish them from covenants in a lease), but it should be noted that the same principles apply whether the land sold is freehold or leasehold: if the vendor is a lessee, and sells part of the land held under the lease, any covenants then entered into are still between vendor and purchaser, not between landlord and tenant.[15]

The enforcement of such covenants is subject to different rules at common law and in equity.[16]

At common law

As between the original covenantor and the original covenantee there is privity of contract, and to that extent the rules are similar to those governing covenants in a lease: thus, unless the covenant is specially worded, the original covenantor remains liable for any breach even if in the meantime he has parted with the land affected *i.e.* he is liable for breaches committed by subsequent owners of the land.[17] Furthermore, the covenant can be enforced not only by the original covenantee himself, but also by any other person with whom it purports to be made (*e.g.* an adjoining owner), even though that other person was not himself a party to the covenant[18] and the benefit of the covenant can be expressly assigned with the land to which it relates, whereupon the assignee will have the same right of action against the covenantor as the covenantee would have had.

If the covenant is taken for the benefit of land owned by the covenantee, the *benefit* of the covenant may pass without express assignment on a transfer of the land. This is a common law rule of some antiquity.[19] It applies equally to positive and to negative covenants, and it does not require that the covenant should also affect land of the covenantor. Originally the covenantee had to have a legal estate in the land, and the transferee had to possess the same estate. For covenants made after 1925 this rule has been

---

[15] See, *e.g.*, *Shiloh Spinners Ltd.* v. *Harding* [1973] A.C. 691.

[16] Fundamental reforms are proposed by Law Commission No. 127 (1984).

[17] LPA 1925, s.79 (p. 133). This provision merely extends the liability of the covenantor: it does not impose liability on his successors (see *Tophams Ltd.* v. *Earl of Sefton* [1967] 1 A.C. 50).

[18] LPA 1925, s.56. The limited scope of this exception to the common law doctrine of privity of contract was established in *Beswick* v. *Beswick* [1968] A.C. 58.

[19] *The Prior's Case* (1368) Co. Litt. 385 a.

somewhat relaxed by section 78 of the Law of Property Act 1925, which enables persons claiming under the original covenantee to enforce the covenant even if they do not hold the same estate as the covenantee: for example, a covenant may be enforced not only by successors in title but also by lessees of the covenantee.[20]

At common law the *burden* of the covenant cannot pass with the land of the covenantor, even though the covenant is clearly intended to regulate the use of the land. Thus, although at common law a transferee of the covenantee's land may be able to enforce the covenant against the original covenantor, neither the original covenantee nor a transferee of his land can enforce the covenant against a subsequent owner of the covenantor's land: the covenant can be enforced only against the original covenantor (or his personal representatives after his death).

Although at common law a subsequent owner of the covenantor's land cannot be made directly liable on the covenants, there are nevertheless some circumstances in which he may in effect become indirectly liable: for example, a chain of indemnity may be created, whereby the covenantor, on later disposing of his land, takes an indemnity[21] from his purchaser against any continuing personal liability on the covenants, and similar indemnities are taken on subsequent dispositions; or a right of re-entry may be reserved by the covenantee in the event of breach of covenant by any subsequent owner of the covenantor's land[22]; or the covenantor may undertake not to dispose of the land without ensuring that the new owner enters into similar covenants with the covenantee and his successors.[23] Another indirect exception to the common law rule derives from the principle of "benefit and burden," under which one who claims the benefit of a grant must accept its burdens. For example it was held in *Halsall* v. *Brizell*[24] that, if a purchaser is given the right to use roads which pass across another's land subject to the obligation to contribute to the cost of maintaining the roads, he may not use the roads without making the contribution, and a subsequent owner of the purchaser's land is in the same position.

---

[20] *Smith* v. *River Douglas Catchment Board* [1949] 2 K.B. 500.

[21] There is no *implied* right of idemnity: *cf*. pp. 135–6.

[22] This is an equitable right (see *Shiloh Spinners Ltd.* v. *Harding*, (note 15). Sometimes a rentcharge is also reserved for this purpose, in which case a supporting right of re-entry is legal (see pp. 30, 143).

[23] For breach of such an undertaking the covenantee may have remedies against both the covenantor and his assignee (see *Esso Petroleum Co. Ltd.* v. *Kingswood Motors (Addlestone) Ltd.* [1974] K.B. 142).

[24] [1975] Ch. 169. See also *E.R. Ives Investment Ltd.* v. *High* [1967] 2 Q.B. 379, and (for an exhaustive analysis of the principle in its various forms) *Tito* v. *Waddell (No. 2)* [1977] Ch. 106.

In equity: the doctrine of Tulk v. Moxhay[25]

Under this doctrine, equity allows both the benefit and the burden of *restrictive covenants* to run with the land of the covenantee and covenantor respectively.

If a restrictive covenant affecting the covenantor's land is taken for the benefit of land belonging to the covenantee, equity is prepared on certain conditions to treat the covenant as creating an interest in the covenantor's land, analogous with a negative easement, and to enforce the covenant by its own remedy of injunction. The covenantee's and covenantor's land may then be regarded as in the nature of a dominant and servient tenement respectively: accordingly, not only will the benefit of the covenant pass with the covenantee's land,[26] but also (of much greater importance) the burden will pass on a transfer of the covenantor's land, and a subsequent owner of that land will be bound by the covenant as if it were a negative easement.

Since the interest arising under this doctrine is merely equitable, however, it cannot be enforced against a subsequent purchaser for value of the legal estate in the covenantor's land who acquires the land without notice, actual or constructive, of the covenant. This rule still applies to covenants created before 1926, but a restrictive covenant created after 1925 (and not being in a lease) is registrable as a land charge under the Land Charges Act 1972.[27] In accordance with the usual rule, registration of the interest will constitute actual notice of its existence to anyone who afterwards acquires the covenantor's land, and failure to register the interest will render it void against a subsequent purchaser of that land (even if he has actual notice of the interest).

The analogy between restrictive covenants and negative easements is not complete, and there are some important differences. Restrictive covenants are more flexible and more extensive than negative easements: since all easements lie in *grant*[28] their subject matter is necessarily limited, and negative easements in particular are confined to rights of light and air flowing to windows or apertures in the dominant building[29]; restrictive covenants on the other hand are not so confined, and there is nothing to prevent the servient owner from covenanting not to build *at all*, or not to carry on any other of a wide range of activities, on his land. Two further important differences are, first, that a restrictive covenant is

---

[25] (1848) 2 Ph. 774. The case itself was decided on very broad principles of equity: the doctrine evolved gradually through subsequent decisions.

[26] This, as we have seen, is also permitted by the common law.

[27] See p. 176.

[28] See p. 113.

[29] The easement of support is also in effect negative.

enforceable only in equity, whereas an easement can (and normally does) constitute a legal interest[30]; and, secondly, that a restrictive covenant can only be entered into expressly, whereas an easement can arise both by implied grant and by prescription, as well as by express grant.[31]

The conditions that must be satisfied in order that a covenant may be enforced under the doctrine of *Tulk* v. *Moxhay* are as follows.[32]

First, the doctrine applies only to restrictive or negative covenants: both at law and in equity the burden of a positive covenant falls on the original covenantor alone.[33] The test for determining whether the covenant is positive or negative is the substance, not the form, of the covenant, and the question is whether performance of the covenant requires expenditure of labour or money. Thus, a covenant to use premises for the purposes only of a private dwelling-house is a restrictive or negative covenant, but a covenant not to allow a building to fall into disrepair is a positive covenant.

Secondly, the covenant must have been taken for the benefit of land retained by the covenantee[34] and capable of being so benefited,[35] and the plaintiff must own some interest in that land. It follows that even the original covenantee cannot rely on the equitable doctrine once he has parted with his land.[36]

Thirdly, if the plaintiff is not the original covenantee, but a subsequent owner of the land, he must prove that the benefit of the covenant has passed to him. This he may do in any of three ways:

1. Assignment

The benefit of the covenant may have been assigned to him, expressly or by necessary implication,[37] at the time when he acquired the dominant land.

---

[30] See p. 116.

[31] It is principally for this reason that the law is reluctant to extend the category of negative easements: see *Phipps* v. *Pears* [1965] 1 Q.B. 76 (and pp. 113–4).

[32] The equitable doctrine is irrelevant where a covenant is enforced against the original covenantor: his liability is contractual, and is enforceable at common law (see p. 137).

[33] Subject to qualifications noted at p. 138.

[34] *Formby* v. *Barker* [1903] 2 Ch. 539, *L.C.C.* v. *Allen* [1914] 3 K.B. 642.

[35] Cf. *Re Ballard's Conveyance* [1937] 1 Ch. 473. *Earl of Leicester* v. *Wells-next-the-sea U.D.C.* [1973] Ch. 110.

[36] *Chambers* v. *Randall* [1923] 1 Ch. 149.

[37] See *Earl of Leicester* v. *Wells-next-the-Sea U.D.C.* above.

2. Annexation

If the terms of the covenant[38] or the surrounding circumstances[39] indicate that the benefit was intended to be taken not only by the original covenantee but also by subsequent owners of the land, the benefit will have passed to the plaintiff without express assignment. Where the plaintiff holds part only of the original covenantee's land the courts have been curiously reluctant to hold that he can enforce the covenant (without express assignment as above) unless it is so worded as to annex the benefit expressly to each part of the land, rather than merely to the land as a whole; it seems now, however, that such annexation can be implied.[40]

3. Scheme of development

When land is developed, *e.g.* by the building of a housing estate, the developer usually requires each purchaser of a plot to enter into restrictive covenants designed to maintain the general character of the estate and the value of the property. In accordance with principles first stated definitively in *Elliston* v. *Reacher*,[41] and since that case considerably extended,[42] these covenants then operate as a kind of local law enforceable at the suit of any plot-owner against any other plot-owner, irrespective of the dates on which they acquired their respective plots: the benefit of the covenants is regarded as running in equity with each plot sold under the scheme, in order to give effect to the common intention and interest of the vendor, the purchasers and their successors. The technicalities mentioned above requiring assignment or annexation of the benefit are thus obviated. It must not be overlooked, however, that the running of the *burden* of the covenants depends on registration: there is no exemption from this requirement for building scheme covenants, and therefore on the sale of each plot the purchaser's covenants must be registered in order to ensure that his successors will be bound.[43]

---

[38] *Rogers* v. *Hosegood* [1900] 2 Ch. 388; *cf.* the common law rule, p. 137.
[39] *Marten* v. *Flight Refuelling Ltd.* [1962] Ch. 115.
[40] *Federated Homes Ltd.* v. *Mill Lodge Properties Ltd.* [1980] 1 W.L.R. 594, applying LPA 1925, s.78 (p. 138 above).
[41] [1908] 2 Ch. 665.
[42] *Baxter* v. *Four Oaks Properties Ltd.* [1965] Ch. 654; *Re Dolphin's Conveyance* [1970] Ch. 654; *Brunner* v. *Greenslade* [1971] Ch. 993.
[43] Failure by the covenantee (*i.e.* the developer) to register might render him liable to purchasers of other plots.

Discharge of restrictive covenants

There are various statutory provisions under which restrictive covenants may be discharged, or modified. In particular, by the Law of Property Act 1925, s.84,[44] the Lands Tribunal has power to modify or discharge a restrictive covenant, with or without the payment of compensation, on various grounds set out in the section, *e.g.* that by reason of changes in the character of the neighbourhood or other circumstances the covenant has become obsolete or would impede some reasonable user of the land.

Apart from these statutory provisions, equity may refuse to grant an injunction for breach of a restrictive covenant if it appears that the covenant is obsolete, or that the plaintiff by acquiescing in previous breaches has waived his rights, or in general that it would be inequitable to enforce the covenant.[45]

Where the fee simple of the benefited and burdened land becomes vested in one person, any restrictive covenants are extinguished unless the common owner recreates them.[46]

---

[44] Applying both to freehold land and to leaseholds if the lease was made for more than 40 years at least 25 of which have expired.
[45] *Chatsworth Estates Co.* v. *Fewell* [1931] 1 Ch. 224, and see *Wrotham Park Estate Co. Ltd.* v. *Parkside Homes Ltd.* [1974] 1 W.L.R. 798 (houses constructed in breach of covenant: damages awarded in lieu of mandatory injunction requiring demolition).
[46] *Re Tiltwood, Sussex*; *Barrett* v. *Bond* [1978] Ch. 269.

17. Rentcharges

A rentcharge is a rent charged upon land, not being a rent payable to a landlord under a lease (a rent payable to a landlord is known as a rent service). To be a legal rentcharge it must be in possession and either perpetual or for a term of years absolute, and it must be created by deed.[1] Any other rentcharge is equitable only.

Legal rentcharges used sometimes to be created upon a sale of land, when the purchaser, instead of paying a lump sum, would covenant to pay an annual sum of money for a fixed term of years or in perpetuity, and the obligation to pay this sum would be charged upon the land. Now, however, the Rentcharges Act 1977 prohibits the creation of any new rentcharge whether at law or in equity, subject to two main exceptions: first, an equitable rentcharge affecting settled land, e.g. a widow's annuity charged on the land under a strict settlement[2]; secondly, an "estate rentcharge," i.e. one created for the purpose of making covenants enforceable against the owner for the time being of the land charged,[3] or for the purpose of meeting or contributing towards the cost of services, repairs or maintenance provided by the rent owner to the land charged.

Remedies for recovery

The owner of a rentcharge has the following remedies for the recovery of the rent if it is not paid.

1. Action on the covenant

The original covenantee, if still the owner of the rentcharge, may sue the original covenantor upon his covenant to pay in the

---

[1] See pp. 30, 25.
[2] See pp. 33, 43.
[3] See p. 138.

deed creating the rentcharge. Such an action against the original covenantor may also be brought by an assignee of the rent-charge if the benefit of the covenant was also expressly assigned to him.[4]

2. Action against terre tenant

At common law the freehold tenant in possession of the land (the *terre tenant*) is personally liable for the rent to the owner of the rentcharge for the time being, and this is so even if the amount of the rent exceeds the current annual value of the land. Moreover, if the land has been split up, the *terre tenant* of any part of the land is at common law liable for the whole of the rentcharge, unless the owner of the rent has agreed to its being apportioned. Under the Rentcharges Act 1977, ss.4–7, however, the Secretary of State now has power to order apportionment on the application of any person whose land is affected.

3. Statutory remedies

By the Law of Property Act 1925, s.121, the owner of a rentcharge is given three statutory remedies for its recovery. First, if the rent or any part of it is 21 days in arrears, the owner of the rentcharge can distrain for it. Secondly, if the rent or any part of it is 40 days in arrears, he may enter and take possession of the land and take the rents and profits until he has raised all the arrears. Thirdly, if the rent or any part of it is 40 days in arrears, the owner of the rentcharge may grant a lease of the land to a trustee upon trust to raise the arrears by mortgaging the leasehold term or any other reasonable means.

4. Re-entry

If the instrument creating the rentcharge so provides, but not otherwise, the owner of a rentcharge which has fallen into arrears may re-enter upon the land and claim the fee simple (or other estate of the grantor of the rentcharge).

The Law of Property Act 1925, s.122, provides that when a rentcharge is charged upon another rentcharge, the owner of the sub-rentcharge may appoint a receiver of the main rent if the sub-rentcharge or any part of it falls 21 days into arrears. The receiver will then obtain payment of the main rent and out of it pay to the owner of the sub-rent what is due to him.

---

[4] *Grant* v. *Edmondson* [1931] 1 Ch. 1.

Extinguishment and redemption

The Rentcharges Act 1977, s.3, provides for the extinguishment
of all rentcharges (subject to the same exceptions noted above) at
the expiry of 60 years after the passing of the Act or after the date
on which the rentcharge first became payable, whichever is the
later.

The Act also contains provisions[5] whereby a landowner may
obtain the discharge of a rentcharge to which his land is subject
upon payment to the owner of the rentcharge of a lump sum
representing the capital value, determined in accordance with a
prescribed formula.

---

[5] ss.8–10, replacing LPA 1925, s.191.

18. Mortgages

A mortgage of land is a transaction by which a borrower of money (the mortgagor) gives security for the loan to his lender (the mortgagee). The mortgagee then has certain rights against the land (*e.g.* a power of sale), by means of which he may raise any sums that become due to him from the borrower. He is not, therefore, restricted to a merely personal action against the borrower, although he does enjoy that right as well as his remedies against the land itself.

Mortgages are most commonly entered into on a purchase of property, when the purchaser borrows the purchase money from a lender such as a building society or a bank. The conveyance by the vendor to the purchaser, and the mortgage by the purchaser to the lender, will both be executed on completion of the purchase (and, as often as not, the money advanced by the purchaser's mortgagee will be paid, not to the vendor, but to the vendor's own mortgagee, in order to pay off the loan with which the vendor himself purchased the property). Second (and subsequent) mortgages may be created if further sums are borrowed on the same security, whether to pay for improvements to the property or for collateral purposes.

Most mortgages are of a legal estate in land—they are made by the freeholder or by a leaseholder. But an equitable interest in land may also be mortgaged; for example if land is settled on A for life with remainder to B in fee simple, it is possible for B to raise a loan for money by mortgaging his equitable interest in remainder under the settlement. It may be assumed that the discussion in the following pages is of mortgages of a legal estate unless the contrary is stated.

Methods of mortgaging

After 1925 if a mortgage is to be a legal mortgage it must be made by demise or by legal charge.[1] If a freehold is being mortgaged by demise the mortgagee will be granted a long term of years, usually for 3,000 years, with a proviso for cesser on redemption, *i.e.* a proviso that the term is to cease when the mortgage is paid off. The corresponding method of mortgaging a leasehold is by sub-demise with a similar proviso—the mortgagee is granted a sub-term of years for a term less by at least one day than that of the leasehold which is being mortgaged (in practice the sub-lease is usually for 10 days less than the leasehold mortgaged).

Both freeholds and leaseholds may be mortgaged by legal charge (or, to give its full title, "charge by deed expressed to be made by way of legal mortgage"), a new form of mortgage introduced by the Law of Property Act 1925. Such a charge gives to the mortgagee the same rights and remedies as if he had a mortgage by demise or sub-demise, but does not technically give to him a term of years in the land. The legal charge has certain advantages over a mortgage by demise or sub-demise. For example, a mortgage of a leasehold created in this way will not be a breach of a tenant's covenant not to sub-let the premises, whereas a mortgage by sub-demise would be.

It will be noticed that whichever method of mortgaging is adopted the mortgagor is left with his legal estate in the land. He may, therefore, create second and subsequent legal mortgages to secure any further loans that may be raised on the same land. Until 1926 this was not possible, because a mortgage of land usually took the form of a conveyance of the mortgagor's whole legal estate in the land to the mortgagee, subject to a proviso for reconveyance on redemption of the mortgage. The Law of Property Act 1925, however, now prohibits this method of mortgaging a legal estate.

An equitable mortgage of a legal estate in land may arise in either of two ways. First a mortgage will not be a legal mortgage unless it is made by deed; but a mortgage which is not made by deed will be a valid equitable mortgage if it constitutes a specifically enforceable agreement to grant a mortgage.[2] For this purpose, it is a sufficient act of part performance[3] of such an agreement if the borrower deposits with the lender, as security for the loan, title deeds relating to the borrower's estate. It follows that in theory a valid equitable mortgage can be made by a mere oral agreement between the parties supported by deposit of title deeds. In practice a mortgagee usually insists upon having at least a written memorandum setting out the terms of the agreement.

[1] LPA 1925, ss.85–87.
[2] See p. 25.
[3] See p. 81.

Temporary loans are often secured by deposit of title deeds accompanied by a "memorandum of deposit," as it is called. Secondly, even if a mortgage is created by deed, the mortgage will be merely an equitable mortgage if it does not show an intention to create a legal estate in the land. Quite commonly the memorandum of deposit to which reference has just been made is under seal, but this document does not create a legal mortgage because it does not show an intention to do so.

A mortgage of an equitable interest in land is itself necessarily equitable. It is usually effected by an assignment (which must be in writing[4]) to the mortgagee subject to a proviso for re-assignment on redemption.

Redemption of mortgages

In the mortgage deed the mortgagor covenants to repay the principal money with interest on a date specified in the deed. This is the legal (or contractual) date of redemption, and at common law once it has passed the mortgagor has no right to redeem his property *i.e.* the mortgagee can in principle "foreclose," and take the property for himself. Equity, however, compels the mortgagee to allow redemption at any time after the contractual date on tender to him of the "price of redemption," *i.e.* the principal money, arrears of interest[5] and the costs of discharging the mortgage. This equitable right of redemption, which arises once the contractual date has passed, was developed by equity into an equitable estate or interest in the land, called the "equity of redemption," which the mortgagor is regarded as having from the moment of the execution of the mortgage deed, and which comprises the mortgagor's entire beneficial interest in the property subject to the mortgage, including not only his equitable right to redeem, but also his general rights of ownership.

It has become the practice to fix the contractual date of redemption very soon (generally six months) after the date of execution of the mortgage.[6] Thereafter, the mortgagor must rely upon his equitable right to redeem. Equity does not attach any time limit to the exercise of this right, but there are various events upon which the right will become extinguished. For example, if the mortgagee sells the land under his power of sale the purchaser will acquire the mortgagor's legal estate free from the equity of

---

[4] LPA 1925, s.53.

[5] *All* arrears must be paid, even though statute-barred; see *Holmes* v. *Cowcher* [1970] 1 W.L.R. 834, and p. 170 below.

[6] Mainly because the mortgagee's statutory powers arise only when the mortgage money has become due (see pp. 155–6).

redemption.[7] Again, if the mortgagee takes possession of the land and remains in possession for 12 years without giving any acknowledgment of the mortgagor's title, the equitable right of redemption will become extinguished.[8] As we shall see later, equity itself, in foreclosure proceedings, may put a period to the equitable right of redemption.[9]

Notice of intention to redeem

Equity has a maxim "he who seeks equity must do equity"; accordingly, equity will not allow the mortgagor to exercise his equitable right of redemption in an unconscionable manner. If the mortgagor were at liberty to repay the mortgage money without prior notice to the mortgagee, the mortgagee might have the money lying idle in his hands for a considerable time before finding a suitable new investment for it. Equity, therefore, requires the mortgagor to give reasonable prior notice to the mortgagee of his intention to exercise his equitable right of redemption, or pay additional interest instead. For a formal legal mortgage six months' notice will usually be required. The giving of notice or the payment of additional interest in lieu is not necessary if the mortgagee has already shown that he wants his money, *e.g.* by giving notice requiring repayment.

Consolidation

Another application of the principle "he who seeks equity must do equity" is in the doctrine of consolidation. In its simplest form this means that if the same person by separate mortgages mortgages two different properties to the same mortgagee, then seeks to exercise his equitable right to redeem one of the properties, the mortgagee can require him to redeem both or neither; otherwise the mortgagor might be able to redeem a property that was a more than adequate security for the loan made on it, leaving the mortgagee with a property that was an inadequate security for the loan made on that property. The right to consolidate has been abolished by statute (now the Law of Property Act 1925, s.93) unless the right is reserved in at least one of the mortgages: this is often done by providing expressly that section 93 shall not apply. Moreover, the right does not

[7] See p. 155.
[8] See p. 170.
[9] See p. 157.

exist unless the contractual date of redemption has passed in both cases.

The right to consolidate exists not only in the simple case mentioned above, but also whenever the following conditions are satisfied[10]:

(i) Both mortgages were made by the same mortgagor.

(ii) Either (a) the equities of redemption (*i.e.* the properties, subject to the mortgages thereon) are in one hand and the mortgages in another single hand, or (b) the position as at (a) has existed at some time in the past since when the equities of redemption have become separated.

Some examples will illustrate the operation of these rules.

Example 1

A mortgages Blackacre to B.

A mortgages Whiteacre to C.

B and C transfer their mortgages to D.

If A then seeks to redeem one of the two properties, D can consolidate, *i.e.* can require A to pay off the mortgages on both properties or not redeem at all.

Rule (ii) above is here satisfied under (ii)(a).

Example 2

A mortgages Blackacre to B.

A mortgages Whiteacre to C.

A sells Blackacre, subject to the mortgage thereon to X.

B and C transfer their mortgages to D.

If X or A seeks to redeem his property (Blackacre or Whiteacre, respectively) D cannot consolidate. Rule (ii) above is not satisfied because there has never been a moment of time when both the properties have been in one hand and both the mortgages in another single hand: the properties had become separated before the mortgages fell into one hand.

Example 3

A mortgages Blackacre to B.

A mortgages Whiteacre to B.

A sells Blackacre, subject to the mortgage thereon, to X.

If X or A seeks to redeem his property B can consolidate. Rule (ii) is satisfied under (ii)(b). It will be observed that in this case, as a condition of paying off the mortgage on his own property, X or

---

[10] *Pledge* v. *White* [1896] A.C. 187.

A can be required to pay off the mortgage on the other property: that mortgage will not then be discharged, but will be transferred to the person making the payment off (*i.e.* X or A, as the case may be).[11]

Preserving the equity of redemption

Equity has evolved a series of rules for the protection of the equity of redemption, which may be regarded as falling under the general principle "once a mortgage always a mortgage." Equity is concerned to ensure that a mortgage shall provide security and nothing more, that it shall not be made irredeemable, and that the mortgagee shall not in any way bring improper pressure to bear on the mortgagor.

It should perhaps be borne in mind that equity's jurisdiction in these matters was established largely at a time when money-lending or usury was regarded as a suspect and undesirable activity. Social and economic circumstances have changed, and it is difficult now to reconcile equity's traditional attitude to mortgages with the transactions into which the vast majority of house-buyers enter so readily with their building society or bank. A further point to notice is that the leading cases in which equity's jurisdiction over mortgages developed were almost without exception cases concerning mortgages of commercial property: the principles applied may be the same as with mortgages of domestic property, but the matters in issue are scarcely comparable.

The main rules are as follows:

1. The substance not the form

Equity will treat as a mortgage any transaction which is in substance intended to provide security for the loan of money, whatever name the parties may give to the transaction. For example, if the lender of money insists upon the transaction being expressed as a conveyance on sale of the property to the lender, with an option to the borrower to re-purchase the property at an enhanced price within a certain time (the difference in price being in fact the interest on the loan), equity will treat this transaction as a mortgage in order that the mortgagor's right of redemption may be preserved: the mortgagor will then have the right to redeem even after the end of the fixed period specified in the deed.[12]

---

[11] See p. 161.
[12] See M. & W. p. 965.

2. Provisions repugnant to the equity of redemption

Equity will treat as void any provision in a mortgage which would or might destroy the equity of redemption. For example, if the mortgage purports to give to the mortgagee an option to purchase the property, the grant of the option is void: otherwise by exercising the option the mortgagee could destroy the mortgagor's right of redemption.[13] Once the mortgage has been created, however, the mortgagor by an independent transaction may validly grant an option to purchase the property to the mortgagee.[14]

3. Postponing the right of redemption

Prima facie, in the absence of evidence of fraud or oppression by the mortgagee, the parties can make what bargain they like as to the earliest possible date of redemption of the property[15]: they are not bound to follow the usual form, by which the contractual date of redemption is made six months after the date of the execution of the mortgage. But equity disallows a postponement which would render the right of redemption merely nominal or illusory, *e.g.* when a leasehold is mortgaged, a provision postponing the right of redemption until the lease itself has almost expired.[16] If a postponement is coupled with a "tie" between the mortgagor and the mortgagee which is void as being in restraint of trade,[17] it seems that the postponement will also be void, *e.g.* where the owner of a petrol station mortgages it to an oil company and agrees to take all his supplies from the company throughout the term of the mortgage, and not to redeem the mortgage for 21 years.[18]

4. Other clogs on the equity of redemption

Any provision in a mortgage is void to the extent that it would prevent the mortgagor on redemption from getting back his property in substantially the same condition as it was in when he mortgaged it. For example, if the owner of a free public-house (*i.e.*

---

[13] *Samuel* v. *Jarrah Timber Corporation* [1904] A.C. 323. The same rule applies if the option is granted on a transfer of the mortgage (*Lewis* v. *Frank Love Ltd.* [1961] 1 W.L.R. 261).

[14] *Reeve* v. *Lisle* [1902] A.C. 461.

[15] *Knightsbridge Estates Ltd.* v. *Byrne* [1939] Ch. 441 (affirmed on different grounds [1940] A.C. 613).

[16] *Fairclough* v. *Swan Brewery Co. Ltd.* [1912] A.C. 565.

[17] This is a common law doctrine based on grounds of public policy.

[18] *Esso Petroleum Co. Ltd.* v. *Harper's Garage* (*Stourport*) *Ltd.* [1968] A.C. 269.

a public-house the owner of which is at liberty to sell any brewer's beers) mortgages it to a brewer, any provision in the mortgage requiring the mortgagor to sell only the mortgagee's beers will be void so far as the restriction purports to continue after the mortgagor has paid off the loan: otherwise having mortgaged a free public-house he would get back a tied one.[19]

5. Collateral advantages

In the absence of evidence of fraud or oppression by the mortgagee, equity has no objection to a provision in the mortgage giving to the mortgagee some collateral advantage, *i.e.* some advantage over and above repayment of the loan with interest.[20] Thus, there is no objection to a provision in the mortgage of a free public-house which requires the mortgagor to sell only the mortgagee's beers *so long as the mortgage lasts*.[21] But if the advantage operates as a clog on, or is repugnant to, the equity of redemption, it will be void. Thus, if the mortgage provides that the property can only be redeemed on payment of a premium, and the amount of the premium is excessive, equity will allow the mortgagor to redeem on repaying the principal plus a reasonable rate of interest.[22]

Mortgagee's remedies

In addition to his right to sue the mortgagor personally for any money that becomes due to him, the mortgagee has (or may have) the following main remedies: a right to take possession of the land; a right of sale; a right to appoint a receiver of the rents and profits of the land; and a right to foreclose. Each of these main remedies must be considered separately.

1. Possession

From the moment that a mortgage is created, a legal mortgagee, whether his mortgage is by demise or by charge, has the right to

---

[19] *Noakes & Co. Ltd.* v. *Rice* [1902] A.C. 24.

[20] *Kreglinger (G. & C.)* v. *New Patagonia Meat and Cold Storage Co. Ltd.* [1914] A.C. 25: *cf. Multiservice Bookbinding Ltd.* v. *Marsden* [1979] Ch. 84 (provisions respecting interest "imprudent" but valid, since not unconscionable).

[21] *Biggs* v. *Hoddinott* [1898] 2 Ch. 307. But note the *Esso* case, above.

[22] *Cityland and Property (Holdings)* v. *Dabrah* [1968] Ch. 166. Under the Consumer Credit Act 1974, ss.137–140, the court has power to relieve any debtor from an "extortionate credit bargain."

take possession of the land.[23] By this means the mortgagee can obtain the rents and profits of the land and can, if necessary, himself grant leases of the land.[24] In principle a mortgagee is entitled to possession regardless of whether the mortgagor is in default,[25] but in practice he will not normally exercise this right except either as a preliminary to selling the property, or as a means of recovering interest on the mortgage debt; and in either case it will usually be necessary for him to bring an *action* for possession against the mortgagor. If the mortgage is of dwelling-house, the court now has a power to adjourn such proceedings or to suspend or postpone the possession order, if it appears that the mortgagor is likely within a reasonable period to pay the amount due or remedy any other default.[26]

Any sums received by a mortgagee in possession must, of course, be set off against the mortgage debt; furthermore, a mortgagee who does take possession is accountable to the mortgagor on the footing of wilful default: he is chargeable, not only for any profits that he does make, but also for any further profits that he ought to have made. For example, if the property is a free public-house and the mortgagee is a brewer, and the mortgagee takes possession of the premises and then grants a lease containing a term which requires the lessee to sell only the mortgagee's beers, the mortgagee will be accountable to the mortgagor for the higher rent he could have obtained if he had let the premises without any such tie.[27] By reason of this strict accountability, a mortgagee will generally prefer to appoint a receiver of the rents and profits rather than himself take possession: he will not then be accountable in this way.

2. Sale

The two principal statutory remedies are the power of sale and the power to appoint a receiver. Both are given by the Law of Property Act 1925, s.101, to every mortgagee whose mortgage is by deed. Thus every legal mortgagee has these powers, and an equitable mortgagee enjoys them if his mortgage is by deed, *e.g.* if

---

[23] An equitable mortgagee probably has a similar right: see M & W. pp. 951–952.
[24] See p. 158.
[25] See *Western Bank Ltd.* v. *Schindler* [1977] Ch. 1. (*Quennell* v. *Maltby* [1979] 1 W.L.R. 318, in which doubt is cast on this principle, can be regarded as confined to its special facts (attempt by mortgagor and mortgagee in collusion to evict mortgagor's statutory tenant)).
[26] Administration of Justice Act 1970, ss.36–39. The Administration of Justice Act 1973, s.8, extends this power to cases where the mortgagor appears likely to bring payment of instalments up to date.
[27] *White* v. *City of London Brewery Co.* (1889) 42 Ch.D. 237.

it was created by deposit of title deeds accompanied by a memorandum of deposit under seal. The statutory powers may be varied or extended by the mortgage.

The power of sale *arises* as soon as the contractual date for redemption has passed or, in cases where the principal is repayable by instalments, as soon as any instalment is due and unpaid.[28] But it does not become *exercisable* until one for three events occurs:

   (i) the mortgagee has served notice requiring payment of the mortgage money and default has been made in payment for three months after such service;

  (ii) some interest is in arrears and unpaid for two months after becoming due; or

 (iii) there has been a breach of some provision contained in the mortgage deed or in the Act which is to be observed by the mortgagor, other than a covenant for payment of the principal money or interest thereon.

The purchaser from the mortgagee is concerned to see that the power of sale has arisen, but not that it has become exercisable; he will get a good title even if the power has not become exercisable,[29] but the mortgagee will then be liable in damages to the mortgagor.

When the mortgagee of a freehold or leasehold sells the land under his statutory power of sale, he conveys to the purchaser the mortgagor's fee simple or leasehold term: the conveyance to the purchaser takes effect subject to rights having priority over the mortgage (unless they are discharged out of the proceeds), but free from all estates, interests and rights over which the mortgage has priority[30]; subsequent mortgages and the mortgagor's equity of redemption are thus overreached[31], as also is any interest created out of the equity of redemption, such as a contract of sale made previously by the mortgagor.[32] After paying off what is due to himself, the mortgagee holds any surplus proceeds of sale upon trust for any subsequent mortgagee, and subject thereto for the mortgagor.[33]

A mortgagee is not a trustee of his statutory power of sale,

---

[28] *Payne* v. *Cardiff R.D.C.* [1932] 1 K.B. 241.
[29] LPA 1925, s.104.
[30] *Ibid.* ss.88, 89, 104.
[31] *Ibid.* s.2(1)(iii).
[32] Whether or not protected by registration (*Duke* v. *Robson* [1973] 1 W.L.R. 267; contrast *Lyus* v. *Prowsa Developments Ltd.* [1982] 1 W.L.R. 1044, in which the sale by the mortgagee was expressly subject to rights created by the mortgagor's contract).
[33] LPA 1925, s.105.

and in general need not exert himself to get the best price obtainable.[34] However, the mortgagee must not deliberately sell at a lower price than he can readily obtain, and he must make a genuine sale: thus he may not sell to himself, directly or indirectly, whether by private treaty or at public auction.[35] Furthermore, the mortgagee is under a duty of care in exercising his power of sale, and may be liable in damages if through his negligence the property is sold for less than it ought to have realised.[36] The duty is owed not only to the mortgagor himself, but also to a guarantor of the mortgage debt, and possibly to subsequent mortgagees and other creditors of the mortgagor.[37]

A mortgagee whose mortgage is not by deed does not have the statutory power of sale, but the court may order a sale upon application by him (or by anyone interested in the equity of redemption, *e.g.* the mortgagor).[38] An equitable mortgagee has the statutory power if his mortgage is by deed. It is generally thought, however, that he cannot pass a legal estate to the purchaser unless there is some conveyancing device in the mortgage which enables him to do this, *e.g.* an irrevocable power of attorney given by the mortgagor to the mortgagee for this purpose.

3. Receiver

A mortgagee whose mortgage is by deed has statutory power to appoint a receiver of the income of the mortgaged property as soon as the contractual date for redemption has passed: the power is not to be exercised, however, until the power of sale has become exercisable.[39] Such a receiver is deemed to be the agent of the mortgagor, who therefore is to be solely responsible for the receiver's acts or defaults unless the mortgage otherwise provides. It is for this reason that a mortgagee who wishes to obtain the profits of the land will generally prefer to appoint a receiver rather than take possession of the land himself: if he appoints a receiver he escapes liability on the footing of wilful default.[40] After paying various outgoings and his own commission the receiver is to apply

---

[34] *Kennedy* v. *De Trafford* [1897] A.C. 180. Building societies are an exception (Building Societies Act 1986, Sched. 4).

[35] Sale to a company in which the mortgagee is the majority shareholder is not necessarily objectionable, provided he otherwise acts reasonably (*Farrar* v. *Farrars Ltd.* (1888) 40 Ch.D.; *cf. Tse Kwong Lam* v. *Wong Chit Sen* [1983] 1 W.L.R. 1349).

[36] *Cuckmere Brick Co. Ltd.* v. *Mutual Finance Ltd.* [1971] Ch. 949.

[37] *Standard Chartered Bank Ltd.* v. *Walker* [1982] 1 W.L.R. 1410.

[38] LPA 1925, s.91.

[39] *Ibid.* ss.101, 109.

[40] See p. 154.

money received by him in payment of the interest accruing due under the mortgage, and, if so directed in writing by the mortgagee, in or towards discharge of the principal money. The residue is to be paid by him to the person who but for the possession of the receiver would have been entitled to receive the income—normally the mortgagor.

A mortgagee whose mortgage is not by deed may apply to the court for the appointment of a receiver.

4. Foreclosure

As soon as the contractual date for redemption has passed,[41] the mortgagee may start foreclosure proceedings in the courts. In such proceedings the court will make a foreclosure order nisi in the first instance, giving to the mortgagor a fixed period (usually six months) within which he must redeem the property, failing which the order will be made absolute, the mortgagor will lose his right of redemption and the mortgagee will become beneficial owner of the property. The court has power to order sale instead of foreclosure,[42] and will generally do so if it appears that the value of the property exceeds the mortgage debt.

By the equitable remedy of foreclosure equity takes away from the mortgagor that which it has itself created, namely, the equity of redemption: foreclosure, therefore, is the mortgagee's counterblast to the mortgagor's equity of redemption. A foreclosure order absolute vests the mortgagor's legal estate in the mortgagee, free from the equity of redemption and free from any subsequent mortgages, which are extinguished.[43] If there are subsequent mortgages, each subsequent mortgagee must be given the right to pay off the plaintiff's mortgage and take a transfer of it, failing which the subsequent mortgagee will lose his security when the order absolute is made. It follows that subsequent mortgagees must be joined with the mortgagor as co-defendants in the mortgagee's foreclosure action. Prior mortgages are unaffected and remain attached to the land.

In exceptional circumstances the court on application may reopen the foreclosure, even though an order absolute has been made, *i.e.* the court may restore to the mortgagor his equity of redemption. Moreover, the foreclosure will automatically be reopened if the mortgagee after foreclosure absolute sues the

---

[41] Or, it seems, if the mortgagor is otherwise in breach of a condition in the mortgage, *e.g.* as to payment of interest, even though the principal sum is not due: see *Twentieth Century Banking Corporation Ltd.* v. *Wilkinson* [1977] Ch. 99.
[42] LPA 1925, s.91.
[43] *Ibid.* ss.88(2), 89(2).

mortgagor on the mortgage debt. For this reason if a mortgagee who has obtained a foreclosure order absolute sells the property he cannot thereafter sue the mortgagor on the mortgage debt; he is not in a position to allow the mortgagor to redeem the property. With this exception a mortgagee's remedies are cumulative, *i.e.* the fact that he has exercised one of the remedies does not prevent him from making use of another if he has not obtained complete redress.

The equitable remedy of foreclosure is available to all mortgagees, legal or equitable.

The power of leasing

The Law of Property Act 1925, s.99, gives power to grant leases of mortgaged land which will be binding upon all persons interested therein. The power is given to the mortgagor, unless the mortgagee has taken possession or has appointed a receiver, in which case the power belongs to the mortgagee. A mortgagee who has appointed a receiver may delegate the power of leasing to the receiver. The leases which the section authorises are agricultural or occupation leases for any term not exceeding 50 years, and building leases for any term not exceeding 999 years. The lease must reserve the best rent that can reasonably be obtained, and no fine may be taken, and other conditions are laid down by the Act.

With the exception of mortgages of agricultural land,[44] the statutory power of leasing can be excluded by the mortgage, and in practice the mortgagor's power is commonly excluded. The statutory power may also be extended by the mortgage.

Quite apart from the statutory power, if either party to the mortgage grants a lease, that lease will be binding upon him, although not upon the other party to the mortgage.

Priority of successive mortgages

1. Mortgages of a legal estate

Where several mortgages of the same land have been created successively, and the security proves inadequate, the question of the priority of those mortgages arises, *i.e.* of the order in which effect will be given to the rights of the several mortgagees. The general rule is "first in time first in right," *i.e.* priority follows the order in which the mortgages were created. There are two main

---

[44] Agricultural Holdings Act 1986, Sched. 14, para. 12.

exceptions to this general rule. To understand these it is first necessary to notice that if a mortgage is protected by deposit of title deeds with the mortgagee[45] it is not registrable under the Land Charges Act 1972, but if it is not so protected then it is registrable under the Act—if it is a legal mortgage it is registrable as a puisne mortgage; if it is an equitable mortgage it is registrable as a general equitable charge.[46] We may now consider the two exceptions.

(i) If the earlier mortgage is an equitable mortgage protected by deposit (and so not registrable) and the later mortgage is a legal mortgage, and the legal mortgagee took his mortgage in good faith and without notice, actual or constructive, of the equitable mortgage, the legal mortgage will rank first. This is not because of any misconduct on the part of the equitable mortgagee, but because in general an equitable interest does not bind a subsequent bona fide purchaser for value of a legal estate (including a legal mortgagee) without notice of the equitable interest. The position of the earlier equitable mortgagee is not, however, as precarious as might at first sight appear, because the fact that the title deeds have been deposited with him will ordinarily ensure that any subsequent mortgagee has notice, actual or constructive, of the equitable mortgage: if the latter inquires for the title deeds he will generally discover the existence of the equitable mortgage, and if he does not inquire he will be fixed with constructive notice of it. But if the legal mortgagee did inquire for the title deeds and was given a false, but credible, explanation of the mortgagor's inability to produce them, he would not be fixed with notice of the equitable mortgage, and would have priority.[47]

(ii) If the earlier mortgage, whether legal or equitable, is registrable, and has not been registered when the later mortgage is created, the later mortgage will have priority. In accordance with the Land Charges Act 1972, s.4, failure to register the earlier mortgage renders it void against a subsequent "purchaser" of the land; the later mortgagee (whether legal or equitable) is within the statutory definition of "purchaser," and it follows that he gains priority, even if he has actual notice of the earlier mortgage.[48] There is, however, a possible conflict between the Land Charges Act 1972, s.4, and the Law of Property Act 1925, s.97, which provides that a registrable mortgage shall rank according to the

[45] Title deeds will normally be held by the first mortgagee, who has the same right to possession of documents as if his security included the fee simple (LPA 1925, s.85(1)).
[46] See p. 175.
[47] *Hewitt* v. *Loosemore* (1851) 9 Hare 449; *Oliver* v. *Hinton* [1899] 2 Ch. 264.
[48] LPA 1925, s.199.

date of its registration as a land charge: if there are two successive mortgages, both of which are registrable, the earlier will rank first if it was registered first, even if it had not been registered when the later mortgage was created. The conflict has yet to be resolved, but it seems that the provisions of the Land Charges Act ought to prevail, on the basis that a charge once rendered void cannot later be revived (at least not without express provision to that effect).

It will be observed that, for the purposes of the Land Charges Act, if the second mortgage is registrable nothing turns upon *its* registration, because failure to register a registrable interest merely renders it void against a *later* purchaser: its priority in relation to an earlier mortgage would not be affected by its non-registration.

2. Mortgages of an equitable interest

The priority of successive mortgages of an equitable interest in any property, real or personal, is governed by the rule in *Dearle* v. *Hall*,[49] as amended by the Law of Property Act 1925, s.137. Under this rule priority generally follows the order in which the respective mortgagees give written notice of their mortgages to the trustees of the settlement or trust under which the mortgaged interest subsists. For example, if by means of a strict settlement, or a trust for sale, land is settled on A for life with remainder to B in fee simple, and B mortgages his equitable remainder first to X and then to Y, the priority of the two mortgages will generally follow the order in which X and Y give written notice of their mortgages to the trustees of the settlement or trust for sale: the first to give notice will rank first. As an exception, if Y when he took his mortgage had actual or constructive notice of the existence of X's mortgage, he cannot gain priority by being the first to give notice: it would be fraudulent for Y to claim priority in those circumstances.[50]

Mortgages of a beneficial interest under a settlement or trust for sale are not registrable under the Land Charges Act 1972, nor is priority affected by deposit of documents of title.

Tacking

Sometimes the rules of priority are affected by the doctrine of tacking. After 1925 only one form of tacking is permitted, namely the tacking of further advances, which is now governed by the Law

---

[49] (1823) 3 Russ. 1.
[50] *Re Holmes* (1885) 29 Ch.D. 786.

of Property Act 1925, s.94. If two successive mortgages of the same land are made to A and B, respectively, and A then makes a further loan to the borrower on the same security, A may sometimes tack (*i.e.* add) this further advance to his original loan, and so claim priority for both his loans over B's mortgage. A prior mortgagee has the right to tack in three cases—(i) if an arrangement has been made to that effect with the intervening mortgagee; (ii) if he had no notice of the intervening mortgage at the time when he made the further advance; (iii) whether or not he had such notice, if his mortgage imposed upon him an obligation to make the further advance. It will be observed that in case (ii) (the ordinary case), notice of the intervening mortgage will be fatal to the right to tack. In general, if the intervening mortgage was registered under the Land Charges Act 1972 at the date of the further advance, registration will constitute sufficient notice to prevent tacking: as an exception, if the prior mortgage was made expressly for securing a current account or such further advances as might be made, registration under the Land Charges Act is not of itself sufficient notice to prevent the prior mortgagee from tacking (unless he actually searches the register). But the prior mortgagee cannot tack if when he made a further advance he had actual notice of the intervening mortgage: for this reason, when a prior mortgage is expressly made to secure a current account or further advances that may be made, a later mortgagee should always give express notice of his mortgage to the prior mortgagee; by so doing he prevents tacking.

Discharge of mortgages

If a mortgage has been created by demise or sub-demise, all that is required, in theory, to discharge the mortgage is an ordinary receipt for the mortgage money, because by the Law of Property Act 1925, ss.5 and 116, the mortgagee's term of years will thereupon become a satisfied term and will cease. In practice, however, reliance is placed, not upon these provisions, but upon a receipt endorsed on or annexed to the mortgage which complies with the provisions of section 115 of the Act. Under this section such a receipt, if it states the name of the person who pays the money and is signed by the mortgagee, will operate to discharge (or "vacate") any mortgage. An endorsed receipt will not vacate the mortgage, however, but will (with certain exceptions) transfer it to the person making the payment if that person is not the person entitled to the immediate equity of redemption.[51]

[51] See p. 151, note 11.

19. Disabilities

Infants

After 1925 an infant or minor, *i.e.* a person below the age of 18 years,[1] cannot hold a legal estate in land, although he may in general own other property, including an equitable interest in land. Land which is held upon trust for an infant for an estate in fee simple or for a term of years absolute is settled land for the purposes of the Settled Land Act 1925, s.1.[2] The legal estate must be vested in the statutory owner by vesting deed or assent, and the beneficial entitlement of the infant will be declared by the trust instrument. The statutory owner has all the powers of disposition of a tenant for life under the Act; the infancy of the person who is beneficially entitled does not, therefore, prevent a binding disposition of the land from being made, and this is why the Act makes the land settled land—an infant cannot make a binding disposition of the property which is vested in him,[3] and it is the policy of the 1925 Acts to keep land alienable at all times.

A purported conveyance of a legal estate in land to an infant alone, or to two or more persons jointly both or all of whom are infants, for his or their own benefit, operates only as an agreement for valuable consideration (whether such consideration has in fact been given or not) to execute a settlement by means of a vesting deed and a trust instrument in favour of the infant or infants, and in the meantime to hold the land on trust for the infant or infants.[4] A conveyance of a legal estate in land to an infant jointly with one or more other persons of full age operates to vest the legal estate in the other person or persons on the statutory trusts,[5] *i.e.* upon trust to sell the land and to hold the net rents and profits pending sale,

---

[1] Family Law Reform Act 1969, ss.1, 12. Before January 1, 1970, the age of majority was 21.
[2] See p. 33, note 2.
[3] A purported disposition is voidable by the infant during minority or within a reasonable time of attaining majority.
[4] SLA 1925, s.27.
[5] LPA 1925, s.19.

and net proceeds of sale after sale, upon trust for the person
or persons of full age and the infant: the beneficial interest of
the infant is, therefore, preserved. Similar provisions apply to
the grant or transfer of a legal mortgage to an infant solely or
jointly with another person.

The appointment of an infant as trustee of any property is
void.[6] The appointment of an infant as executor is not void,
but is suspended during his minority[7]: other arrangements are
then made for the administration of the deceased's estate to be
undertaken during the minority, but the infant is entitled to a
grant of probate on attaining majority.

By a curious provision of the Administration of Estates Act
1925, s.51(3), if an infant dies without having married and
entitled at his death to a vested equitable interest in fee simple
in land, or to an absolute interest in property settled to
devolve with such land or as freehold land, he shall be deemed
to have had an entailed interest in the property. In the result,
the land upon the infant's death reverts to the grantor (*i.e.* the
person who gave the land to the infant) or, if he is dead, his
estate, because the notional entail comes to an end.

Persons suffering from mental disorder

Under the Mental Health Act 1983 the court has wide
powers of disposition over the property of a person who is
suffering from mental disorder, and may appoint a receiver to
exercise these powers on its behalf. So long as a receivership is
in force the patient has no power to make an *inter vivos*
disposition of his property, although he may make a valid will
during a lucid interval. If no receiver has been appointed, the
position with regard to a disposition of his property by a
person suffering from mental disorder is as follows:

(i) It is *valid* if the disposition is made for valuable
consideration and the other party has no notice of the
disability.
(ii) It is *voidable* if it is made for valuable consideration
and the other party has notice of the disability.
(iii) It is *void* if the disposition is gratuitous.

Other persons and bodies

Married women, traitors and felons, aliens, corporations and

---

[6] *Ibid.* s.20.
[7] Supreme Court Act 1981, s.118.

charities were all formerly subject to particular disabilities, but with slight exceptions these disabilities have now been abolished by various statutes. A few vestiges remain, *e.g.* a charity may not even now dispose of land which forms part of its endowment without special permission, unless it is one of the privileged charities that are exempt from the restriction.

20. Acquisition of title under the Limitation Act 1980

All statutes of limitation have as their object the extinction of legal claims or titles which the claimant or owner has failed to pursue or protect within due time. Different periods of limitation may be prescribed for different causes of action, but in each case at the end of the prescribed period the action becomes statute-barred.

With respect to actions to recover possession of land, the basic provision is now contained in section 15(1) of the Limitation Act 1980, which provides that no action shall be brought by any person to recover any land after the expiration of 12 years[1] from the date on which the right of action accrued to him or, if it first accrued to some person through whom he claims, to that person. In general, the only person who can bring an action to recover possession from a "squatter," *i.e.* some other person who has wrongfully taken possession of land, is someone who is himself entitled to possession. Accordingly, as we shall see, the Act contains detailed provisions governing the rights of action of persons who are not immediately entitled, and whose interests might be prejudiced by the inactivity of the owner in possession.

The effect of lapse of time under the Act is twofold: first, the title of the former owner is extinguished[2]; secondly, the squatter acquires a good possessory title to the land. In considering both negative and positive aspects, however, it must be remembered that title to land in England means title to a particular estate or interest. It follows, first, that where several persons own different estates or interests in the same land, separate rights of action to recover possession of the land may accrue at different times to different owners; and, secondly, that the nature and extent of any title acquired by a squatter can only be determined by reference to the particular estate owners who have become statute-barred.

---

[1] 30 years when the action is brought by the Crown or a spiritual or eleemosynary corporation sole, 60 years for actions by the Crown to recover foreshore.
[2] s.17.

It is, of course, rare for one person actively to dispossess another of his land. Questions are most likely to arise under the Limitation Act where there is a misunderstanding as to the correct boundaries of land, and one person takes possession of part of another's land in the mistaken belief that it is his own.

ACCRUAL OF RIGHT OF ACTION

Interests in possession

If the person bringing an action to recover land has an interest in possession, and has been dispossessed, the right of action is deemed to have accrued on the date when he was dispossessed. If he has merely discontinued his possession, no right of action is deemed to have accrued unless and until *adverse possession* has been taken by some other person.[3] In either case, it will be appreciated, the effect of these provisions is that if the owner is to recover the land, and prevent his title being extinguished, he must bring his action within 12 years from the date on which adverse possession was taken.

Future interests

If a succession of interests subsists in land and adverse possession is taken during a preceding interest, the owner of a future interest may generally bring an action to recover the land within 12 years from the date when adverse possession was taken or six years from the date when his future interest fell into possession, whichever period last expires.[4] For example, if land is settled on A for life with remainder to B in fee simple, and adverse possession of the land is taken by a squatter during A's life interest, when A dies B may bring an action against the squatter within 12 years from the date when the squatter took possession of the land or six years from the death of A, whichever is longer.

This special rule has no application if adverse possession has been taken before the future interest is created. For example, in the above illustration if adverse possession had been taken by the squatter before the land was settled on A and B, neither A nor B could bring an action to recover the land from the squatter after the expiration of 12 years from the date when the squatter took

---

[3] Sched. 1, paras. 1, 8.
[4] s.15(2); Sched. 1, para. 4.

possession, because the settlor, through whom each would claim, would himself then be barred. Again, the special rule has no application to the owner of an interest which falls into possession on the determination of an entailed interest.[5] For example, if land is settled on A in tail with remainder to B in fee simple, and S takes adverse possession of the land during the currency of the entailed interest, B must bring his action within 12 years from the date when adverse possession was taken. Yet B cannot sue until his remainder falls into possession, so that he may well be barred by the Act before he has any chance to sue.

Finally, where a person is entitled to an interest in possession and at the same time he is also entitled to a future interest in the same land, and his right to recover the interest in possession becomes barred under the Act, no action may be brought by that person or by any person claiming through him in respect of the future interest unless in the meantime possession of the land has been recovered by a person entitled to an intermediate interest.[6] For example, if land is settled on A for life with remainder to B for life with remainder to A in fee simple, and S takes possession of the land and holds it for 12 years during A's lifetime, no action can be brought by A's personal representatives in respect of the fee simple remainder unless after A's death possession of the land has been recovered by B.

Settled land and land held on trust

The provisions of the Act are applied[7] to equitable interests in land, including interests in the proceeds of sale of land held upon trust for sale, in like manner as they apply to legal estates, and accordingly a right of action to recover the land is, for the purposes of the Act, deemed to accrue to a person entitled in possession to such an equitable interest in the same way as it would have accrued if his interest had been a legal estate in the land. However, the title of a tenant for life or statutory owner of settled land to the legal estate is not to be extinguished so long as the right of action to recover the land of any person entitled to a beneficial interest has not accrued or has not been barred by the Act. Similarly, when land is held upon trust, including a trust for sale, the right of the trustees is not to be extinguished so long as the right of action to recover the land of any beneficiary has not accrued or has not been barred. For example, if land is settled on A for life with remainder

---

[5] s.15(3).
[6] s.15(5).
[7] s.18.

to B in fee simple, and S takes adverse possession of the land and holds it for 12 years during A's lifetime, A's right to the beneficial life interest will become extinguished, but his title to the legal estate (vested in him as the "tenant for life" of the Settled Land Act) will not, because no cause of action has yet accrued to the remainderman B.

The Act also provides[8] that possession of settled land, or land held on trust for sale, by a beneficiary who is not solely and absolutely entitled shall not bar the title of a tenant for life, statutory owner, or trustee, or of any other beneficiary. Moreover, trustees cannot acquire a squatter's title against their own beneficiaries.[9] A somewhat curious consequence of these provisions is that, as co-ownership of land now involves a statutory trust for sale,[10] one co-owner cannot, by ousting his fellows, acquire a squatter's title to the land.[11] He will be a beneficiary under the trust for sale and usually a trustee as well.

Leaseholds generally

If a squatter takes possession of land after a lease of it has been granted, the landlord may sue the squatter to recover the land within 12 years after the determination of the lease. For example, if shortly after the fee simple owner has granted a lease for 50 years to a tenant a squatter takes possession of the land and holds it for 12 years, the tenant becomes statute-barred, so that the squatter will be entitled to remain in possession of the land for the rest of the lease; but the landlord will have 12 years from the determination of the lease within which to sue the squatter for recovery of the land.[12]

A lessee under a lease for a fixed term cannot acquire a squatter's title against his own landlord by virtue of his possession of the land during the currency of the lease. If, for example, shortly after a lease for 50 years has been granted the lessee begins to withhold payment of his rent and continues to do so for 12 years, he does not thereby acquire a squatter's title against his landlord. The landlord at any time may require the tenant to pay rent for the remainder of the leasehold term. He may also sue the tenant for arrears of rent so far as the Act allows: he may generally recover up to six years' arrears by action or distress,[13] but in the

---

[8] Sched. 1, para. 9.
[9] s.21.
[10] See Chap. 9.
[11] *Re Landi* [1939] Ch. 828.
[12] As to the other rights of the landlord, see pp. 173–174.
[13] s.19.

case of agricultural holdings the right of *distress* is limited to one year's rent.[14]

Similarly, a tenant at will cannot acquire a squatter's title against his landlord merely by remaining in possession without paying rent: time does not begin to run in his favour until the tenancy is determined by the landlord; but in the case of a tenancy at sufferance (which is not really a tenancy at all and amounts to adverse possession) time begins to run from its commencement.[15]

If a person wrongfully claims to be entitled to the reversion upon a written lease at a rent of at least £10 per annum (other than a lease granted by the Crown) and demands payment of the rent from the tenant, and the tenant pays the rent to that person for 12 years, the person to whom the rent has been paid acquires a possessory title to the reversion.[16]

Periodic tenancies

The Act provides[17] that a tenancy from year to year or for any other period not granted in writing shall for the purposes of the Act be deemed to be determined at the expiration of the first year or other period of the tenancy, and that accordingly the right of action of the person entitled to the land shall be deemed to have accrued at the date of such determination or on the date of the last receipt of rent. If, for example, a tenant under a yearly tenancy which has not been granted in writing remains in possession without paying rent for 13 years from the commencement of the tenancy, he will acquire a squatter's title against the landlord. But the payment of rent or the giving of a written acknowledgement of the landlord's title before the landlord becomes barred will start the 12-year period running afresh.

If a periodic tenancy is granted in writing time does not begin to run against the landlord until the tenancy is determined.

Rentcharges

The Act[18] defines land as including rentcharges and provides more specifically that in relation to rentcharges references in the

---

[14] Agricultural Holdings Act 1986, s.16.
[15] As to tenancies at will and at sufferance see pp. 86–7. Until August 1, 1980 a special rule applied to tenancies at will but this was abolished by the Limitation Amendment Act 1980.
[16] Limitation Act 1980, Sched. 1, paras. 6, 8(3).
[17] Sched. 1, para. 5.
[18] s.38.

Act to the possession of land shall be construed as references to the receipt of the rent, and references to the date of dispossession of land shall be construed as references to the date of the last receipt of rent. In consequence of these provisions if a rentcharge is unpaid for 12 years it becomes extinguished; and if a person wrongfully claims to be entitled to the rentcharge, and the rent is paid to him for 12 years, the former owner of the rentcharge becomes statute-barred and the claimant acquires a possessory title to the rentcharge.

Mortgages

Both the mortgagor's right of redemption, and the mortgagee's rights to recover principal and interest and to foreclose, may be extinguished by lapse of time.

1. Right of redemption

The Act[19] provides that when a mortgagee of land has been in possession of the mortgaged land for a period of 12 years no action to redeem the land of which the mortgagee has been so in possession can thereafter be brought by the mortgagor or any person claiming through him.

2. Rights of mortgagee

An action to recover any principal sum of money secured by a mortgage on any property, real or personal, and a foreclosure action in respect of land, must be brought within 12 years from the date when the right to receive the money, or the right to foreclose, accrued (*i.e.* the contractual date of redemption). In general, a mortgagee may not recover more than six years' arrears of interest payable under a mortgage.[20]

Disabilities

If on the date when a right of action accrues the person to whom it accrues is under disability (infancy or unsoundness of mind), the action may be brought at any time before the expiration of six years from the date when the person ceased to be under disability or died, whichever event first occurred, notwithstanding that the

---

[19] s.16.
[20] s.20(5), but see *Holmes* v. *Cowcher* [1970] 1 W.L.R. 834 (p. 148 above).

period of limitation has expired; there is a proviso that no action to recover land or money charged on land shall be brought after the expiration of 30 years from the date on which the right of action accrued, and in any event there is no extension of time unless the disability subsisted at the date of the accrual of the cause of action.[21]

When a right of action which has accrued to a person under disability accrues on the death of that person while still under disability to another person who also is under disability, no further extension of time is to be allowed by reason of the disability of the second person. Successive disabilities without a break of the *same* person, however, rank as one disability, *e.g.* where someone is an infant at the date of the accrual of the cause of action to him and later becomes of unsound mind before attaining his majority.

Acknowledgement and part-payment[22]

Where there has accrued a right of action (including a foreclosure action) to recover land, and the person in possession of the property acknowledges the title of the person to whom the right of action has accrued, or in the case of an action by a mortgagee the person in possession makes any payment in respect of the mortgage debt, whether of principal or interest, the right is deemed to have accrued on and not before the date of the acknowledgement or payment. For example, if a mortgagor in possession of the mortgaged land makes a payment of interest to the mortgagee, the mortgagee may bring a foreclosure action within 12 years from the date of that payment: he is not limited to 12 years from the contractual date of redemption, as he otherwise would have been.

Where a mortgagee is by virtue of the mortgage in possession of the mortgaged land, and he either receives a sum in respect of the principal or interest of the mortgage debt or he acknowledges the title of the mortgagor, an action to redeem the land may be brought at any time before the expiration of 12 years from the date of the payment or acknowledgement.

For the above purposes an acknowledgement must be in writing and signed by the person making the acknowledgement. Any such acknowledgement, and any such payment as has been mentioned, may be made by the agent of the person by whom it is required to be made, and must be made to the person whose title or claim is being acknowledged or his agent. There are detailed provisions as

[21] s.28.
[22] ss.29–31.

to the effect of acknowledgement or part-payment on persons other than the maker or recipient, *e.g.* where one of two or more mortgagees in possession gives an acknowledgement of the mortgagor's title.

Once the right of a person to bring an action to recover land has become barred, however, and his title to the land has been extinguished, no acknowledgement or payment given or made thereafter will revive his right to recover the land.

Fraud and mistake

Where in the case of any action for which a period of limitation is prescribed by the Act the action is based upon the fraud of the defendant or his agent (or any person through whom he claims or his agent), or any fact relevant to the right of action has been deliberately concealed by any such person, or the action is for relief from the consequences of mistake, the period of limitation does not begin to run until the plaintiff has discovered the fraud or mistake or could with reasonable diligence have discovered it. This provision, however, has no application to an action against a bona fide purchaser for value of property who was not a party to any fraud and did not at the time of the purchase know or have reason to believe that any fraud or mistake had occurred.[23]

ADVERSE POSSESSION

The essence of the acquisition of title under the Limitation Act is adverse possession. For this purpose, possession is only adverse if it is inconsistent with the title of the true owner. It follows, as we have seen,[24] that during the subsistence of a tenancy or licence the tenant or licensee cannot be regarded as having adverse possession against his landlord or licensor: only when the tenancy is determined, or the licence is revoked, can time begin to run in favour of the former tenant or licensee.

Where the owner has not recently been in occupation of the land, and has no present use for it, it may be a difficult question to decide whether acts done by another person in relation to the land amount to possession and, if so, whether such possession is adverse in the sense indicated above. The acts done must generally be such as to *exclude* the true owner[25]: casual acts of trespass from

---

[23] s.32.
[24] At pp. 168–9.
[25] Acts done in relation to part may indicate possession of the whole: see *Higgs* v. *Nassauvian* [1975] A.C. 464.

time to time are insufficient for this purpose, and it must be clear that the squatter has the intention to dispossess the owner.[26] In the case of boundary disputes, fencing is the most obvious evidence of adverse possession.[27] In other cases confusion has arisen because in determining whether adverse possession has been taken the courts have sometimes applied two different criteria—one objective, with respect to the acts done by the squatter, the other subjective, with respect to the purpose for which the owner intends to use the land—and only where the former is inconsistent with the latter, it has been held, does the squatter have adverse possession.[28] Indeed the courts went so far as to hold that where the owner had no present use for the land the squatter's possession must be *deemed* to be with the owner's implied licence[29]—and of course a licensee cannot acquire title under the Limitation Act. The implication of such a licence as a matter of *law* is now negatived by the Limitation Act 1980, but without prejudice to any finding of *fact* that a person's occupation of land is by implied permission of the owner.[30]

NATURE OF POSSESSORY TITLE

Possession of land of itself gives a better right to the land than that of anyone else except a person who can prove a better title to it. It follows that if the only person who can prove a better title to the land is statute-barred, the possession of the squatter gives a title to the land which is good against the whole world. It is upon this principle that the squatter's title depends; there is no transfer, notional or otherwise, of the title of the former owner[31] to the squatter. Thus the squatter is not a purchaser for value of the land and cannot claim to be entitled as such to take free from equitable interests (such as restrictive covenants) of which he has no notice.[32] Again, if a squatter takes possession of land which has been let under a lease and acquires a good squatter's title against the lessee, the landlord cannot directly sue the squatter upon the tenant's covenants in the lease;[33] but if the landlord has a right to

---

[26] *Powell* v. *McFarlane* (1977) 38 P. & C.R. 452.
[27] But note *George Wimpey & Co.* v. *Sohn* [1967] Ch. 487 (fencing intended to exclude public).
[28] *Leigh* v. *Jack* (1879) 5 Ex.D. 264, *Williams Bros. Direct Supply Ltd.* v. *Raftery* [1958] 1 Q.B. 159.
[29] *Wallis's Cayton Bay Holiday Camp Ltd.* v. *Shell-Mex and B.P. Ltd.* [1975] Q.B. 94; distinguish *Treloar* v. *Nute* [1976] 1 W.L.R. 1295.
[30] Sched. 1, para. 8(4).
[31] Which is extinguished: see note 2.
[32] *Re Nisbet and Potts' Contract* [1906] 1 Ch. 386.
[33] *Tichborne* v. *Weir* (1892) 67 L.T. 735.

re-enter for breach of the tenant's covenants in the lease the squatter may deem it wise to perform those covenants in order to escape ouster by the landlord;[34] and, if the lease provides for payment of a reduced rent if the tenant performs the tenant's covenants in the lease, and the squatter chooses to pay rent at the reduced rate, he will then be estopped from denying his liability on the other covenants in the lease.[35] It also follows that if a squatter obtains a squatter's title against a lessee, and the lessee later acquires the reversion, he can at once oust the squatter: the lease has become merged in the reversion, by virtue of which the former tenant is now claiming possession.[36] Equally, if in similar circumstances the tenant surrenders the lease to his landlord, the landlord can at once oust the squatter.[37]

Even before a possessory title has been completed, *i.e.* before the former owner has become statute-barred, a squatter who takes possession of another's land at once acquires an interest in it which he can assign *inter vivos* or dispose of by his will, and which will pass to his statutory next of kin on his intestacy. An assignee from a squatter can add his own period of possession to that of his predecessors, and the title of the former owner will become extinguished after a total of 12 years.[38] Moreover, if a squatter is himself ousted by another squatter, the second squatter, in defending an action brought by the former owner of the land, can add to his own period of possession that of the squatter whom he has ousted. The first squatter could, however, recover the land from the second squatter if he brought an action against him before the expiration of 12 years from the date when the second squatter took possession: the defendant could not plead *jus tertii*, *i.e.* that the land belonged to a third party, not to the plaintiff.[39]

If a squatter abandons possession, and after an interval a second squatter takes possession, the second squatter has no right to add to his own period of possession that of the first squatter.[40]

---

[34] A squatter has no claim to relief against forfeiture (*Tickner* v. *Buzzacott* [1965] Ch. 426).

[35] *Ashe* v. *Hogan* [1920] I.R. 159.

[36] *Taylor* v. *Twinberrow* [1930] 2 K.B. 16.

[37] *Fairweather* v. *St. Marylebone Property Co.* [1963] A.C. 510.

[38] *Asher* v. *Whitlock* (1865) L.R. 1 Q.B. 1.

[39] See M. & W., pp.103–104, 1036.

[40] Limitation Act 1980, Sched. 1, para. 8(2).

21. Registration

THE CENTRAL LAND CHARGES REGISTER

Provision is made by the Land Charges Act 1972[1] for the registration of certain rights against land[2] in five registers kept by the Land Registry, namely the registers of *pending actions* (including bankruptcy petitions), *annuities* (*i.e.* certain annuities created before 1926), *writs and orders affecting land* (such as writs of execution and bankruptcy receiving orders), *deeds of arrangement* executed by debtors, and *land charges*. Of these, the last-mentioned are by far the most important category.

Register of land charges

Land charges comprise six classes, of which mention need be made only of classes C, D and F.

Class C

(i) Puisne mortgage, i.e. a legal mortgage not protected by deposit of title deeds with the mortgagee.

(ii) Limited owner's charge, i.e. a charge given by statute to a tenant for life or statutory owner who discharges inheritance tax or certain other liabilities.

(iii) General equitable charge, i.e. any equitable charge which is not registrable in any other class, is not protected by deposit of title deeds, and does not arise, or affect an interest arising, under a trust for sale or strict settlement. A common example is an equitable mortgage of a legal estate in land which is not protected

---

[1] This repealed and re-enacted most of the provisions of the Land Charges Act 1925.
[2] Other than registered land.

by deposit of title deeds. On the other hand, a mortgage or other charge of an equitable (*i.e.* beneficial) interest under a trust for sale or settlement is not registrable.

(iv) Estate contract, i.e. a contract to convey or create a legal estate made by a person who at the date of the contract owns a legal estate or is entitled to have such an estate conveyed to him. This important class includes contracts of sale, agreements for a lease, options to purchase and similar rights.[3]

Class D

(i) Inland Revenue charge, i.e. a charge on land for inheritance tax.

(ii) Restrictive covenant, i.e. a covenant (other than one between lessor and lessee) restrictive of the user of land and entered into after 1925.

(iii) Equitable easement, i.e. an easement, right or privilege over land created after 1925 and being merely an equitable interest.[4]

Class F

A charge affecting any land by virtue of the Matrimonial Homes Act 1983.

Registration and failure to register

In general registration of a registrable interest constitutes actual notice of the interest to all persons who acquire the land or any interest in it.[5] Failure to register the interest renders it void against a subsequent "purchaser,"[6] and where an interest is void by reason of non-registration a purchaser "shall not be prejudicially affected" by notice of it.[7]

The definition of "purchaser" differs with the type of land charge: for the purposes of Class C land charges (other than estate contracts entered into after 1925) and Class F land charges,

---

[3] As to the nature of equitable interests arising under such transactions, see pp. 25–6.
[4] Distinguish *E.R. Ives Investments Ltd.* v. *High* [1967] 2 Q.B. 379, *Shiloh Spinners Ltd.* v. *Harding* [1973] A.C. 691.
[5] LPA 1925, s.198.
[6] LCA 1972, s.4.
[7] LPA 1925, s.199.

"purchaser" means purchaser for value of any interest in the land, whether legal or equitable; for the purposes of Class D land charges, and estate contracts entered into after 1925, "purchaser" means purchaser of a legal estate for money[8] or money's worth (which does not include marriage consideration). In either case a mortgagee or lessee is a "purchaser" for this purpose; but, if the narrower definition applies, only if he obtains a legal estate.

These provisions have been applied rigorously by the courts, and the consequences of failure to register are likely to be drastic. They can be understood by considering a basic example. Suppose that L, by an instrument in writing but not under seal, has leased land at a rent to T for seven years. The purported lease is void at law,[9] but it constitutes a valid equitable lease[10] enforceable not merely against L personally (whose liability is contractual) but also against anyone acquiring the land from L except a purchaser without notice. Suppose that L now sells and conveys the land to P, expressly subject to T's lease (and probably at a lower price because P is not getting vacant possession). On general principles P should be bound by the lease—and he will be, if T has registered it as an estate contract: but if T has failed to register it, the lease will be void against P, and the fact that P had notice of it will not prejudicially affect him. If P then evicts T, and T sues L for breach of contract, L has no defence to T's action and is liable in substantial damages,[11] notwithstanding that T's loss was caused, on one view, by his own default[12] in failing either to require the lease to be made under seal, or to register it (if unsealed); or, on another view, by P's default in breaking his agreement with L to take the property subject to the lease.[13]

The result can scarcely be regarded as either just, expedient or even necessary. It could be avoided if P were held directly liable to T on either or both of two well recognised grounds: first, that P became a constructive trustee for T when he acquired the land expressly subject to T's interest[14]; secondly, that an injunction lies

---

[8] See *Midland Bank Trust Co. Ltd.* v. *Green* [1981] A.C. 513, in which the House of Lords held that an unregistered option was void against a "purchaser", although the transaction had the sole collusive purpose of defeating the option, and was at a gross undervalue (land worth £40,000 "sold" to owner's wife for £500).

[9] LPA 1925, s.52.

[10] Under the principle discussed at p. 85.

[11] *Wright* v. *Dean* [1948] Ch. 686, *Hollington Bros. Ltd.* v. *Rhodes* [1951] 2 T.L.R. 691 (*sed quaere* as to measure of damages).

[12] Or that of his solicitor: see *Midland Bank Trust Co. Ltd.* v. *Hett, Stubbs & Kemp* [1979] Ch. 384.

[13] P may be liable to indemnify L if T sues L.

[14] *Binions* v. *Evans* [1972] Ch. 359 (see p. 131, note 11), *Lyus* v. *Prowsa Developments Ltd.* [1982] 1 W.L.R. 1044 (see p. 155, note 32).

against P to restrain him from wrongfully causing a breach of contract between L and T.[15] Neither of these solutions is inconsistent with the Land Charges Act, s.4, or with the Law of Property Act, s.199: the fact that T's equitable lease is void as an estate contract should not prevent its enforcement on some other ground or by some other means; and P is "prejudicially affected," not by mere notice, but by his agreement to take the land subject to T's interest.

If T were in occupation P would in any event have *constructive* notice of the lease,[16] but that of itself would be insufficient to raise a constructive trust of the kind suggested. P accordingly would be protected by the Law of Property Act 1925, s.199, and would be bound, if at all, only to the extent of any *legal* rights which T might have as a periodic tenant, by virtue of his occupation of L's land and payment of rent.[17] Of course if P were himself to accept rent from T, or in any other way deal with him as tenant, an estoppel would arise and the lease would be binding despite non-registration.[18]

System of registration

Registration of a registrable interest is against the name of the estate owner of the land affected, and not against the land itself. This is a serious defect in the system; it is not possible to ascertain what interests have been registered in respect of a particular plot of land since 1925 (when interests such as restrictive covenants and equitable easements created after 1925 became registrable) unless the names of the estate owners for that period are known. Although the deeds produced by a vendor to a purchaser as proof of title should reveal charges created during the period for which the title is adduced,[19] and might also refer to earlier charges, there is a very real risk that both vendor and purchaser might be unaware of certain registered charges affecting the title. To meet this difficulty, the Law of Property Act 1969, s.25, provides for the payment of compensation where a purchaser of any estate or interest has suffered loss by reason that the estate or interest is affected by a land charge[20] of which he had no knowledge, and which was registered against the name of any estate owner who

---

[15] See *Swiss Bank Corpn.* v. *Lloyds Bank Ltd.* [1979] Ch. 548.
[16] See p. 27, note 9.
[17] See pp. 84–86.
[18] *Taylor Fashions Ltd.* v. *Liverpool Victoria Trustees Co. Ltd.* [1982] Q.B. 133.
[19] See p. 26, note 8.
[20] Other than a local land charge.

was not a party to any transaction, or concerned in any event, comprised in the title which the purchaser was entitled to require. Compensation is payable to the purchaser by the Chief Land Registrar, and is recoverable by proceedings in the High Court.

Searches

Personal search may be made of the registers, but in practice official certificates of search are generally obtained by or on behalf of prospective purchasers. These are certificates of search made by responsible officials of the registry. Such a certificate is conclusive in favour of a purchaser. Moreover, if the purchaser completes his transaction before the expiration of 15 working days after the date of the certificate, he will not be affected by any entry in the register which is made after the date of the certificate, unless it is made in pursuance of a priority notice which had already been entered on the register before the certificate was issued.[21]

Priority notices

Any person who intends to take a registrable interest, *e.g.* a restrictive covenant, may lodge a priority notice on the register not less than 15 working days before the date of creation of the registrable interest. If he then registers his charge within 30 working days of the entry of the priority notice, the registration will date from the time when the interest was created.[21] The object of this procedure is to ensure that where the creation of a registrable interest is to be followed immediately by some other transaction, such as a mortgage of the land affected, registration is effective against a party to that other transaction.

LOCAL LAND CHARGES

The Local Land Charges Act 1975[22] makes provision for the registration of certain charges in registers kept by local authorities, *i.e.* county councils and district or borough councils. As defined by the Act, local land charges include various charges arising by statute in favour of a local authority or other public body, such as charges for securing money recoverable in respect of highways and public health matters, and prohibitions or restrictions on the use of

[21] LCA 1972, s.11.
[22] Repealing and replacing provisions in the Land Charges Act 1925.

land imposed by a local authority or government department; they also include any other charge or matter which is expressly made a local land charge by any statutory provision.[23]

Local land charges affect both unregistered and registered land. They are registered against the land, not against the name of the estate owner. Failure to register a charge does not affect its enforceability, but if a purchaser suffers loss by reason of a charge not being registered, or not being disclosed on an official search of the register, he is entitled to compensation payable by the registering authority.

REGISTRATION OF TITLE TO LAND

Quite different from the system of registration of charges referred to above is that of registration of title to land, which is governed by the Land Registration Act 1925.[24] This system is much more ambitious, and is designed to replace the traditional method of establishing title to land. The process of investigating the title of a vendor or mortgagor normally involves examining and interpreting an assortment of documents, some of them perhaps obscure or inconclusive, followed by enquiries and requisitions as to matters arising on the documents or otherwise; and the same elaborate ritual will be repeated on the occasion of every successive disposition of the land. The Land Registration Act 1925, without wittingly changing the substantive law of property,[25] seeks to cheapen and simplify conveyancing by greatly facilitating proof of title; where the title to land has been registered, reference need only be made to the register to ascertain what estate and appurtenant rights the proprietor has in the land, the nature of his title, any restrictions on his powers of disposition, and incumbrances such as mortgages and restrictive covenants affecting the land.

The title deeds of an estate owner in unregistered land are replaced, in the case of registered land, by a land certificate which is issued by the registry and which contains particulars corresponding to those contained in the three parts of the register itself. A conveyance of registered land is effected by a simple statutory form of transfer, and the particulars in the register and in the land

---

[23] For an example of a *private* charge, see the Rights of Light Act 1959, s.2 (p. 124, note 51).

[24] As amended by the Land Registration Act 1986.

[25] The underlying structure of the land law is the same, whether the title to the land is registered or unregistered: changes made by the LRA 1925 are ostensibly procedural only, although important differences of substance have also emerged.

certificate are then amended by substituting the name of the transferee as registered proprietor.

The title of the proprietor is in effect guaranteed by the state inasmuch as, should an error occur in the register, application may be made for rectification, and compensation is payable out of public funds in respect of any loss caused.

Compulsory registration

In certain areas, including the Greater London area and many boroughs and urban districts throughout the country, registration of title is compulsory.[26] When an area is declared a compulsory area the title to the fee simple must be registered upon the occasion of the first conveyance on sale thereafter, and the title to a leasehold must be registered when a lease for more than 21 years is granted or an existing lease having more than 21 years to run is assigned on sale. If application for registration is not made within two months of such a transaction, the transaction becomes void as to the legal estate.

The register

This is divided into three parts:

(i) *The property register,* which describes the land and the estate (*e.g.* the fee simple) the title to which is registered, and any interests, such as easements, which are known to be appurtenant to the land.

(ii) *The proprietorship register,* which states the kind of title (*e.g.* absolute) which has been granted and the name and address of the proprietor; it also contains a note of any *cautions, inhibitions* or *restrictions* which have been entered.

(iii) *The charges register,* which consists of entries of mortgages and other interests adverse to the land; *notices* are entered in this part of the register.

---

[26] The compulsory areas as at Feb. 1, 1978, are designated in the Registration of Title Order 1977, and some additional areas have been designated since then. In other areas registration is voluntary, but voluntary registration is now restricted to certain cases specified by the registrar (Land Registration Act 1966).

Rights in registered land

Rights in land the title to which has been registered fall into three classes, namely registered interests, overriding interests and minor interests.

Registered interests

These are the legal estates the title to which has been registered under the Act. The only interests in respect of which title may be registered are the legal estates in land, *i.e.* the fee simple absolute in possession and the term of years absolute.[27] Title to a lease, however, may not be registered if the lease was granted for a term of 21 years or less or it is a mortgage term with a subsisting right of redemption.

1. Nature of title

Upon application for registration of the title to a *freehold*, the registrar may grant any one of three titles, namely absolute, qualified and possessory. If an absolute title is granted, the title of the proprietor to the fee simple is guaranteed, subject only to interests entered on the register, overriding interests (unless the register states that there are no such interests affecting the land) and, where the proprietor is not entitled for his own benefit, minor interests of which he has notice. Registration with qualified title has the same effect, subject to some possible adverse interest which is *specified* in the register. Registration with possessory title has the same effect, except that no guarantee at all is given as to the absence of adverse interests subsisting at the date of first registration.

Title to a *leasehold* may be absolute, qualified, possessory or good leasehold. Absolute, qualified and possessory titles have the same effect as the corresponding freehold titles, except that the registered proprietor is, of course, subject to all the obligations of the lease. Absolute leasehold title guarantees the title of the landlord to grant the lease as well as the title of the leasehold proprietor to the lease itself. When good leasehold title is granted no guarantee is given with regard to the landlord's right to grant the lease, but in other respects the title is the same as absolute title.

---

[27] Title to a legal interest such as a rentcharge (either perpetual or for a term of years) may also be registered.

2. Conversion of title

The registrar has power to upgrade titles, and on application by the proprietor must upgrade:

(i) good leasehold to absolute title, if satisfied as to the freehold and any intermediate leasehold title;

(ii) possessory to absolute or good leasehold title, if satisfied as to the title, or if the land has been registered with possessory title for at least 12 years and the proprietor is in possession;

(iii) qualified to absolute or good leasehold title, if satisfied as to the title.

Overriding interests

These are interests which are not required to be noted on the register but which will bind a purchaser of the land, whether or not he has notice of their existence. All registered land is deemed to be subject to any overriding interests subsisting in reference thereto and falling within the categories listed in section 70 of the Land Registration Act 1925. The most important overriding interests are set out in the following paragraphs of section 70(1):

(*a*) Easements, profits, public rights, etc.

(*f*) Rights acquired or in the course of being acquired under the Limitation Acts.

(*g*) The rights of every person in actual occupation of the land or in receipt of the rents and profits thereof, save where inquiry is made of such person and the rights are not disclosed.

(*k*) Leases granted for a term not exceeding twenty-one years.

Paragraph (*g*) calls for further comment. The rights to which it refers are confined to those of a proprietary character, and do not include personal rights, such as those created by a mere licence, which are not binding on third parties.[28] Interests arising under a contract of sale, or an informal lease, or an option or a right of pre-emption, are included,[29] with the result that whereas in the case of unregistered land such rights would not bind the land unless they

---

[28] *Strand Securities Ltd.* v. *Caswell* [1965] Ch. 958; *National Provincial Bank Ltd.* v. *Ainsworth* [1965] A.C. 1175.

[29] *Bridges* v. *Mees* [1957] Ch. 475; *Woolwich Equitable B.S.* v. *Marshall* [1952] Ch. 1; *Webb* v. *Pollmount Ltd.* [1966] Ch. 584; *Kling* v. *Keston Properties Ltd.* (1985) 49 P. & C.R. 212.

were registered under the Land Charges Act 1972, they will be binding as overriding interests if the title to the land is registered— provided that the person entitled is in actual occupation.[30] The rights of a beneficiary under a trust may also constitute an overriding interest under this paragraph,[31] notwithstanding that the Land Registration Act expressly provides that persons dealing with a registered estate shall not be affected with notice of a trust express, implied or constructive.[32]

For the purposes of paragraph (g) there is no requirement that the occupation of the person entitled should be such as in the case of unregistered land would constitute constructive notice of the interest in question. The unfortunate and doubtless unforeseen result is to complicate conveyancing, and to compound the difference between the two systems, registered and unregistered.[33]

Minor interests

These comprise all interests in registered land other than registered interests and overriding interests. They fall into two classes:

(a) Interests, such as those of beneficiaries under a settlement or trust for sale, which (as in the case of unregistered land) are capable of being overreached, and which when overreached do not bind a purchaser even if they have been protected by some kind of entry on the register.

(b) Interests, such as those created by estate contracts or restrictive covenants, which will bind a purchaser if they have been protected by an appropriate entry on the register, but not otherwise.

Minor interests may be protected by the entry of restrictions, notice, caution or inhibition on the register.

Restrictions are appropriate to protect any minor interest of class (a) above. They are entered at the request of the registered proprietor and indicate, *e.g.*, that capital money is to be paid to the trustees of the settlement or trust for sale.

---

[30] If he is not in actual occupation, they will constitute minor interests only, and as such require protection by notice or caution.

[31] *Hodgson* v. *Marks* [1971] Ch. 918; *Williams & Glyn's Bank* v. *Boland* [1981] A.C. 487.

[32] s.74. With respect to beneficial interests under a strict settlement, however, s.86(2) provides that these shall take effect as minor interests *and not otherwise*.

[33] *Cf. Caunce* v. *Caunce* [1969] 1 W.L.R. 286 (p. 57 above). A possible further difference, in relation to the overreaching of beneficial interests under a trust for sale, was scotched by *City of London B.S.* v. *Flegg* [1987] 2 W.L.R. 1266 (see p. 58 above).

Notice is the primary method of protecting interests which are not capable of being overreached (class (b) above) and which, in the case of unregistered land, would be registrable under the Land Charges Act 1972.

A *caution* against dealings with the land may be lodged by any person interested in registered land. This entitles the cautioner to be notified by the registrar of proposed dealings with the land, and to object within a specified period. A caution is frequently lodged as a means of protecting a minor interest, such as that of a purchaser under an estate contract,[34] where the cautioner is unable to register a notice because the registered proprietor has not furnished his land certificate.[35]

An *inhibition* may be entered in pursuance of an order of the court or of the registrar in circumstances such as the bankruptcy of the registered proprietor. Its effect generally is to prevent dealings with the land until further order.

Dispositions of registered land

Ownership of a legal estate in registered land is vested in the proprietor by virtue of registration, and his powers of disposition are those conferred by the Act, including such powers to transfer the legal estate and to grant leases, easements and other rights over the land as ordinarily attach to estate ownership of unregistered land.[36] Any disposition of registered land requires completion by registration, otherwise it will create a minor interest only, which takes effect only in equity and requires protection by notice or caution.[37] Thus, the grant of a lease of registered land must itself be registered, provided that the lease is capable of registration.[38]

A disposition for value of registered land, when registered, confers on the transferee or grantee the legal estate or interest disposed of together with all appurtenant rights, subject to any incumbrances and other entries appearing on the register, and subject to any overriding interests, but free from all other estates and interests whatsoever.[39] Minor interests are thus overridden by

---

[34] It may also be used to protect the interest of a person beneficially entitled under a trust for sale (*Elias* v. *Mitchell* [1972] Ch. 652.).

[35] Notices must be entered on the charges register, and accordingly on the land certificate.

[36] LRA 1925, s.18 (freeholds), s.21 (leaseholds).

[37] *Ibid.* s.101.

[38] See p. 182.

[39] LRA 1925, s.20 (freeholds), s.23 (leaseholds). Dispositions in the latter case are also subject to obligations incident to the lease.

a registered transfer or other disposition for value of registered land, whether or not the purchaser has express, implied or constructive notice of them, unless they are protected by some entry on the register, such as a restriction in the case of beneficial interests under a trust, or a notice or caution in the case of other minor interests.[40] It must however be remembered that if a person entitled to a minor interest is in actual occupation of the land his rights are effectually upgraded to the status of an overriding interest, and accordingly have the protection afforded by the Act to any such interest.[41]

Mortgages of registered land

Mortgages may be effected in any of three ways:

(i) Registered charge. This may be in any form (and may or may not contain a demise), but it must be by deed and must be registered in the charges register. The land certificate is deposited at the registry, and a charge certificate is issued to the chargee. The priority of successive registered charges is governed by the order of registration, not of creation.[42] A registered chargee has all the powers of a legal mortgagee.

(ii) Unregistered mortgage. Registered land may be mortgaged in the same way as if it were unregistered. Such mortgages take effect as minor interests only, and require protection by notice or caution.

(iii) Deposit of land certificate. The land certificate takes the place of title deeds, and accordingly a lien or mortgage may be created if the registered proprietor deposits the certificate with a lender of money as security for the loan.[43] This in itself affords *de facto* protection, since without the land certificate no disposition of the land can be registered, but the mortgage may also be protected as a minor interest by notice or caution.

Rectification and indemnity

The title of the registered proprietor arises not from any

---

[40] *Ibid.* s.59(6). As to the meaning of "purchaser," see *Smith* v. *Morrison* [1974] 1 W.L.R. 659; *Peffer* v. *Rigg* [1977] 1 W.L.R. 285.
[41] See pp. 183–184.
[42] See pp. 159–160 with respect to mortgages of unregistered land.
[43] As to the efficacy of this method, see *Barclays Bank Ltd.* v. *Taylor* [1973] Ch. 63.

conveyance or transfer to him but from registration, and the title so registered is guaranteed by the state. Clearly, however, provision must be made for cases in which it subsequently appears that the wrong person has been registered as proprietor, or in which adverse claims are held to prevail over his title. Accordingly the Act provides that in certain circumstances the register may be rectified, and that an indemnity may be paid out of state funds to any person who suffers loss when rectification is either granted or, notwithstanding some error or omission in the register, refused.

The register may be rectified pursuant to an order of the court or by the registrar, subject to an appeal to the court, where *e.g.* the court has decided that any person is entitled to any estate, right or interest in the land, or an entry has been obtained by fraud, or in any other case by reason of an error or omission in the register it may be deemed just to rectify it.[44] Where the registered proprietor is in possession, however, rectification will not be ordered[45] (except to give effect to an overriding interest or an order of the court) unless the proprietor has caused or substantially contributed to the error or omission by fraud or lack of proper care, or unless for some other reason it would be unjust not to rectify the register against him.[46]

Any person who suffers loss as a result either of the register being rectified, or of some error or omission in the register which is not rectified, is entitled to be indemnified under the Act.[47] No indemnity can be recovered, however, if either the applicant or a person from whom he derives title (otherwise than under a disposition for value which is registered or protected on the register) has caused or substantially contributed to the loss by fraud or lack of proper care.[48] It has also been held that a proprietor is not entitled to an indemnity if the register is rectified merely to give effect to an overriding interest which is in any event binding on him.[49]

The amount of the indemnity recoverable under the Act in respect of the loss of an estate or interest is its value at the time of rectification or, where the register is not rectified, at the time when the error or omission which caused the loss was made. The period of limitation for claims to an indemnity is six years. For the purposes of the Limitation Act 1980 the cause of action does not arise until the claimant knows or ought to know of the existence of

---

[44] LRA 1925, s.82(1) and (2).
[45] And see *Freer* v. *Unwins Ltd.* [1976] Ch. 288 (rectification not retrospective).
[46] LRA 1925, s.82(3).
[47] *Ibid.* s.83(1) and (2).
[48] *Ibid.* s.83(5).
[49] *Re Chowood's Registered Land* [1933] Ch. 574.

his claim but, subject to certain exceptions, if the claim arises from the registration of land with an absolute or good leasehold title it must be brought within six years from the date of such registration.[50]

---

[50] As to the consequences where rectification is refused despite an error in the register, see *Epps* v. *Esso Petroleum Co. Ltd.* [1973] 1 W.L.R. 1071.

22. Devolution on Death

When a person dies, the whole of his property, including both realty and personalty, devolves on his personal representatives, *i.e.* passes to them by operation of law. These personal representatives may be executors or administrators. An executor is a person appointed by the will of the deceased to execute the terms of the will. An administrator is a person appointed by the court to administer the deceased's estate when he has died intestate or when he has died testate but without leaving an executor who is able and willing to act. An executor who is willing to act must obtain a grant of probate from the court, and is then said to prove the testator's will; but the will, not the probate, is the source of his authority, and he becomes executor immediately upon the death of the deceased. An administrator is appointed by the grant of letters of administration by the court, and he owes his position entirely to this grant.

There are a very few exceptions to the rule that a deceased person's property devolves upon his personal representatives. Amongst these is an entailed interest which the deceased owner has not barred during his lifetime or by his will: this passes directly to the heir.[1]

The duties of personal representatives are:

(i) to collect the assets belonging to the estate,
(ii) to pay the funeral, testamentary and administration expenses and the deceased's debts, and
(iii) to distribute any surplus amongst the persons entitled under the deceased's will or the law of intestacy.

Testamentary liberty

Many systems of law, and in particular those, such as the Scots law, which are derived from the Roman Law, do not allow

---

[1] See pp. 5, 18.

complete testamentary liberty: a man may dispose of only part of his estate by his will, and the rest goes to certain relatives prescribed by law. English law has never adopted this position, and in general it has allowed complete testamentary liberty, although originally the law of curtesy and of dower made some provision for a surviving husband or wife.

Curtesy was a life estate in his wife's lands which the law on certain conditions gave to a surviving husband. The wife had to be seised of the land for an estate of inheritance, and it was necessary that issue of the marriage capable of inheriting the land should have been born alive. In the period immediately before 1926 the husband had no claim to curtesy if his wife had disposed of the land *inter vivos* or by her will. Curtesy still applies after 1925 when a wife is a tenant in tail in possession at her death and has not barred the entail by her will.

On much the same conditions the law gave to a surviving wife a life estate in one-third of her husband's lands, and this was known as her dower. In this case the birth of issue capable of inheriting was not required, but it must have been possible for such issue to be born; *e.g.* if land had been granted to A and the heirs of his body by his wife Mary, a wife other than Mary could not claim dower out of the land in question. The widow's dower might be assigned to her by metes and bounds, *i.e.* one-third of the land might be allocated to her for life. Alternatively, by agreement with the heir or other person entitled to the land she might be given the right to receive one-third of the rents and profits of the land. After the Dower Act 1833, a wife could not claim dower if the husband had disposed of the land *inter vivos* or by his will, or if he had made a declaration by deed or by will barring the wife's right to dower. A claim to dower cannot arise on a death after 1925.[2]

The Inheritance (Provision for Family and Dependants) Act 1975

The effect of this Act[3] is significantly to restrict the testamentary liberty allowed at common law. Under the Act, certain close relatives and dependants may apply to the court on the ground that the disposition of a deceased person's estate by his will (or by the rules of intestacy) fails to make reasonable financial provision for the applicant.

---

[2] There is one exception of a transitional character relating to a person who was of full age and of unsound mind at the end of 1925 (AEA 1925, s.51(2)).

[3] Repealing and replacing the Inheritance (Family Provision) Act 1938.

The persons who can apply include a wife or husband, a former spouse who has not remarried, a child of any age (including an illegitimate child and a child *en ventre sa mère*), any person treated by the deceased as a child of the family,[4] and any person who was being maintained wholly or partly by the deceased immediately before his death. Applications must be made within six months from the date on which representation was first taken out, but the court has a discretion to extend this period.

Special provisions are made with respect to the rights of a party to a marriage where a decree of divorce, nullity or judicial separation has been made. First, if a party to the marriage dies within 12 months from the date of the decree, and no financial prövision or property adjustment order has been made under the Matrimonial Causes Act 1973, the court may treat the decree as not having been granted; secondly, on or after granting the decree the court may with the agreement of both parties order that neither party shall be entitled on the death of the other to apply under the 1975 Act.

"Reasonable financial provision" means,[5] in the case of a husband or wife of the deceased,[6] such provision as it would be reasonable in all the circumstances of the case for a husband or wife to receive, whether or not that provision is required for his or her maintenance, having regard in particular to what the applicant might reasonably have expected to receive if the marriage had ended by divorce, not by death.[7] In all other cases provision is confined to maintenance only.

In determining whether reasonable provision has been made for the applicant and, if not, whether to make any of the orders authorised by the Act, the court is required to have regard to certain matters. These include the financial resources and needs of the applicant, and of any beneficiary of the estate; any obligations and responsibilities which the deceased had towards the applicant or towards any beneficiary; the size and nature of the estate; any physical or mental disability of any applicant or of any beneficiary; any other matter, including the conduct of the applicant or any other person, which in the circumstances of the case the court may consider relevant; and (where the applicant is a spouse or former spouse) the age of the applicant, the duration of the marriage, and the contribution made by the applicant to the welfare of the family of the deceased.

---

[4] See *Re Callaghan* [1985] Fam. 1; *Re Leach* [1986] Ch. 226.
[5] As defined in s.1(2).
[6] Except where a decree of judicial separation was in force at the date of death.
[7] s.3(2). See *Re Besterman* [1984] Ch. 458.

The orders which the court can make include orders for periodic or lump-sum payments, the transfer or settlement of specific property, and the variation of settlements.[8] For this purpose recourse can be had not only to property of which the deceased was possessed at his death, but also (subject to certain conditions) to property of which he was joint beneficial owner: the *jus accrescendi* prevents any share in such property from passing under the will or intestacy of a joint owner, and the whole beneficial interest accordingly remains vested in the surviving joint owner or owners, but for the purposes of making financial provision under the Act the court has power to order that the deceased's severable share shall be treated as part of his net estate to such extent as appears to be just in all the circumstances of the case. Furthermore, if within six years before his death the deceased has with intent to defeat a claim under the Act disposed or contracted to dispose of property for less than full value, the court has power to order the recipient[9] to provide money or property for the purpose of making financial provision under the Act.

Orders made under the Act may direct how the burden of any provision shall be shared between beneficiaries of the deceased's estate. In the event of any subsequent change in the circumstances of the case the court has wide powers to vary or discharge any order for periodical payments.

---

[8] There are also powers to vary and discharge maintenance agreements and orders made under the Matrimonial Causes Act 1973, and to treat certain applications under the 1973 Act as applications under the 1975 Act.

[9] Whether or not he still has the property.

23. Wills

The common law recognised at an early date the right to dispose of personalty by will, but it was not until the Statute of Wills was passed in 1540 that wills of land became possible, and then only to a limited extent. In the course of time these limitations ceased to apply, and for long both personalty and realty have been freely disposable by will.

Dispositions by will differ from dispositions *inter vivos* in two important respects. First, a will has no effect until the testator dies,[1] whereas a deed of grant normally takes effect forthwith upon execution.[2] Secondly, a will unlike a deed is not an instrument of transfer: land disposed of by will, so far as it is available in the course of due administration of the deceased's estate, is transferred to the persons entitled by written assent[3] executed by the personal representatives, the will itself operating merely as a trust instrument behind the "curtain" of the assent.[4]

In general if a will is to be valid the testator must be of full age and of sound testamentary capacity, and the will must be executed with the formalities prescribed by section 9 of the Wills Act 1837.[5]

Formalities

By section 9, (a) the will must be in writing; (b) it must be signed by the testator or by some other person in his presence and by his

---

[1] Two consequences of this are discussed at pp. 195 and 203.

[2] *i.e.* upon being signed, sealed and delivered (but if it is delivered as an *escrow, i.e.* subject to some condition, it will not take effect until the condition is fulfilled).

[3] An assent by personal representatives is not required to be made under seal (LPA 1925, s.52(2)(a)).

[4] In favour of a subsequent purchaser an assent by a personal representative in respect of a legal estate is to be taken as sufficient evidence that the assentee was the person entitled to the estate (AEA 1925, s.36(7); *cf.* the "curtain" principle discussed at p. 41 in relation to settlements.

[5] As substituted by the Administration of Justice Act 1982, s.17, in respect of deaths after December 31, 1982.

direction; (c) the testator must have intended by his signature to give effect to the will; (d) the testator must make or acknowledge his signature in the presence of two witnesses present at the same time; and (e) each witness must then either attest and sign the will, or acknowledge his signature, in the presence of the testator (but not necessarily in the presence of any other witness). An attestation clause, *i.e.* a clause by which the witnesses certify that the will has been signed in their presence and that they have signed in the presence of the testator, is commonly included, but is not required by section 9.

Any mark made by the testator counts as his signature for this purpose if it was designed to fulfil the function of a signature, *i.e.* to authenticate the document.

The "presence" referred to in the section is physical presence and mental presence. Physical presence means the ability to see what is being done if one chooses to look. Mental presence means the mental capacity to understand the character of the act. Thus, although an infant can be a good witness, it is essential that he should be old enough to understand the character of the act of witnessing. A blind man cannot be a witness, because the nature of his disability is inconsistent with the act of witnessing.[6]

Privileged testators

Certain privileged testators may make valid wills although they are under full age and without complying with the formalities prescribed by section 9.[7] Such a will may even be made by word of mouth, in which case it is called a nuncupative will. A privileged testator is one who at the time of making the will is in one of the following categories:

    (i) A soldier in actual military service.
    (ii) A mariner or seaman at sea.
    (iii) A member of the Royal Navy or Royal Marines so situated that had he been a soldier he would have been in actual military service.

"Soldier" includes members of the Royal Air Force and women members of the Army and R.A.F. The words "in actual military service" mean that the soldier must be serving *in connection with* hostilities, whether those hostilities have broken out, or are apprehended, or have concluded. Thus a soldier is in actual military service as soon as he receives mobilisation orders even if

[6] In *Gibson* [1949] P. 434.
[7] Wills Act 1837, s.11, as amended by the Wills (Soldiers and Sailors) Act 1918.

he has not yet joined his unit, and a member of an army of occupation is in such service even though hostilities have long since concluded.

The words "at sea" in the expression "mariner or seaman at sea" refer to the status of the mariner or seaman: they do not require that he should in fact be at sea at the time of making the will. Thus a member of the crew of a ship is "at sea" while he is on shore leave.[8]

Members of the Royal Navy are included with merchant seamen in the second category mentioned above; the third category is limited to them and members of the Royal Marines. One effect of the third category is to make a member of the Royal Navy or Royal Marines a privileged testator from the moment that he receives mobilisation orders in connection with hostilities, even if he has not yet joined his ship; as we have seen, a soldier is in actual military service as soon as he receives mobilisation orders.

A will made by a privileged testator remains valid indefinitely[9]; the validity of a soldier's will is accordingly not limited to the duration of his military service.

Revocation

Since a will has no effect until the testator dies, it can be revoked at any time in any of three ways, namely by a later will or codicil, by marriage or by destruction.

1. Later will

A later will (or codicil) revokes an earlier will if it shows an intention to that effect. Such an intention is clearly shown if the later will contains a clause expressly revoking all earlier wills.[10] The formal phrase "This is the last will and testament of . . . " does not of itself show an intention to revoke earlier wills.[11] If a later will does not show an intention to revoke an earlier will in its entirety, the two documents will be read together and the earlier will be revoked only so far as it is inconsistent with the later. For example, if the same property is specifically devised to different persons in the two wills, but the devise in the second will is

---

[8] But see *Re Rapley* [1983] 1 W.L.R. 1069.

[9] Unless and until revoked.

[10] But a revocation clause in a standard printed form of will may be disregarded if the court is satisfied that the testator did not in fact intend to revoke other wills (*Re Phelan, decd.* [1972] Fam. 33, in which each of a series of wills disposed of different properties).

[11] *Simpson* v. *Foxon* [1907] P. 54.

contingent upon the devisee attaining a certain age, the gift to the devisee under the earlier will is not revoked unless and until the contingency is fulfilled.[12]

2. Marriage

By section 18 of the Wills Act 1837,[13] a will is revoked by the testator's marriage, subject to two exceptions:

(i) If by a disposition in his will a testator exercises a power of appointment, that disposition is not revoked by his subsequent marriage, unless the property appointed would in default of appointment pass to his personal representatives.

The underlying reasons for this exception, and for the rule itself, are the same: the will is revoked by the testator's marriage because it was made before he had acquired family responsibilities with respect to his property; but property over which he merely has a power of appointment is not his property and therefore not property to which his family would have any claim on his death, except (in effect) where the instrument creating the power contains a gift over in favour of his estate in the event of his failing to exercise the power.

(ii) Marriage to a particular person does not revoke a will if it appears from the will that at the time it was made the testator expected to marry that person, and intended that the will should not be revoked by the marriage. This exception applies also to a specific disposition in a will, where it appears that the testator intended that the disposition should not be revoked by the marriage.[14]

3. Destruction

A will is revoked by burning, tearing or otherwise destroying it done by the testator, or by some other person in his presence and at his direction, with the intention of revoking it.[15] Thus, there must be both the fact of destruction (not *e.g.* merely writing "these are revoked" across the document)[16] and the intention to revoke. Destruction of that part of the will which contains the signatures is sufficient.

If a testator keeps his will in his own possession and at his death the will cannot be found, the presumption is that he has destroyed

---

[12] *Duffield* v. *Duffield* (1829) 1 D. & C. 268.
[13] As substituted by the Administration of Justice Act 1982, s.18(1).
[14] Nor is any other disposition revoked in such case, unless it appears that the testator intended it to be revoked by the marriage.
[15] Wills Act 1837, s.20.
[16] *Cheese* v. *Lovejoy* (1877) 2 P.D. 251.

the will with the intention of revoking it, but this presumption is rebuttable by evidence to the contrary.[17] Furthermore, if a will has been mutilated or destroyed without the testator's authority, or has been accidentally destroyed or lost, extrinsic evidence is always admissible to prove the contents of the will; for example the will may be proved by means of a copy or the oral testimony of one who can swear to the contents of the document.[17]

Revival

Revival means restoring a revoked will to life without the necessity of executing a new will in the same terms.

A will that has been revoked by destruction cannot be revived. A will that has been revoked by another will or by marriage can be revived either by re-execution of the document or by the execution of a further will or codicil showing an intention to revive the revoked will; but a revoked will cannot be revived in any other way, and, in particular, if an earlier will has been revoked by a later will the revocation of the later will will not of itself revive the earlier will.[18]

Conditional revocation

The revocation of a will may be conditional, in which case it will not take effect unless the condition is fulfilled. The doctrine of dependent relative revocation is a particular application of this principle: if a will (or part of it) is revoked for the purpose only of substituting some other will for it, and that other will is not in fact brought into existence, the revocation does not become effective. An obvious illustration is when a testator who has given instructions for the preparation of a new will destroys an existing will, but dies before he is able to execute the new document; the inference in such a case will generally be that he destroyed the old will for the purpose only of substituting the new will,[19] in which case the destruction will not revoke the old will. Again, if an earlier will is revoked by a later will, and the testator destroys the later will in the mistaken belief that he will thereby revive the earlier will, the later will is not revoked. A further illustration appears under the next heading.

---

[17] *Sugden* v. *Lord St. Leonards* (1876) 1 P.D. 154.
[18] Wills Act 1837, s.22.
[19] A mere intention to make a new will is insufficient for this purpose (*Re Jones* [1976] Ch. 200).

Alterations

An alteration made in the document before its execution is part of the will. However, as there is a presumption that an alteration was made after execution, it is desirable (although not legally necessary) that any such alteration should be initialled by the testator and witnesses; otherwise when the time comes to prove the will it may be impossible to rebut the presumption.

An alteration made by the testator after the execution of the will is not generally part of the will, unless the alteration has itself been executed as a will, for which purpose initialling by the testator and witnesses is sufficient. There is, however, an exception where a testator *obliterates* words so effectively that the original wording is no longer "apparent," because in this case probate will be granted of the will with a blank for the obliterated words, so that the alteration will be effective even if it has not been executed as a will.[20] The original wording is not "apparent" unless it is visible to the eye, with or without the aid of a magnifying glass, strong light or the like. The court will not tamper with the document in an endeavour to read the original words, *e.g.* by removing a piece of paper which has been pasted over certain words. Moreover, extrinsic evidence is not in general admissible to prove the original wording, and for this reason an infra-red photograph of the document (which might reveal the original wording) cannot be given in evidence. When, however, a testator obliterates words and *substitutes* others in the mistaken belief that the substituted words will be effective, the doctrine of dependent relative revocation applies and extrinsic evidence, including an infra-red photograph,[21] is admissible to prove the original wording.

Gifts to witnesses and their spouses

Section 15 of the Wills Act 1837 provides that any gift by will to a person who attests the will as a witness, or to the husband or wife of such a witness, shall be void. The spouse of a witness does not fall within this rule unless he or she was married to the witness at the date of the execution of the will, and the rule is excluded if the will is confirmed by a codicil which is not attested by the beneficiary or his or her spouse. By the Wills Act 1968, the attestation of a will by a beneficiary or the

---

[20] Wills Act 1837, s.21. The obliterated words are regarded as revoked by destruction.

[21] *In b. Itter* [1950] P. 130.

spouse of a beneficiary shall be disregarded if the will is duly executed without his attestation and without that of any other such person.

Section 15 has been applied to a charging clause in a will allowing the trustee of the will to charge for his services as a trustee; such a trustee cannot charge for his services if he or his spouse has attested the will.[22] On the other hand, the rule has been held inapplicable to a witness who was appointed trustee after the testator's death; he was therefore held entitled to charge for his services under a charging clause in the will.[23]

Criminal homicide

At common law a person who criminally causes the death of another forfeits any benefit that he would have taken under that person's will or intestacy. Under the Forfeiture Act 1982, however, the court has power to modify the effect of the forfeiture rule in cases other than murder, if satisfied that the justice of the case so requires. The Act also provides that the forfeiture rule shall not preclude anyone from applying for provision to be made out of a deceased person's estate under the Inheritance (Provision for Family and Dependants) Act 1975.

Lapse

In general, a gift by will lapses and fails if the donee predeceases the testator. This is a common law rule, and applies in the absence of contrary intention. A further special case of lapse arises under section 18A of the Wills Act 1837,[24] whereby any devise or bequest to a spouse lapses if his or her marriage to the testator is dissolved, annulled or declared void, unless a contrary intention appears by the will. When a gift lapses the property falls into the residuary estate,[25] unless the gift itself is of residue, in which case there is an intestacy with regard to that property, and it passes to the testator's statutory next of kin.

The general rule of lapse is subject to the following exceptions:

    (i) If a gift is made in discharge of a moral obligation—as in one case,[26] where a woman who had promised to pay her

[22] *Re Pooley* (1888) 40 Ch.D. 1.
[23] *Re Royce's Will Trusts* [1959] Ch. 626.
[24] Inserted by the Administration of Justice Act 1982, s.18(2).
[25] Wills Act 1837, s.25.
[26] *Re Leach* [1948] Ch. 232.

son's debts left a legacy to one of his creditors—then if the donee predeceases the testator the property goes to the donee's estate.

(ii) By section 32 of the Wills Act 1837, if property is left by will to any person in tail and the donee predeceases the testator, leaving issue living at the testator's death who are capable of inheriting under the entail, there is no lapse and the property goes as if the donee had survived the testator and died immediately afterwards. The result is that the property passes to the donee's heir in tail.

(iii) By section 33(1)[27] of the same Act, if a gift is made to a child or more remote descendant of the testator, and the intended beneficiary dies before the testator, leaving issue who are living[28] at the testator's death, then the gift takes effect as a gift to those issue, in equal shares *per stirpes*.[29]

(iv) By section 33(2),[30] if a gift is made to a class of persons consisting of children or remoter descendants of the testator, and a member of the class dies before the testator, leaving issue living[30a] at the testator's death, the gift takes effect as if the class included the issue of the deceased member (again taking in equal shares *per stirpes*). Suppose, for example, that T has three children, A, B and C, and by his will gives property "to all my children equally." T dies, survived by A and B; C has predeceased T, but has himself left children D and E who survive T. In accordance with section 33(2), the property will be divided into three shares: one third will go to A, one third to B, and the remaining one third to D and E (who accordingly will take one sixth each). If, on the other hand, the gift were to T's children "jointly," no question would arise in relation either to lapse or to section 33(2): the surviving children A and B alone would be entitled, by virtue of the *jus accrescendi*.

Commorientes

If there is no evidence as to which of two persons survived the

---

[27] As substituted by the Administration of Justice Act 1982, s.19 (and applying unless a contrary intention appears by the will).

[28] Or *en ventre sa mère*.

[29] See p. 209.

[30] See note 27.

[30a] See note 28.

other, then for the purposes of succession to property the presumption is that the younger survived the elder.[31]

The will and its construction

It must be conclusively presumed that the deceased's testamentary wishes are those which he has set out in the written will. Extrinsic evidence is not admissible to add to, vary or contradict the written instrument. But, provided that the testator's true intentions are sufficiently clear from the will itself, the court may sometimes be able to correct obvious mistakes[32]; and now, by the Administration of Justice Act 1982, s.20, the court has a general power to rectify a will in order to carry out the testator's intentions, if it is satisfied that the will fails to do so in consequence of a clerical error or a failure to understand his instructions.[33]

Once it has been determined that a written instrument is to be regarded as the last will and testament of the deceased, the question of construction arises, *i.e.* it becomes necessary to determine the *meaning* of the instrument. The primary rule here is that the words must be given their ordinary grammatical meaning. But this rule may be departed from in certain circumstances, *e.g.* where the ordinary meaning of the words would give rise to an absurdity. In general, the same canons of construction apply to a will as apply to any other written instrument, and the topic is not one that can be considered at length here. We must, however, consider briefly the question how far extrinsic evidence is admissible to assist the court in its task of construction. The general rule is that such evidence is not admissible, but there are two main exceptions to this rule:

(a) Under what is sometimes called the *armchair principle*, evidence is always admissible as to what the facts were at the date when the testator executed the will, in order that the court may be able, as it were, to seat itself in the testator's armchair and look at the will through his eyes. Extrinsic evidence is accordingly admissible to show the meaning of the terms which had a special meaning for the testator by reason of the locality in which he lived or the trade at which he worked or by reason of family usage. For example, in one case,[34] where the testator left everything to "mother," evidence was admitted to show that in the testator's family he referred to his wife as "mother."

[31] LPA 1925, s.184. For an exception see p. 211.
[32] See *Re Phelan*, note 10.
[33] Application must be made within six months of representation first being taken out, but the court may extend this period.
[34] *Thorn* v. *Dickens* [1906] W.N. 54.

(b) Extrinsic evidence is admissible to resolve an *equivocation*, *i.e.* a difficulty which arises when an attempt is made to put into operation the provisions of the will because it is found that there are two or more persons or things which equally well answer some term of the will. But extrinsic evidence is not admissible to *create* an ambiguity which does not exist if the words are given their normal meaning. For example, if a testator makes a gift by will to "my niece," and he has only one legitimate niece, there is no ambiguity, because the reference must be taken as being to the legitimate niece;[35] extrinsic evidence is therefore inadmissible to show that the testator intended to benefit an illegitimate niece—to admit the evidence would be to admit it in order to *create* an ambiguity.[36] But if the gift is to "my nephew" and the testator has two nephews, both by legitimate relationship, extrinsic evidence is admissible to show which of those two nephews he intended to benefit; there is a genuine equivocation. In such a case if the evidence, when admitted, shows that the testator intended to benefit a third, and illegitimate nephew, that illegitimate nephew will take; once the evidence has been admitted, the full consequences of its admission must be accepted.[37]

The application of these rules is now subject to the Administration of Justice Act 1982, s.21, under which extrinsic evidence, including evidence of the testator's intention, may be admitted to assist in the interpretation of a will where any part is meaningless, or where the language is ambiguous either on the face of it or in the light of surrounding circumstances.[38]

Extrinsic evidence is not admissible to resolve a *contradiction*; if a contradiction cannot be resolved by reference to the instrument as a whole, the later provision in the will prevails over the earlier.[39] Thus if a gift is expressed as "one thousand pounds (£10,000)" it takes effect as a gift of ten thousand pounds. One troublesome form of contradiction is now disposed of by statute: if a will gives property absolutely to a spouse, but purports also to give an interest in the same property to issue, the gift to the spouse is to be treated as absolute notwithstanding the purported gift to issue.[40]

The following additional rules may also be noticed:

---

[35] This presumption no longer applies in relation to dispositions made after December 31, 1969 (Family Law Reform Act 1969, s.15).

[36] *Re Fish* [1894] 2 Ch. 83.

[37] *Re Jackson* [1933] Ch. 237.

[38] Previously it was doubtful whether evidence was admissible to resolve patent, as well as latent, ambiguities (see *Doe d. Gord* v. *Needs* (1836) 2 M. & W. 129).

[39] The opposite rule applies to gifts by deed.

[40] Administration of Justice Act 1982, s.22 (applying except where a contrary intention is shown).

1. A will speaks from the death

A will speaks from the death with regard to the property disposed of by it, *i.e.* it is to be construed as if it had been executed at the moment of death, unless a contrary intention appears.[41] For example, a gift of "all my realty" prima facie means all the realty that the testator has at the date of his death. But the court may find evidence of a contrary intention when there is a specific gift of property which is not liable to increase or decrease (*e.g.* "my piano"); in such cases the reference is generally taken to be the property described which the testator possessed at the date of making the will. The gift is then said to be adeemed, and it fails, if the testator afterwards disposes of that property; for example, if the gift is of "my piano" and the testator after executing the will disposes of the piano, the legatee will get nothing[42]—he will not get another piano which the testator purchases in substitution, unless after that purchase the will containing the specific bequest is confirmed by codicil.[43]

2. The class closing rules

When a will contains a gift to a class of persons there are somewhat elaborate rules for deciding what members of the class are intended to be benefited. For example, if the will gives property to "John's children," a question of construction may arise as to whether the testator intended that the property should go only to such of John's children as were living at the date of the testator's death, or that it should go to all John's children whether born before or after that date. The prima facie rule[44] for immediate class gifts is that if there is any member of the class living at the testator's death the gift includes only those members then living; but if there is no member of the class then living the gift includes later-born members. A similar rule applies to conditional gifts: if the gift is to "John's children who attain 21", and at the testator's death a child of John has already attained 21, the gift prima facie is taken to include only those children of John then living who attain 21; but if no child of John has already attained 21 at the testator's death, the class remains open until a member attains 21, and the gift includes John's children *then* living

[41] Wills Act 1837, s.24.
[42] *Re Sikes* [1927] 1 Ch. 364.
[43] *Re Reeves* [1928] Ch. 351 (gift of "all my interest in my present lease" of certain property held to cover a new lease of the property, the will having been confirmed by codicil after the grant of the new lease).
[44] Commonly referred to as the rule in *Andrews* v. *Partington* (1791) 3 Bro.C.C. 401.

who attain 21. There are further rules applying to gifts in remainder and gifts of reversionary interests.

These highly artificial rules are ostensibly designed to implement the testator's intention so far as practicable, and accordingly they give way to any contrary intention expressed in the will, as where a gift is expressed to be made to "all John's children *whenever born.*"[45] They have the advantage of sometimes enabling trustees to distribute property earlier than would otherwise be possible; they might also sometimes prevent an infringement of the perpetuity rule (although since the Perpetuities and Accumulations Act 1964[46] came into force they are effectually redundant for that purpose).

3. Appointments under powers of appointment

If a testator is the donee of a *general* power of appointment which he can exercise by his will, and he leaves a will which does not contain an express appointment under the power, but which contains a general devise or bequest, there is an implied appointment in favour of the general devisee or legatee.[47] For example, if the testator in his will says "I leave all my property to A," A will take not only the testator's own property but also any property over which the testator had a general power of appointment.

A general devise or bequest does not impliedly exercise a *special* power possessed by the testator.

4. Gift "to A but if he dies without issue then over to B"

Originally a gift in these or similar terms was construed as showing an intention to give a fee tail in the property to A. But this construction was abolished by section 29 of the Wills Act 1837, which provided, in effect, that under such a gift the property should go initially to A and that its final destination should be decided according to whether or not A had any issue living at the date of his death. If at his death A has issue then living the property forms part of his estate in fee simple or, if it is personalty, absolutely. But if at his death he has no issue living, the property goes over to B for a similar estate or interest. An exception to this rule was enacted by the Conveyancing Act 1882, with regard to land, and by section 134 of the Law of Property Act 1925, with regard to all property. Under this exception if at any time during

[45] *Re Edmondson's W.T.* [1972] 1 W.L.R. 183.
[46] See p. 73, note 22.
[47] Wills Act 1837, s.27.

A's lifetime any of his issue attain the age of 18, the gift over to B at once fails, with the result that the property then belongs to A in fee simple or absolutely. This provision applies to deeds as well as to wills, and it applies whatever interest is granted to A unless it be an entailed interest. Thus section 134 applies if the property is given "to A for life," or "to A in fee simple," with a gift over to B if A dies without issue.

5. The rule in Wild's Case

Before 1926 if a testator gave land to A "and his children," a question of construction arose as to whether the effect was to pass the *fee simple* to A and his children jointly, or (on the basis that "and his children," were used as words of limitation) to pass a *fee tail* to A.[48] The prima facie rule established in *Wild's Case*[49] was that if A had no children at the date when the will was made he would take a fee tail, but if he had a child at that date he would take the fee simple jointly with such of his children as were living at the testator's death. After 1925 the second branch of the rule remains unaffected, but the first branch cannot apply, since informal expressions are no longer effective to create an entailed interest: it is uncertain what the precise effect is in such case, but it may be assumed that A takes the fee simple.[50]

24. Intestacy

SURVIVALS OF THE OLD LAW

On a death intestate before 1926 the deceased's realty went to his heir, ascertained by applying the old common law canons of descent, whereas his personalty went to his statutory next of kin under the old Statutes of Distribution. Since 1925 the general rule is that succession to both realty and personalty is governed by the provisions of the Administration of Estates Act 1925. As an exception, an unbarred entail still devolves upon the heir, ascertained by applying the old realty canons of descent. For this reason some knowledge of the old law is still required today. Another reason is that the word "heir" or "heirs" may be used as a word of purchase[1] in a post-1925 instrument, in which case the reference must be taken to be to the heir as ascertained under the old law: there is no heir under the Administration of Estates Act 1925. An unbarred entail can, of course, devolve only upon an heir found amongst descendants of the original tenant in tail,[2] and the following summary is confined to the rules applicable to finding an heir amongst descendants.

(i) Descent is traced from the last purchaser of the land, *i.e.* from the person who last acquired the land otherwise than by descent on intestacy. When considering the descent of an unbarred entail this rule presents no difficulty, because the last purchaser is always the original tenant in tail.

(ii) Males are preferred to females in the same degree.

(iii) An elder male is preferred to a younger male in the same degree.

(iv) Amongst females there is no preference for an elder over a younger, and all females in the same degree take equally as coparceners.[3]

[1] See p. 9.
[2] See p. 5.
[3] See p. 53.

(v) If a person would have been heir (including co-heir) but for the fact that he is dead, then if that person has left issue, those issue, or such of them as are preferred under the above rules, have the right to represent their deceased parent.

In the following examples M stands for male and F for female.

Example 1

T, the original tenant in tail, has four children, M1, F1, M2, F2, born in that order, all of whom survive him. The males are preferred to the females, and the elder male to the younger male, so that M1 is the sole heir.

Example 2

The facts are the same, except that M1 has predeceased T, leaving two children, a son and a daughter, both of whom survive T. M1's son, being preferred to his sister, has the right to represent his deceased father and is therefore the sole heir. Had M1 left only a daughter, she would have had the right to represent her deceased father, and she therefore would have been sole heir. It will be observed that in consequence of rule (v), the whole of the elder son's line is preferred to the younger son and his line.

Example 3

T, the original tenant in tail, has had two children, F1 and F2, both of whom survive him. The two daughters together constitute the heir, taking between themselves as coparceners. There is no preference for an elder female over a younger female.

Example 4

The facts are the same as in example 3, except that F1 has predeceased T, leaving two children, a son and a daughter, who survive T. F1's son, being preferred to his sister, has the exclusive right to represent his deceased mother. It follows that he and F2 together constitute the heir.

Example 5

T, the original tenant in tail, has two sons, M1 and M2, both of whom survive him. M1 therefore becomes the sole heir and enjoys the land in tail. Later M1 dies, a bachelor, without having barred the entail. Upon the death of M1 the land devolves upon M2. This example shows how necessary it may be to remember the rule that descent is to be traced from the last purchaser, *i.e.* the original tenant in tail.

When a female tenant in tail dies without having barred the entail, a surviving husband can claim curtesy, on the usual conditions,[4] but on the death of a male tenant in tail a surviving wife cannot claim dower.

In the above examples it has been assumed that the descent of the entail has not been restricted by the instrument creating it. A tail male cannot, of course, be inherited by a female descendant.

MODERN LAW

Under the provisions of the Administration of Estates Act 1925, the whole estate of the deceased, including both realty and personalty, is held upon a statutory trust to sell it, except that "personal chattels" (as defined by the Act) and reversionary (*i.e.* future) interests are not to be sold without special reason. Out of the proceeds of sale the deceased's personal representatives are to pay the funeral, testamentary and administration expenses and the deceased's debts. What is left over is called by the Act "the residuary estate," and it is this which goes to the statutory next of kin as defined by the Act. In prescribing the rights of the next of kin the Act accords priority first to the widow or widower, and secondly to issue; only if the deceased left no issue is any other class of relative entitled; and only if the deceased left neither surviving spouse nor issue is there a possibility of any class more remote than parents or brothers and sisters (or their issue) being entitled.

Surviving husband or wife

The rights of a surviving spouse must be met in full before other relatives can receive anything. The surviving spouse is entitled to:

> (i) The "personal chattels" absolutely. These are defined in detail by the Act and include, broadly, all personal chattels not used for business purposes, but excluding money and securities for money.

[4] See p. 190.

(ii) A statutory legacy, free of death duties and costs, with interest at six per cent. per annum from the date of the death to the date of payment. If the deceased left surviving issue who attain a vested interest (under rules to be given hereafter), the amount of this legacy is £75,000; otherwise it is £125,000.[5]

(iii) An interest in one-half of the rest of the residuary estate. If the deceased left surviving issue who attain a vested interest, the spouse's interest is for life only; otherwise it is an absolute interest, *i.e.* the spouse becomes absolute owner of that one-half of the rest of the residuary estate.

(iv) If the deceased left no surviving issue who attain a vested interest, no parent, no brother or sister of the whole blood who attains a vested interest, and no issue (who attain a vested interest) of a deceased brother or sister, the surviving spouse takes, not the limited interest described above, but the whole of the residuary estate absolutely.

Surviving issue

Subject to the rights of any surviving spouse, the residuary estate goes to the surviving issue, if any, on the statutory trusts. These statutory trusts are as follows:

1. The *per stirpes* rule

Issue of a child who has predeceased the intestate take between them the share that their deceased parent would have taken. Thus, if the intestate has had two children, one of whom has predeceased the intestate leaving two children who have survived the intestate, then (subject to the next rule) the two children of the deceased child will take between them the one half-share that their deceased parent would have taken if he had survived the intestate.

2. The vesting rule

No person attains a vested interest unless and until he attains the age of 18 or marries under that age. Thus, if the intestate has had two children, both of whom survived the intestate, and one of these children attains 18 (or marries under that age), but the other

---

[5] The legacy and the rate of interest were fixed at these amounts by the Family Provision (Intestate Succession) Order 1987 and the Intestate Succession (Interest and Capitalisation) Order 1983 respectively.

dies under 18 without marrying, the child who attains 18 (or marries under that age) takes the entire residuary estate, subject to the rights of any surviving spouse.

In addition to these rules there are two *hotchpot rules* which apply to issue:

3. Inter vivos advancements

If the deceased has made an *inter vivos* advancement to a *child* of his, and that child claims a share of the estate on intestacy, he must bring into account the value of the advancement, unless the circumstances indicate a contrary intention on the part of the deceased. An advancement is a gift of property which is designed to set up, or advance, the child in life. The value of property which is to be brought into hotchpot under this rule is to be ascertained at the date of the deceased's death.

4. Gifts by will

Where the deceased has died partially intestate, there is hotchpot under the rule given above and, in addition, any benefit conferred by the will upon a *child* or *remoter issue* of the deceased must be brought into hotchpot. This again is subject to any contrary intention that the deceased may have shown.

A simple illustration may be given of hotchpot under rule (3) above. Suppose that the deceased has left two surviving children, C1 and C2, but no surviving spouse, and that during his lifetime the deceased made an *inter vivos* advancement of £1,000 to C1, and that the residuary estate is worth £5,000. If C1 wishes to claim a share of the residuary estate (as obviously he will on the facts given) he must bring the amount of his advancement into hotchpot. This makes the residuary estate worth £6,000, which is then divided equally between C1 and C2. C1, therefore, brings in £1,000 in order to take out £3,000. Needless to say, C1 is not, in fact, required to hand over a cheque for £1,000; the necessary calculation is made on paper and the actual residuary estate of £5,000 is distributed as to £2,000 to C1 and £3,000 to C2.

Other relatives

The order of succession, if there are no surviving issue who attain a vested interest, is as follows:

(i) The deceased's parents absolutely in equal shares.
(ii) Brothers and sisters of the whole blood on the statutory trusts.
(iii) Brothers and sisters of the half blood on the statutory trusts.
(iv) Grandparents absolutely in equal shares.
(v) Uncles and aunts of the whole blood on the statutory trusts.
(vi) Uncles and aunts of the half blood on the statutory trusts.

If there are no relatives in the above list, the Crown or the Duchy of Lancaster or Cornwall is entitled to the residuary estate as *bona vacantia*. The Crown in its discretion may then make provision out of the estate for dependants of the deceased who are not amongst the statutory next of kin referred to above.

The "statutory trusts" mentioned above in relation to classes (ii), (iii), (v) and (vi) are the same as those for issue; but there are no hotchpot rules.

As already indicated,[6] relatives in classes (iii) to (vi) above cannot take if the deceased has left a surviving spouse, because in default of issue, parents, brothers and sisters of the whole blood and issue of a deceased brother or sister of the whole blood (taking under the *per stirpes* rule) the entire residuary estate goes to the surviving spouse absolutely.

Relatives in any given class take to the total exclusion of relatives in a lower class. If, for example, the deceased has left a surviving parent, no interest in the estate will be taken by brothers or sisters or by remoter relatives.

Special rules applicable to spouses

1. Commorientes

If there is no evidence as to whether the intestate survived his or her spouse, the intestate's estate is to be distributed on the basis that the spouse predeceased the intestate, so that effect is not given to the rights of a surviving spouse. This exception to the normal *commorientes* rule[7] applies only for the purposes of the law of intestacy and only as regards spouses.

---

[6] At p. 209.
[7] See pp. 200–1.

2. Redemption of life interest

When a surviving spouse is entitled to a life interest under the law of intestacy (*i.e.* when there are surviving issue), the spouse may elect to take, instead of the life interest, a lump sum of money calculated in accordance with provisions made under the Act. The right must generally be exercised within 12 months of the first grant of representation, but the court may extend the time on certain grounds.

3. Option to purchase house

A surviving spouse is given the right to purchase from the estate at its true value any dwelling-house in which the surviving spouse was resident at the date of death of the deceased. There are certain exceptions to the right, *e.g.* it does not apply where the house is leasehold and the lease will come to an end within two years of the death of the deceased or the landlord has the right to determine the lease within that time. The right must be exercised within the same time as the right mentioned in paragraph 2 above, but here again the court may extend the time on certain grounds.

4. Hotchpot

In cases of partial intestacy the amount of the statutory legacy conferred upon the spouse (but not any other interest to which he or she is entitled) must be diminished by the value of any benefit (other than a specific bequest of personal chattels) conferred upon the spouse by the will. There is no other hotchpot provision applicable to a spouse.

5. Separation

If the parties are separated by judicial decree, the estate of the intestate devolves as if the spouse were dead.[8]

Adopted children

An adopted child is to be treated in law as the legitimate child of the adopters, and not as the child of any other person.[9] It follows

---

[8] Matrimonial Causes Act 1973, s.18(2).
[9] Children Act 1975, s.8; Adoption Act 1976, s.39. In the case of a death intestate before January 1, 1976, similar provisions in the Adoption Act 1958 continue to apply.

that the adopted child and the adoptive parents and their children can take under the intestacy of each other.

Legitimated children

Where a child is legitimated by the subsequent marriage of his or her parents the rules of intestacy apply as if the child had been born legitimate.[10]

Illegitimate children

In general illegitimate children had no rights under the law of intestacy, and such expressions as "child" and "children" did not include illegitimate children, unless a contrary intention appeared. With respect to deaths after 1969, however, the Family Law Reform Act 1969, s.14, provides that where either parent of an illegitimate child dies intestate, that child (or, if he is dead, his issue[11]) can take under the intestacy as if he had been legitimate; and if an illegitimate child dies intestate, each of his parents can take under the intestacy as if the child had been born legitimate.

Much more radical reforms are made by the Family Law Reform Act 1987,[12] which removes virtually all distinctions affecting the property rights of illegitimate persons and their next of kin, in relation to both testate and intestate succession (including devolution of an entailed interest).

---

[10] Legitimacy Act 1976, s.5. In the case of a death intestate before January 1, 1976, the provisions of the Legitimacy Act 1926 continue to apply.
[11] *i.e.* legitimate issue: the Act does not generally abolish the distinction between legitimate and illegitimate birth for the purposes of intestacy.
[12] ss.18–21. The Act comes into force on a day to be appointed.

Index

Accumulation rule, 76 *et seq.*
Administrators, 189
Agricultural holdings,
  fixtures, 14, 15
  security of tenure, 110, 111
Assent, 47, 193
  settled land, 34, 44

Barring of entail, 17 *et seq.*
Base fee, 17 *et seq.*
Benefit and burden, 138

Cestui que vie, 5
Charge by way of legal mortgage, 30, 147
Commons, 124, 125, 126
Commorientes, 200, 201, 211
Constructive notice, 26, 27, 56, 57, 178, 184
Contracts for disposition of land, 25, 26, 80, 81
Conversion, doctrine of, 46, 60
Co-ownership, 53 *et seq.*
  co-parceny, 53, 54, 206, 207
  determination of, 64, 65
  joint tenancy, 53 *et seq.*
    joint tenants for life, 38, 54
  partition, 65
  severance, 62, 63, 64
    words of, 61
  tenancy in common, 53 *et seq.*
  trust for sale, statutory, 54, 56, 59
  trustees, 54, 55, 56
  undivided shares, 54
  union, 64, 65
Co-parcenary. *See* Co-ownership.
Copyhold, 3, 4
Covenants concerning land, 133 *et seq.*, 143
  building scheme, 141
  discharge of, 142
  indemnity, 135, 136, 138

Covenants concerning land—*cont.*
  in leases, 133–6
  restrictive covenants, 26, 113, 139 *et seq.*
"Curtain" principle, 41, 42, 47, 193
Curtesy, 190, 208
Customary rights, 128

Derogation from grant, 96, 117
Descent, canons of, 45, 53, 206, 207, 208
Devolution on death, 189 *et seq.*
Disabilities, 162 *et seq.*
  infants or minors, 33, 162, 163
  mental disorder, 163
Disentailing assurance, 17, 18, 19
Distress, 89, 90, 144, 168
Dower, 190

Easements, 30, 112 *et seq.*, 139, 140, 183
  acquisition of, 116 *et seq.*
  conditions of, 112, 113
  continuous and apparent, 118
  equitable, 116, 176
  express grant of, 116
  extent of, 115, 116, 117, 120
  extinguishment of, 126, 127
  implied grant of, 117–9
  implied reservation, 117
  intended easements, 117
  light, rights of, 113, 115, 117, 118, 119, 124
  natural rights, 114, 115
  necessity, of, 117
  prescription, 119 *et seq.*
  reservation of, 116, 117
  support, right of, 113, 114, 115
  way, rights of, 115, 116, 117, 123
Ejectment, 7
Entailed interest. *See* Fee tail.
Entry, right of, 30, 89 *et seq.*, 136, 138, 144
Equity, 23 *et seq.*

Equity—*cont.*
  equitable easement, 116, 176
  equitable estoppel, 26, 130, 131
  equitable interest, 23 *et seq.*, 30, 81
  equitable lease, 85
  equitable mortgage, 147, 148
    of redemption. *See* Mortgages.
Escheat, 5
Estate, doctrine of, 4 *et seq.*
Estoppel, equitable, 26, 130, 131
Estovers, 20
Executors, 189

Fee simple, 4, 5, 28, 29
  rights of beneficial owner, 12 *et seq.*
Fee tail, 5, 6, 28, 45
  barring of, 17 *et seq.*
  devolution of, 53, 206–8
  special, 10, 19
Fines and recoveries, 17
Fishing rights, 15, 16
Fixtures, 13–5
Foreshore, 15, 165
Freehold estate, 7
Freehold tenure, 3, 4

Heirs, 4, 5, 206

Infants, 33, 162, 163
Intestacy, 206 *et seq.*
  adopted children, 212, 213
  canons of descent, 4, 5, 53, 206–8
  hotchpot rules, 210, 212
  illegitimate children, 213
  issue, rights of, 209, 210
  per stirpes rule, 209
  relatives entitled (other than issue),
    210, 211
  spouse, rights of, 208, 209, 211, 212
  statutory trusts, 209, 211
  trust for sale, statutory, 208
  vesting rule, 209, 210

Joint tenancy. *See* Co-ownership.

Land, definition of, 13
Landlord and tenant. *See* Leaseholds.
Leaseholds, 5, 7, 29, 82 *et seq.*
  assignment, 94, 99, 100
  enfranchisement, 108, 109
  enlargement of lease, 94
  equitable lease, 85
  essentials of lease, 83, 84
  fixtures, 14, 15
  forfeiture, 88 *et seq.*
  leases for lives, *etc.*, 87

Leaseholds—*cont.*
  legal estate, as, 28–30, 84, 85
  merger, 94
  notice to quit, 85, 86, 87
  obligations of landlord and tenant, 95
    et seq.
  option to purchase reversion, 74, 75,
    134
  periodic tenancies, 85, 86
  perpetually renewable leases, 87, 88
  quiet enjoyment, covenant for, 95, 96
  rent restriction. *See* Security of
    tenure, below.
  repair, covenant to, 98, 99
  reversionary lease, 30, 88
  security of tenure, 82, 101 *et seq.*
    agricultural holdings, 110, 111
    assured tenancy, 106
    business premises, 109, 110
    enfranchisement, 108, 109
    farmworkers' dwellings, 106, 107
    long tenancies of dwelling-houses,
      107, 108
    protected shorthold tenancy, 104
    protected tenancy, 102
    regulated tenancy, 101 *et seq.*
    restricted contract, 104, 105
    secure tenancy, 105, 106
    statutory tenancy, 102, 103, 104
  sub-lease, 95, 136
  surrender, 93
  tenancy at sufferance, 87, 169
  tenancy at will, 86, 87, 169
  "usual covenants," 98
  waste, 22, 97, 98
  yearly tenancies, 85, 86
Legal charge, 30, 147
Licences, 83, 113, 129 *et seq.*
Life estate, 5
  right of beneficial owner, 19 *et seq.*
Limitation of actions, 165 *et seq.*
  accrual of right of action, 166 *et seq.*
  acknowledgment of title, 171, 172
  adverse possession, 166, 172, 173
  disabilities, 170, 171
  fraud, 172
  future interests, 166, 167
  leaseholds, 168, 169, 172–4
    periodic tenancies, 169
    tenancies at will, 169
  licences, 172, 173
  mistake, 172
  mortgages, 170, 171, 172
  part-payment, 171, 172
  possessory title, 165, 173, 174
  rentcharges, 169, 170

Limitation of actions—*cont.*
  settled land, 167, 168
Limitation, words of, 9 *et seq.*, 205

Minerals, 4, 21, 22
Mortgages, 164 *et seq.*
  by demise, 146, 147
  collateral advantages, 153
  consolidation, 149, 150, 151
  deposit of title deeds, 147, 148
  discharge of, 161
  equitable, 147, 148
  equity of redemption, 26, 151 *et seq.*,
    157
  fixtures, 14
  foreclosure, 157, 158
  leases of mortgaged land, 158
  legal charge, 30, 147
  mortgagee,
    liability of, to account, 154, 156
    remedies of, 153 *et seq.*
  possession, mortgagee's right to, 153,
    154
  priority, 158 *et seq.*
  receiver, mortgagee's power to
    appoint, 157, 157
  redemption, 148, 149
  registration, 159, 175, 176
  sale, mortgagee's power of, 154–6
  tacking, 160, 161

Navigation, rights of, 16
Notice, doctrine of, 26, 27, 56, 57,
    178, 184

Overreaching, 27, 40, 47, 48, 58, 155,
    184

Part performance, doctrine of, 81
Perpetual trusts, rule against, 76
Perpetuities, rule against, 66 *et seq.*
  age reduction, 68, 72, 73
  capacity to have children, 68, 72
  class gifts, 69, 70, 73
  exceptions, 74, 75
  lives in being, 67, 68, 69, 73
  "wait and see," 67, 73
  options, 74, 75
  perpetuity period, 67, 69, 72, 74
  powers of appointment, 70, 71, 72
  subsequent interests, 70
Per stirpes rule, 200, 209
Personal representatives, 189
  special, 44
Personalty, 7, 8, 46, 60
Planning, 12, 13

Power of appointment, 70, 71, 72, 204
Prescription. *See* Easements and
    Profits.
Privity of estate, 134, 135
Profits, 124 *et seq.*
Protector of settlement, 17, 18
Public rights, 127
Pur autre vie, life estate, 5
Purchase, words of, 9, 11, 206

Realty, 7, 8
Re-entry. *See* Entry, right of.
Registration of charges, 27, 31, 175 *et
    seq.*
  local land charges, 179, 180
  priority notice, 179
  searches, 179
  system, 178
Registration of title, 180 *et seq.*
  cautions, 184, 185, 186
  compulsory, 181
  dispositions of registered land, 185,
    186
  indemnity, 187, 188
  inhibitions, 185
  land certificate, 180, 181, 185, 186
  leases, 182, 183, 185
  minor interests, 184, 185, 186
  mortgages, 186
  notices, 185, 186
  overriding interests, 183, 184, 185,
    186, 187
  rectification, 186–8
  register, 181
  registered interests, 182
  retrictions, 184, 186
  titles, nature and conversion of, 182,
    183
  voluntary, 181
Remainder, 6, 29
Rentcharge, 30, 33, 43, 44, 138, 143–5
Restrictive covenants. *See* Covenants
    concerning land.
Reversion, 6, 29
Reversionary interest, 6
Riparian rights, 15, 16

Security of tenure. *See* Leaseholds.
Settled land. *See* Settlements, strict.
Settlements, 6, 29, 32 *et seq.*, 162, 167
Settlements, strict, 32 *et seq.*
  ad hoc, 50, 51
  "curtain" principle, 41, 42, 47
  discharge, deed of, 45, 46
  duration of, 43 *et seq.*
  imperfect, 41, 42, 43

Settlements, strict—*cont.*
 improvements to settled land,
  36
 leases of settled land, 36
 marriage settlements, 51, 52
 mortgages of settled land, 36
 overreaching, 40
 "settled land," 32, 33
 statutory owner, 35, 162
 tenant for life,
  as trustee, 37, 38, 39
  death of, 44
  definition, 34, 35
  joint, 38, 54
  powers of, 35, 36, 37
  premature determination of
   interest, 44
  trust instrument, 33, 34
  trustees, 34, 38, 39, 40, 42, 44, 45
  vesting instruments, 33, 34
Socage, 3
Spes successionis, 9

Tenancies. *See* Leasehold.
Tenancy in common. *See* Co-
 ownership.
Tenant for life. *See* Settlements,
 strict.
Tenure, doctrine of, 3, 5
Term of years (*see also* Leasehold), 28,
 29, 30
Timber, 20, 21
Treasure trove, 12
Trusts, 23, 24, 184
 resulting, 56, 57
Trusts for sale, 32, 33, 46 *et seq.*

Trusts for sale—*cont.*
 ad hoc, 50, 51
 consents, 48, 49
 co-ownership, 54 *et seq.*
 creation, 46, 47
 intestacy, 208
 overreaching, 47, 48, 58
 powers of trustees, 49, 50
 settlements, 46 *et seq.*

Undivided shares. *See* Co-ownership.
Uses, 23

Vesting instrument. *See* Settlements,
 strict.
Villeinage, 3

Waste, doctrine of, 19, 20, 22, 87, 97
Water rights, 15
Wills, 193 *et seq.*
 alterations, 198
 class-closing rules, 203, 204
 commorientes, 200, 201
 construction, 201 *et seq.*
 formalities, 193, 194
 lapse, 199, 200
 nuncupative, 194
 powers of appointment, 204
 privileged testators, 194, 195
 revival, 197
 revocation, 195, 196, 197
  conditional, 197
  dependent relative, 198
 witnesses, 194, 198, 199
Words of limitation, 9 *et seq.*, 205
Words of purchase, 9, 11, 206